# Resolving Personal
# and Organizational Conflict

# Resolving Personal and Organizational Conflict

## Stories of Transformation and Forgiveness

Kenneth Cloke

Joan Goldsmith

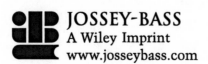

**JOSSEY-BASS**
A Wiley Imprint
www.josseybass.com

Jossey-Bass books and products are available through most bookstores. To contact Jossey-Bass directly, call (888) 378-2537, fax to (800) 605-2665, or visit our website at www.josseybass.com.

Substantial discounts on bulk quantities of Jossey-Bass books are available to corporations, professional associations, and other organizations. For details and discount information, contact the special sales department at Jossey-Bass.

**Library of Congress Cataloging-in-Publication Data**

Cloke, Ken, date.
   Resolving personal and organizational conflict: stories of transformation and forgiveness/Kenneth Cloke, Joan Goldsmith.—1st ed.
      p. cm.
   Includes bibliographical references and index.
   ISBN 0-7879-5060-2 (alk. paper)
   1. Conflict management.   I. Goldsmith, Joan.   II. Title.

HM1126.C56   2000
303.6'9—dc21                                                                    00-035738

FIRST EDITION
*HB Printing* 10 9 8 7 6 5 4 3 2 1

When you are in the middle of a story it isn't
a story at all, but only a confusion; a dark
roaring, a blindness, a wreckage of shattered
glass and splintered wood; like a house in a
whirlwind, or else a boat crushed by icebergs
or swept over the rapids, and all aboard
powerless to stop it. It's only afterwards
that it becomes anything like a story at all.
When you are telling it, to yourself or to
someone else.

Margaret Atwood, *Alias Grace*

# Contents

Preface      xi

1    The Hidden Meaning of Conflict Stories      1
2    Transforming Stories to Resolve Conflict      35
3    Stories Unheard and Untold      59
     *All in the Family*      66
     *Date Rape: Getting to No*      73
     *The Fatherless Child*      81
4    Stories That Sacrifice Life      87
     *The Frightening Possibility of Success*      95
     *Resigned to Being Different*      102
     *Addicted to Defeat*      115
5    Stories That Hold Organizations Hostage      124
     *Conflict on Board*      130
     *School for Scandal*      145
     *Communication Down the Drain*      156
6    Stories of Boundary Violations      166
     *Sex, Lies, and Mediation*      173
     *Neighbors in Spite*      188
     *An "F" in Problem Solving*      194

Conclusion: Living Happily Ever After      207
Index      209
About the Authors      217

*This book is dedicated to the gifted storytellers in our lives: our uncles, Ron Rodecker and Milton Goldsmith, who taught us to listen for the deeper truths hidden in the tale.*

# Preface

*History is always an invention; it is a fairy tale built upon certain clues. The clues are not the problem . . . [t]hese clues are pretty well established; most of them can literally be laid on the desktop for anyone to handle. But these, unfortunately do not constitute history. History consists of the links between them, and it is this that presents the problem. And the link is especially opaque . . . because the only thing that anyone—and that includes me—can use to fill in the gaps between history's clues is themselves.*
PETER HOEG, *THE HISTORY OF DANISH DREAMS*

When we were children, the words "Once upon a time" elicited our undivided attention and signaled the beginning of a journey promising adventure, romance, and hidden wisdom. In stories we found lessons to guide us as we grew up and engaged a sometimes strange and hostile world. We learned from Homer, Aesop, Andersen, and the Grimm brothers, from Aladdin and Scheherazade, from Cinderella, Snow White, and the Knights of the Round Table, and from a multitude of historic legends, religious parables, cultural myths, family legends, and mysteries we whispered to each other as children.

Just mentioning these stories immediately evokes mystery, imagination, and reverie. As we think of them, we retreat for a moment into childhood. We open ourselves and become relaxed yet fully attentive. We prepare to listen to tales that lull us to sleep, assuage our impatience, divert our attention, soothe our fears, and heal our wounded feelings.

These magical stories of mystery and adventure charm our imaginations, yet they also carry vital information, somehow helping us bond with our peers and parents and understand the world, including our own secret selves. Most of the stories we were told as children centered on heroic combat with forces of evil, romantic fantasies of true love, riddles and paradoxes that addressed our baser instincts. They were noble and patriotic, brave and true, alluring and beautiful. They mostly ended with evil vanquished, love triumphant, and everyone decent living happily ever after.

Although these stories were instructive in many ways, they did little to prepare us for the heroic task of reconciling our differences. They did not always teach us how to empathize with our opponents, how to apologize and take responsibility for our mistakes, how to remain vulnerable and open in the face of criticism and attack, how to be honest and committed and still keep love alive, how to compromise and negotiate in ways that allow everyone to win, or how to work together to resolve the petty, pointless conflicts that fill our lives.

If we relied only on childhood stories and fantasies, we would be ill equipped to overcome obstacles and challenges in our friendships, families, neighborhoods, schools, workplaces, and communities when they are torn apart by conflict, violence, or pain—other than to engage in a heroic struggle to the death. The difficulty, of course, is that in the stories the knight doesn't die or return missing a leg. The hero doesn't experience post-traumatic stress disorder. The princess is never actually raped by the ogre. The evil upstart is not finally promoted. Everyone follows the leader. So what is the point of listening to stories if they are so unrealistic? Between blind faith and an equally blind rejection, there is a third path that we can follow in listening to stories.

## The Stories We Tell

Consider not just the fairy tales of our youth but also the thousands of stories we all tell each other as adults about the conflicts we experience in the course of our daily lives. As we shift our attention from fictional tales to real-life descriptions of conflict, we can see that these stories also present us with unique opportunities for learning, growth, and change. These opportunities emerge when we listen carefully to stories of conflict—not as descriptions of literal truth but as fairy tales and metaphors for reality—in precisely the same way we listened as children and now "listen to" novels, poems, and songs.

In their structures, stories of conflict carry deep assumptions about the nature of the world. They reveal hidden truths about us as well as about our enemies. If we hear stories of conflict in this way, we can be rational and critical and at the same time touched and emotionally responsive. We can admire the structures of these stories and mine them for the jewels of insight they contain.

We all have stories to tell about our lives, our conflicts, our enemies, our agonies, our pain. We also have stories, although fewer, about the magic of forgiveness and transformation, about responsibility and learning, and about how difficult yet how easy it is to reach resolution. Every person, in every conflict, has a story that reveals the hidden fulcrum on which his or her fate rests. Every tale that is told, every story that captivates, is a search for that fulcrum.

The hidden fulcrum appears to us as a choice. Every conflict we encounter asks us to choose how we will behave and who we will be in the presence of our adversary. Each choice has consequences for ourselves and for the feelings, thoughts, and energies that shape who we are. Every story we tell about our conflicts is a mirror reflecting our choices and revealing our deeper issues, hidden interests, secret opportunities, and transformational possibilities. Every story allows us to pinpoint possibilities for personal and organizational learning, which are always present when we face our conflicts directly and openly, with honesty and empathy.

## About the Stories in This Book

Over the past twenty years, we have professionally mediated thousands of conflicts and have been intensely interested in how what we do moves people in conflict—subtly, sublimely, and almost by magic—from stubbornness, hostility, and fear to listening, collaboration, and forgiveness. It is difficult to catch these moments or be very precise about how our work is done, because analysis and observation are only part of the process. The other part is intuition, which means entering conflict curiously, as though it were a story about our own lives, except that in it we appear in all the roles—as dragon, princess, and prince.

All the stories told in this volume are true—or, rather, they reflect what people actually said and did during mediations we conducted. We have, of course, altered names, genders, ages, and so on in order to protect our clients' identities and privacy. The stories in this book, whether literally true or not, were chosen because each one provides insights into the deeper environment of conflict. The stories narrated here represent a small sample of those we have been told. We share them in the hope that you will become as fascinated as we have been by each story of conflict and by how it turned into a story of resolution.

Throughout the book, we refer to how a deeper understanding of the narrative structure and metaphorical reasoning of conflict stories can be used by mediators as a guide to the invention and application of practical methods and techniques. In our own efforts to help people overcome impasses and become more open to resolution, transformation, and forgiveness, we are guided by the deeper meanings contained in the stories people tell about their conflicts.

We hope you will follow the journey we took through the resolution process to the sudden, seemingly magical appearance of creative ideas and unique opportunities for learning and change. We hope you will notice the extraordinary capacity of people who are stuck in conflict to grow beyond their experiences and learn to alter their lives.

## How to Read This Book

As you plunge into these narratives and stories of conflict, imagine yourself not only as the mediator but also as each of the combatants. Ask what you would have done in their place. If you had been the conflict resolver, how might you have used a comment or question to deepen the conversation? We invite you to evaluate these narratives critically, to search for our mistakes and failures. In this way, you will learn more about how to apply an understanding of conflict stories to the disputes you face in your own work and life.

As the mediators in these narratives, we endeavored to help people communicate what was wrong honestly and empathetically, without sinking into the trap of demonization and victimization. We tried to encourage people to identify ways of building sustainable, supportive relationships in their families, communities, and organizations. We wanted to model, by the quality of our presence, their own potential for listening and creative problem solving.

This quality of presence and involvement arises almost automatically when we listen to fairy tales, and so we invite you to read these narratives and stories in a similar way, as tales of conquest—not of others, but of the conflicts that keep you trapped. We go further and invite you to hear as fairy tales all the stories of conflict that you will ever be told, not because they are untrue but because their truths are hidden deep within their narrative structure. Then, if you silently repeat the words "Once upon a time" immediately before hearing someone tell you a story about conflict, you will be listening in exactly the right frame of mind.

## Structure of the Book

What makes conflict stories fascinating is the fact that every human being is different, every conflict is different, and both storyteller and conflict are changing at every moment. Each mediation is a story in itself. From all the stories we have heard, we have selected a few of the most instructive to study in this volume.

We use the terms *mediator* and *conflict resolver* interchangeably to include not only professional mediators but also ombudsmen, facilitators, conciliators, counselors, lawyers, peer coaches, and anyone else who is trying to find a way of ending destructive conflicts. We include in this category managers in public and private sector organizations, school principals, teachers, professionals in higher education, union stewards, community leaders, neighbors, and family members—in short, anyone who finds him- or herself stuck in a conflict story and would like to find a way out.

We are less concerned with the specific content of the disputes we describe than with the process of resolution, less interested in the obvious than in the hidden nature of conflict, for stories of conflict contain a richness and variety that will always keep conflict resolvers guessing. We want to illustrate this richness and variety and search out the reasons why we all tell conflict stories in similar ways, reveal the narrative structure and metaphorical clues hidden in every conflict story, discover the trail of bread crumbs leading to its center, and from there, come to resolution, transformation, and forgiveness. We pay less attention to solutions than to identifying a broad set of methods and skills you can use to support people in locating the solutions they need. Our focus is less on how to moderate anger than on how to transform it into awareness, dialogue, and reconciliation.

Chapters One and Two offer a framework for understanding and working with stories of conflict. The twelve conflict narratives that follow in Chapters Three through Six are organized according to the function these stories play in maintaining and resolving conflicts. In Chapter Three, the stories of conflict center on incomplete communication—that is, communication that is either not heard or not acknowledged by the parties to the conflict. Chapter Four features conflict stories in which the narrators are willing to sacrifice some important part of their lives in order to maintain or protect their stories. In these cases there is usually a deeper story undergirding the surface tale, a sadder one that concerns who the narrator is or is not as a person. In Chapter Five we explore the price paid by organizations and the people who work in them, who may not have directly contributed to a conflict but are being held hostage by it. Usually, however, the organization has nurtured a culture that rewards the kinds of behavior that have produced the conflict and penalizes the people who try to resolve it. In Chapter Six we investigate conflicts in which boundary violations have taken place and then have been justified, rationalized, disguised, accentuated, or covered up by stories. Often these stories reflect a blindness that is both external and internal, an insensitivity to the pain of others that always reflects a deeper, internal vulnerability.

As you read these narratives and the stories of conflict they reveal, notice whom you like, whom you don't, and why. Notice which memories get stimulated from your own past, which feelings and stories arise within you, and how you might apply their lessons, not only to working with others in resolving conflicts but also in addressing the conflicts in your own life. Try to bring to these stories the same level of curiosity and openness that carried you into the fairy tales that filled your childhood. Use these stories as scalpels to examine your own open wounds and unresolved conflicts, and as mirrors to reflect your own emotions and possibilities and not just the pain, passion, and possibilities of others.

## Rethinking Success and Failure

In each narrative, we investigate what worked, what didn't, and why. For this reason, we have included not only our successes but also our half-successes and failures. Having said this, we add that in conflict resolution we believe it makes no sense to speak of success and failure. These terms place too great an emphasis on settlement as opposed to resolution, and on outcomes as opposed to learning.

Winston Churchill once defined success as moving from failure to failure with undiminished enthusiasm. A similar definition might be applied in all mediations, which begin at impasse (a sort of failure) and then, often for no definable reason, move to resolution. One way of transforming failure into success is to shift our thinking about the nature of conflict and about what the words *success* and *failure* mean to us. Statements about success and failure are not so much about what people have done as about how they feel about what they have done and about who they think they are. For example, someone's failure as a disciplinarian may indicate his or her success as a nurturer, and vice versa. The terms *success* and *failure* are deceptive because the effect of success is generally repetition, whereas failure results in rethinking, experimentation, and creativity, all of which promote learning and growth. So which is the success and which the failure?

If your goal as a conflict resolver is to increase your learning, then neither success nor failure, as a concept, prove particularly helpful. There is a subtle, intangible danger that arises whenever you define success as simply settling a conflict. When you are interested only in settlement, you link your definition of success to choices that rightfully belong to others. In this way, your desire for success can lead you to subtly coerce others into accepting solutions that are not workable or that they do not own. In a more delicate sense, focusing on success and failure is a distraction from being fully present with the story and the conflict.

We hope that as you read these narratives and stories, you will be led to create your own internal definition of success. As we mediated these disputes, what mattered most to us was not whether the technique or question we were using was right or wrong but whether we were willing to learn, experiment, and take risks, without fear of failure.

In this sense, failure means trying too hard to succeed, whereas success means being willing to accept the possibility of failure. We hope these examples from our experience will encourage you to develop your own strategies. We encourage you to test your approach against our experience. In the process, we hope you will succeed and overcome your fear of failure. We also hope your inevitable failures will turn into lessons that make it possible for you to succeed with others.

## Listening to What Is Said Without Words

We have tried to describe, in words, how the people in each of our mediations struggled with issues of rage and fear, revenge and forgiveness, guilt and shame, frustration and release, and how they progressed toward resolution, transformation, and forgiveness. Often, however, these shifts took place in silence, without words. Over the years, we have become increasingly fascinated with the common thread of emotion and conflict that binds us all, and with the inexplicable, elusive alchemy that makes the process of mediation so profound and potent a source of change. In every alchemical reaction, there is a magic elixir or potion, a philosophers' stone, that transmutes lead into gold. In mediation this elixir is not scientific, reductionist, or rational so much as artistic, holistic, and intuitive. We have been frustrated by our inability to explain with any reasonable degree of precision how even the simplest resolutions occur, or to capture in descriptive terms the quality of the transformational experience. We have found it necessary to search for a deeper meaning than what can be conveyed through analysis, and we have found it in stories. It is through stories that science becomes magical, that impasse and hatred are transformed into resolution and forgiveness. This happens when, as Lao-tzu wrote, we

Take time to listen to what is said without words,
To worship the unnameable,
To obey the law too subtle to be written.

Our message to you is to follow your intuition, to be guided by stories and by your responses to them. Follow with empathy and imagination into their deepest, darkest caves, and be willing to risk being deeply, painfully honest about what you see. If you do, you will light a way to extraordinary opportunities for growth, change, deeper and more satisfying relationships, and learning. We have found that the path to transformation leads directly through our conflicts. May you find yourself in the pages that follow, and may you discover in the process that all the roles and behavior in all the stories we tell already exist within you.

## An Expression of Thanks

We have been fortunate in being able to work with people who invited us into their deepest, darkest spaces and showed us what it means to be honest, empathetic, courageous, and vulnerable in the face of adversity. In the process, we have discovered through others many of the lessons we needed to learn in our own lives. For these lessons, we profoundly thank the people with whom we mediated.

In twenty years of professional work as conflict resolvers, we have had many mentors, teachers, and wise friends, from whom we have learned at first hand how to listen, how to hear, and how to understand and learn from the people we have met and from the stories they have told. Each of these people deserves our thanks. We especially want to acknowledge the courage of our many mediation colleagues, who struggle every day to help people stuck in conflict give birth to stories of resolution, transformation, and forgiveness.

We especially want to thank those who helped us discover our inner voices and our own discerning sense of truth, who held special keys to our understanding of our own subterranean stories, and who were our teachers and guides. Our most profound thanks to our parents, Shirley and Richard Cloke and Miriam and Len Goldsmith, for enabling us to appreciate our own stories of conflict, and for giving us the courage to search for paths to resolution, transformation, and forgiveness.

We thank our dear friend, Warren Bennis, for helping to bring this book to life. We have been honored to have as partners in this endeavor our outstanding proofreader, Miriam Goldsmith, and indexer, Carolyn Thibault. They have believed in this book and worked closely with us to shape it. Our staff—Matt Kramer, Grace Silva, Solange Raro, and Anne Roswell—did not let us down for a minute; we are sure they have stories of their own to tell about this process.

Finally, we want to thank the many individuals whose stories of struggles, defeat, and triumph appear in these pages. We narrate their stories out of a desire to learn, and we honor them on behalf of everyone in conflict whose distress, as a result of this telling, may be tempered. These individuals took a risk in choosing to work with us. In the process they confronted unimagined dangers and cut through Gordian knots. They had the courage to tell their stories and discover their meaning.

June 2000

Kenneth Cloke
Joan Goldsmith
*Center for Dispute Resolution*
*Santa Monica, California*

# Resolving Personal
# and Organizational Conflict

# Chapter One

# The Hidden Meaning of Conflict Stories

*Between the conception*
*And the creation*
*Between the emotion*
*And the response*
*Falls the Shadow.*
T. S. ELIOT, *THE HOLLOW MEN*

An ancient piece of Jewish wisdom asks, "What is truer than the truth?" It answers, "The story." How is it possible for a story to be "truer than the truth"? Stories contain not only the truth of factual description, of events, people, and places, but also fragments of the storyteller's truth. They expose the Shadow that falls between emotion and response.

Stories open up parts of ourselves that we have hidden or shielded from view. They present masks to the outside world that provide us space to hide behind, yet in their conception and design they reveal who we really are. Stories are expressions of our deepest desires, and for this reason they encourage us to become more human, even to ourselves. They are, as Franz Kafka wrote, "an axe to break the frozen sea within."

Stories are impressive fabrications. They are, as someone described novels, "lies in search of a higher truth." They are designed, woven, and polished in the subconscious mind of the storyteller, the artist, the sculptor, the poet who created them. They are hardy yet delicate, true yet false, external yet internal, factual yet symbolic,

1

unresolved yet resolvable. They seem impervious yet are easily malleable, to last forever and yet change in the telling.

Whenever events occur, stories take shape that surround and profoundly alter the way they are experienced. Hard facts mix with the soft human material of the artist, who is at the same time canvas and painting, marble and sculpture, music and instrument. Once the story is shaped and refined, once it has become coherent and whole, the artist experiences an inner need to tell it to others, perhaps as a way of confirming a timeless, universal human connection. Stories are a set of instructions for figuring out who people really are and how to respond to anger, pain, fear, and shame.

Stories are a method of learning and a means of play. They pass important cultural information from generation to generation. For this reason, they command our immediate attention and invoke deep listening. We have learned to anticipate the captivating, deeply satisfying experience of listening to fables, myths, and fairy tales, although none of them are about real life or even about us.

## The Power of Stories

Why do we listen so closely to stories? What is it about them that delights, enchants, and transports us? What is the strange hidden power of stories? Why do they induce such deep states of listening?

Stories invite the listener to jointly experience an event with the storyteller. They elicit a sympathetic vibration, an empathic discovery of what it must have felt like to live the event being narrated. They encourage a deep level of communication and promote a sense of community by bringing people together, through imagination and empathy, to collectively define the meaning of the world in which they live. Listening changes people. The Native American novelist Leslie Marmon Silko describes the process this way:

> At Laguna Pueblo . . . [stories express] an understanding of the original view of creation—that we are all part of a whole; we do not differentiate or fragment stories and experiences. . . . So in the telling . . . the storytelling always includes the audience, the listeners. In fact, a great deal of the story is believed to be inside the listener; the storyteller's role is to draw the story out of the listeners.

In stories, we both lose and find ourselves. At some deep place within them, we both discover and create who we are. Even a fairy tale that concerns princesses, dragons, and knights in shining armor somehow seems to be about us or parts of ourselves that we are able to bring to life by listening deeply, as though the story was about us. We willingly suspend our disbelief in the story's truth or falsity and thereby access its deeper truths.

The same process takes place in mediation. We have realized, in the course of listening to tens of thousands of stories about conflict over the last twenty years, that every story about conflict is, at one level, a fairy tale. Each tale of conflict, in the way it is told, has the power to keep people locked in combat, and it has an equal power to free them from suffering. Each story can lead them closer to anger or forgiveness, toward impasse or resolution, into stasis or transformation.

Every party to a conflict, on hearing his or her opponent tell a story describing how awful he or she was, or how he or she caused the conflict, finds it difficult to suspend disbelief and examine the story for its deeper truths. Often he or she is unable to set aside, even for a moment, judgments about the factual truth or falsity of the story to search for its metaphorical truths. This party cannot feel empathy for his or her opponents or experience with them the emotions described in the story. He or she is unable to reach across the barrier of opposition to discover something in and about the story that bridges the distance from the other party or parties to the conflict.

Yet every authentic story reverberates powerfully inside us. Whenever a story touches us deeply, we identify acutely with the experience of the speaker, and the story becomes one that is also about us. Even if it is told in a way that casts us as the villain, we can recognize from the structure of the story that our "villainy" is only the flip side or mirror image of our opponent's pain. Mediators can encourage people to discover these hidden meanings for themselves.

When we work with schools, organizations, and communities attempting to resolve cross-cultural conflicts or address issues of bias and prejudice and celebrate their diversity, we often use stories to evoke empathy and compassionate listening. We ask people to find someone in the audience who is completely different from them.

We ask women and men, blacks and whites, gays and straights to find each other. Then we ask them to tell each other a story about a time when they felt discriminated against for any reason.

Some people's stories describe racial, gender-based, or cultural discrimination; other stories are about being too short or too tall or funny-looking, or about being called a name as a child. Ancient, profound, deeply painful stories are remembered and exchanged as the storytellers relive their shame and sadness amidst tears and rage. Although people are very different, as their stories unfold they discover that the experience of discrimination is remarkably similar despite their differences.

For example, one African American woman told of driving through an upper-class neighborhood and repeatedly being stopped and questioned by police. A Latino man told of being expelled from school as a child on his first day because he had only recently arrived in the United States and could not speak English. An elderly woman with a thick accent spoke of growing up Jewish in prewar Germany and of being discriminated against in the United States because of her accent. A Caucasian male engineer told us he could not think of a time when he had felt discriminated against. After a few minutes of listening to other people's stories, he shared a repressed memory of being teased unmercifully. Forty years later, he blushed as he recalled the pain their ridicule had caused him.

The experience of discrimination can be understood by everyone, even if, by comparison, it looks trivial. Through this exercise, people often experience a deep sense of relief, letting go of burdens they have been carrying for years. They are grateful for the opportunity to articulate memories they have not shared before, and they are deeply appreciative of their partners for listening carefully and compassionately to their stories. There is often surprise among storytelling partners that their experiences are remarkably similar despite differences in age, gender, sexual orientation, and ethnic, racial, or other backgrounds. As a result, people can identify powerfully across the apparent abyss of their differences. They can see that the purpose of discrimination is to shame and divide them and prevent them from discovering the similarities in their stories.

It then becomes possible for those who have discovered their own emotional pain to understand the deeper damage done to others by repeated, even harsher experiences of prejudice. After considering what they have gone through, they can empathize with what it may feel like to experience discrimination not as a single event but as a daily occurrence for thirty or forty years. Although people are listening to stories about other people's lives, no one ever appears bored, and attention never wavers.

Storytelling has the potential to carry us, listeners and storytellers alike, to a new place in our relationships with one another and with ourselves. Simply exchanging personal details and trivia about our lives helps us become more compassionate, recognize ourselves in others, and deepen our relationships.

## Conflict Stories and Reality

Moments of incredible intimacy, insight, and empathy often occur in storytelling, uniting people so opposite that they might otherwise dislike each other. We need to ask why it is so much more difficult to make the same connections when we hear our adversaries tell stories about their conflicts with us.

What are conflict stories, and what is the source of their power? From the point of view of the people involved in conflict, stories are an effort to mend the fabric of their perceived reality—to create a consistent, sequential version of upsetting, unexpected, seemingly contradictory facts or events. We tell stories to integrate our experiences into a matrix, system, or pattern of thought that reinforces, justifies, and defends our identities. Whenever significant conflicts occur in our lives, we immediately create stories about what has happened, in an effort to make sense out of our conflicts. We tell stories to rationalize what we have said or done, to justify our roles, to express our injured feelings, to defend our positions, or to prove that we were right.

For example, we were recently in the company of a two-year-old girl who fell down, skinned her knee, and cried inconsolably for several minutes. A short while later, she relayed to her grandmother the story of what had happened: she had fallen down, hurt herself, cried, and was now all better. It was clear that for her the story was a kind of bandage or medication, a salve not for her scraped knee but for her injured self. As she told her story, the event simultaneously grew more distant and became more permanent. She later repeated the story several times—to her father, her aunt and uncle, and everyone else who came within range. By the fourth or fifth telling, a painful memory had been replaced by a story about pain, bravery, and recovery, in the same way that a photograph both stimulates and substitutes for detailed recollection.

The stories we tell ourselves and others create causal connections between seemingly disparate, unconnected events that might otherwise frighten us with their irrationality and threaten the safety with which we try to fill our lives. As we tell these stories, we link random events in a seemingly logical, purposeful sequence. Doing so allows us to feel protected, good about ourselves, and less anxious about the world. Stories allay our fears, quell our anxieties, soothe our pains, and alleviate our shame. They deny the inevitability of death, or they tell us we are lucky not to have been more badly injured.

We continuously search out, manufacture, and process reality through stories. We use stories to make the world's sudden, irregular events consistent with our continuous, regular inner lives—with our beliefs, feelings, actions, and attitudes. Stories are how we learn to avoid danger, avert failure, and prepare for unexpected contingencies by imagining how we might respond successfully to them.

When others are angry with us, for example, we can easily become frightened. We assuage our fears by manufacturing images and stories that give us permission to pull away, or to cause the others harm. We do this because we would feel guilty if we did not first cast our opponents as unworthy of our company. In this way, we create them in the image of our own fear. Thus, the stories we tell others and the ones we tell ourselves recreate the world as an externalized self-image.

At the same time, our *authentic* selves, our inner sense of truth, our core integrity, and our natural capacity for empathy are often sacrificed. Stories give meaning and identity to our lives, but they do so in a social context that produces and conveys social meaning. We tell them for a purpose, yet our purpose causes us to lose track of the actual experience from which we shaped the story, with its plot, its characterizations, and its descriptions of feelings.

When there is a tenuous relationship between who we really are and who our stories say we are—between what actually happened and the tales we weave to cover, protect, and deflect from some vulnerable space within—we become confused and disoriented. When we tell false stories, or stories about a false self, we lose connection with who we really are. Only by listening carefully to our own stories and making explicit the hidden assumptions that buttress our tales can we observe how we have brought together the elements that created our stories. Through self-observation and discovery, we can understand why we have created a story and how it melds our assumptions and expectations with our experiences. From there we can discover alternative stories, including those told by our opponents, that are as accurate and inaccurate as our own.

When, as mediators, we try to decide which of two conflict stories is true and which is false, we forget that these stories, like novels and fairy tales, are fictions that are designed to reveal larger truths. In this sense, all stories are true, perhaps not factually but as expressions of how we feel at the time we describe it, about what has happened to us. They express true needs, emotions, interests and desires, however false the facts may be. By following the clues hidden in stories, we can discover the truths they symbolize.

## Stories Within Stories

In every conflict story there are three separate stories that describe vastly different truths. There is an *external story* that is told for public consumption. Beneath it, there is a second, *internal story* that is constructed to protect the ego. Beneath that, there is a third, *core story* that explains why the storyteller found it necessary to invent the other two stories.

All three stories reveal common themes and similarities in language, yet the purpose and method of each story are different. In external stories, the focus is on demonizing the other person, characterizing what he or she did as wrong or harmful, so these stories are told in an angry or pained tone of voice. In internal stories, the focus is on excusing ourselves, justifying our actions and inactions, and our tone conveys guilt or shame. Core stories connect the other two stories. They focus on accepting responsibility for the conflict and being who we really are. The tone in these stories is centered, authentic, honest, and self-aware. The mediator's role is to diminish, reframe, or remove the demonizations and negative characterizations in external stories, to extract, bypass, or question the justifications and excuses in internal stories, and to encourage the parties to discover their core stories and reveal them to each other. It is the search for these core stories that forms the center of our work. They are the fulcrum tipping impasse and stasis toward resolution and transformation.

As people in conflict discover and tell their core stories to each other, bridges are erected, permitting empathy, understanding, forgiveness, and reconciliation to cross between them. External stories, by contrast, build invisible boundaries that defend and protect the parties against those they have chosen to describe as enemies, keeping them locked in position. Internal stories isolate them even more, protecting them against their own vulnerability, guilt, and shame. Internal and external stories both work to keep core stories well hidden.

In Buddhism, there is a practice known as "Three objects, three poisons, three seeds of virtue." These three consist of what we try to minimize, what we try to maximize, and what we do not care about minimizing or maximizing. They can also be thought of as negative, positive, and neutral. In conflict resolution terms, they translate into, "You're wrong," "I'm right," and "Who cares." These three positions correspond roughly to the external, internal, and core stories if we change the last statement to "I do care, but I don't want to admit it."

When core stories are finally revealed, it is almost as if a direct channel were opened between the parties, revealing their authentic selves. Their tone and the quality of energy flowing between them shifts dramatically, allowing new possibilities to emerge. They connect with each other at a deep level because they have dropped their conflict masks and protective stories and revealed who they really are.

## Listening for the Core Story

All stories bypass our rational thought processes. They speak to us directly through fantasy, emotion, heart, and spirit. The subconscious mind does not distinguish between metaphor and reality, between what is true and what is intensely imagined, whether as wish or fear. It is to this nonrational, subconscious mind that stories communicate. When conflict stories are told, these deeper issues, feelings, needs, and wants are revealed, even when the storytellers want them hidden.

For example, we mediated a claim of sexual harassment involving a man and a woman who had worked together for several years. At first they were unwilling to speak to each other about what had happened and sat frozen in silence. We asked the woman to tell her story and reveal her experience. We asked the man to listen with empathy and an open mind, without being distracted by thoughts about how he was going to respond when his turn came.

Instead of describing this man as evil, the woman spoke honestly about her fears and about the pain she had felt as she went to her car and found his unwanted love notes and requests for dates. She spoke graphically of her aborted efforts to tell him she did not want to see him. She described his silent staring and persistence in following her around the building where they worked. She painted a clear picture of his harassing behavior and her feelings of being hounded by him. She acknowledged her ineffectiveness in communicating her desire that he stop. Finally, with our assistance, she turned to him, told him she was miserable, and, in tears, asked him to please stop. At the end of her story, they both cried. The man, for the first time, understood the pain he had caused and was profoundly ashamed of his behavior. He apologized from his heart, saying he knew he could never make up for what he had done. He said he had fallen in love with her. He admitted not noticing her fear or registering her rejection. He thanked her for opening his eyes and promised he would respect her wishes. He said he would never speak to her again unless she spoke first. In response, she told him she understood his anguish and accepted his apology, although what he had done still was not okay. With authenticity and emotional honesty, each was able to hear what the other felt and, on that basis, resolve the conflict. They were both released from the burden of carrying their stories alone and from the hostile external stories they had created of evil, cruelty, harassment, and fear. They were also able to transcend the internal stories they had told themselves in order to exonerate their own behavior. The woman, for instance, had told herself that she was justified in not directly asking the man to stop, because he was so insensitive he would never listen. She admitted wanting to keep her feelings of fear and revulsion to herself because in her culture it would have been highly inappropriate for a woman to speak so directly to a man. The man, in turn, had told himself that he did not need to acknowledge the woman's subtle signals, because she was behaving politely toward him. He admitted being unable to hear the word *no* and placing his need for affection over her need for safety. As they each revealed their core stories and mistaken assumptions, they were able to see together the events and actions that these assumptions had precipitated, and they were able to acknowledge the anguish and pain they felt as a result. Through their tears, they told each other that they finally understood each other in a genuine way and could now begin to heal. The healing process accelerated as they created a new, third story—not of fear and pain but of learning, listening, and improved understanding. Then they agreed to tell this story to their colleagues at work.

## The Dangers in Mediating Conflict Stories

The parties in mediation tell their stories not just to friends, colleagues, or mediators but also to the very people they have accused of evil, the people who have justified their rage and have served as explanations for their fear. In organizational mediations, as one person tells his or her story, others are inspired to join in and tell their own stories of the same experience or events. As everyone recounts some version of what happened, a composite or collective story emerges, one that is truer and more accurate than any of the others. Objective truth, in this sense, is an amalgam of all the possible subjective truths that can be told; it cannot be found in one story before the others have been told. Here are some of the dangers in mediating conflict stories.

### Unpredictability

Mediation is rarely a simple process in which the antagonists spin narratives for the mediator and their open-minded, actively listening opponents. It works archeologically, excavating deeper stories that may be entirely different from or even contradictory to the one that lies just beneath the surface. It is an adventure, a hunt for hidden treasure that even the storytellers may not know is there. This story does not have a safe, predetermined ending, so one danger is unpredictability: anything can happen.

## Collusion

Every form of vulnerability is loaded with fear, reluctance, and mistrust, making vulnerability especially risky in the presence of conflict. Most people are reluctant to explore or share their core stories. They feel frightened, shy, or embarrassed, and committed to the tales they have constructed and to the beliefs anchored in their version of what happened. Moreover, their opponents find it difficult to hear their deeper, more vulnerable stories. They fear being manipulated into a powerful form of empathy, or being pressured to surrender an important interest, or being called on to reveal their own inner selves. For this reason, another danger is that the parties on both sides of a conflict may collude or conspire to defend their stories against other, less flattering versions and to keep communication superficial by staying with superficial stories.

## Seduction

Storytelling is a fluid art. Stories change as feelings, interests, and needs shift. People tell stories as a way of encouraging their listeners to respond supportively and sympathetically. Storytelling is sometimes used to manipulate, win over, or hypnotize listeners into supporting the storyteller's feelings. Stories are designed, and other people's actions are coordinated, in such a way as to elicit the desired emotional responses. To quote the philosopher Ludwig Wittgenstein, "every word strikes an emotional note," and this is particularly true of conflict stories. The danger for the mediator is of being seduced by a highly emotional internal story. A rich narrative has the power not only to attract the storyteller's antagonist but also to trigger memories, unresolved issues, feelings, and incomplete episodes in the life of the mediator. Thus, all the parties to the mediation process may succumb to the intensity or tragic beauty of a story told with deep, absorbing emotion.

## Undue Influence

Every time we enter a conflict, the conflict enters us, and every story we hear is changed by the way we hear it. In this way, our own stories have an impact on the stories told by others, and this is true even when our "story" about mediation is that we should not get involved in trying to understand the stories of parties who are in conflict.

Instead of denying our influence, we can use it to enhance learning. Every story we hear contributes to our personal and professional growth, so it is possible for mediators to use storytelling to reveal openings for our own learning, resolution, and transformation.

## The Context of Narrative Communication

The context of a narrative communication is its framework: the big picture, the environment that surrounds it. The context assigns meaning, both for the speaker and for the listener, and every communication takes place within a context. Therefore, to understand the meaning of any communication, it is necessary to be aware of the visible and invisible contexts in which it takes place. What is actually understood by speaker and listener alike depends on the degree of awareness and attention that each can bring to bear on the invisible context. Thus, whenever anyone tells a story, the listener has a choice: to focus on the literal meaning of the story and ignore its hidden contextual elements, or to search out the contextual elements and hear a more complex but clearer story.

Because conflict stories often carry strong emotions, they require mediators to elucidate the context, which is rarely explicit. By addressing contextual elements, mediators support the storytellers in understanding and defusing the story, because when the context is uncovered, a new story emerges from underneath the words, leading the listener to the core story.

One way of elucidating the context is for the mediator to elicit background information that explains why a speaker is upset. The mediator can unhook the past from recent events or reframe accusations as statements of the speaker's own pain. In these ways, the mediator creates an environment in which the story can be heard, digested, and explored.

Given that the key contextual element in most conflict stories is the antagonistic relationship between speaker and listener, the mediator can also ask questions that reveal problems in the relationship, the history of the relationship, and expectations for the relationship. This process will reveal what each of the parties is responsible for in their dysfunctional relationship. Moreover, the mediator can ask questions that clarify the background of each person, the environment in which troubling incidents have taken place, and any organizational structures and systems that have added meaning to the communication.

In addition, the mediator can focus on the communication process—on how the message is being delivered, on the speaker's tone of voice, energy level, and body language, and on the medium of communication that was used. The mediator can also check on what the listener has heard—on what was understood, on what was internalized, and on what was missed. The mediator can ask questions of the speaker as well, to explore his or her intentions, discover the speaker's hoped-for impact on the listener, assess the actual emotional impact on the listener, and compare it to the impact the speaker desired. This process encourages resolution by revealing the parts of the story that were acceptable or agreeable to the listener and by focusing the listener's attention on elements that he or she missed. The speaker can also be led to recognize, for example, that a communication was ineffective because it did not take account of the listener's context, or because it was actually incongruent with the context and therefore sent a mixed message.

By openly identifying the contextual patterns in conflict stories, mediators enable parties to pay attention to the hidden elements that define the meaning of their communications. This process encourages them to act strategically and thereby increase the effectiveness of their communications. Because they learn to avoid using inconsistent and incongruent communications that distort their messages, they decrease the level of their conflict.

## Key Components and Functions of Conflict Stories

Every conflict story reveals key components and functions—justifications, defenses, and expectations—that harden and intensify every time the story is told. As mediators, we rarely stop to analyze or reveal the components that keep these stories locked in place, nor are we conscious of the functions that these components play in maintaining stability and security in the storyteller's life. Without this kind of analysis, there is a danger that we will let people fall into the trap of telling their stories to a sympathetic listener who does not empathically challenge their views but merely reinforces their positions, thereby blocking resolution of their conflicts.

Understanding a story's key components and functions allows the mediator to support the parties in releasing their external and internal stories and allowing their core stories to emerge. As you read the following two sections, consider the effects that these ideas could have on the conflicts you are mediating.

## Components

Not every conflict story contains every one of the following components, but most contain one or more, which can be identified through questions and used to create an opening to the core of the conflict:

- *The storyteller is a victim, more acted on than acting.* Who is the victim in the story? Who is the actor? Who is acted on? Why is the story told in this way? In telling it this way, what does the storyteller expect to gain from the listener?
- *The opponent is the creator, initiator, and cause of the conflict.* What would happen to the story if the opponent were not the cause of the conflict? What reaction would the listener have if the storyteller began by taking responsibility for everything that has happened?
- *Whatever the storyteller has done is presented as rational and just.* In the story, does the speaker include a description of the mistakes she has made? Does she describe her own irrational actions or fears? If not, why not? What does she think would happen if she did?
- *Whatever the opponent has done is presented as irrational and unjust.* In the story, does the opponent do anything right? Is there a way of rationally explaining what the opponent has done? If not, why not? Why is it difficult for the

storyteller to admit that his opponent may have done something right?

- *The symbolic and metaphorical content of the story points to the real meaning that it has for the storyteller.* In the story, what symbols and metaphors are used? What real meanings do they reveal?

- *Both parties' stories about the conflict are metaphorically true.* How do the metaphors used by the storyteller express a deeper truth about the conflict? What is the metaphorical truth of the opponent's story?

- *The story links perceived facts in such a way as to favor the storyteller, while facts inconsistent with the story are denied, dismissed, or disconnected.* What facts have been left out of the story? Why? What would happen to the story if they were inserted?

- *The conflict story, in its imagery and language, reveals a set of emotional assumptions that have more to do with the underlying conflict than with the event itself.* What images are implicit in the story? What are the storyteller's emotional assumptions? What words does she use to describe her opponent? Is it possible to find different words that have the same meanings but are positive or neutral? Why were these words not chosen?

- *Stories about the opponent are actually about the storyteller—about what he admires in others but lacks in himself, or what he dislikes and rejects in others but is simultaneously drawn to in himself.* What can the storyteller learn about himself from what he dislikes or admires in others? What does the story say about what he has done, and what does it reveal about what he has not done?

## Functions

Understanding the role the story plays, both in the life of the storyteller and in the conflict, may reveal openings that allow the mediator to break its hold. The key functions of the conflict story operate on many levels, both for the storyteller and for the listener:

- *The conflict stories people tell create their lives; in a story's telling, the conflict is created.* What aspects of the story have shaped or created the speaker's life? How? How has the telling of the story helped create or deepen the conflict?

- *Stories are rituals designed to comfort the storyteller with their familiarity.* Does the storyteller appear to be comforted by the story? How? Why is this important?
- *The more a story is repeated, the more it is believed to be true.* How often has the conflict story been repeated? Has it changed as it has been repeated? How? Why?
- *Conflict stories maintain the self-image and self-esteem of the storytellers.* How has the self-image of the storyteller been enhanced or bolstered by the story? What would happen to the storyteller's self-esteem if the opponent's story were accepted?
- *Stories indirectly help fulfill wishes, dreams, and expectations, or they explain why wishes, dreams, and expectations have not been fulfilled.* Are there any wishes, dreams, or expectations expressed in the story? What are they? How would the story change if these wishes, dreams, and expectations became realities? Is the story primarily about the opponent or about the storyteller's wishes, dreams, and expectations?
- *Most stories that people tell about themselves are compensatory, and the satisfaction that storytellers take in these stories reveals their underlying needs and interests.* Does the story reveal an underlying need or interest on the part of the storyteller? What parts of the story provide the greatest emotional satisfaction? Why? What are each party's underlying needs or interests? How are underlying needs and interests revealed in each party's story?
- *Most stories told about others are relational. Thus the storyteller creates others as a way of creating herself through her relationships with them.* How does the storyteller's narrative create the other person? What impact does her description of the other person have on her self-definition? On her relationship with the other person?
- *Stories create listening and produce powerful bonds with listeners, even when the listeners are opponents.* How could the storyteller use his story to create a bond with his opponent in the conflict? Could he tell the same story without the device of a victim or a demon? Without one who is good and another who is evil? Without a predefined notion of right and wrong?

- *Conflict stories can all be retold to end with the words "and they lived happily ever after" and describe a full resolution of the conflict.* How could the parties tell their stories so as to have them end in this way? What would they have to give up in order to do so? What would a happy ending do to their relationship?

## The Language of Metaphor

The language of metaphor, allusion, and symbolism is exactly opposite to the language of fact, attribution, and logic. Factual and logical accounts are linear, temporal, unchanging, causal, local, and specific. Metaphorical and symbolic descriptions are circular, timeless, always changing, without cause, universal, and general. Metaphors are images we use to try to make sense of the world by comparing it with something we understand. Mediators can discover the hidden contexts of conflict stories from the metaphors that the parties use in telling them.

Logic is automatic and predictable, whereas metaphor is accidental and chaotic. In metaphor, events are linked symbolically, not because one action leads causally to another but because it is associated with another action through *meaning.* The meaning of any metaphor is implicit rather than explicit, based on feeling rather than reason and on something other than what is literally being said.

Meaning often is evident through tone of voice, feeling, intensity, or sensation rather than through data, reasoning, or precise definitions of words. Metaphor, in this sense, is the language of art and of the unconscious. It is the stuff of dreams used by mediators to reach the inner self and bypass the logical, rational barriers that keep others at a distance.

For example, consider the stories told by a divorcing couple who disagree about who will get the family home. To each spouse, the house is described as more than just a residence. Its meaning to each party is often revealed through the use of metaphors that identify deeper conflicts lying below the surface. For one of the spouses the house symbolizes security in old age, whereas for the other it represents an investment or opportunity to turn a profit. It may represent a lost childhood, a broken promise, a hope for reconciliation, or a weapon of revenge. It may be a hedge against fate, a way of saying no, or the equalizer in a perceived power imbalance. It may represent a memory of martyrdom, a way of holding on to being right, or memories of being together. It can hold many meanings other than its ordinary meaning as a place to live.

Metaphorical elements occur in workplace conflicts as well. For instance, in one mediation we conducted, an employee kept repeating statements about his supervisor: "She's always telling me what to do," "I feel powerless when I'm around her," "She is so punishing," and "She's too controlling." When we repeated to the employee the words he had used in describing his relationship with his supervisor, he realized for the first time that he felt like a child when confronted by her. "Oh my God," he said, "it's my mother!" With this insight, he discovered why she was a problem in his life. As a result of this insight, he was able to see that the problem was mostly his. We were then able to assist him in reaching an agreement with his supervisor on what they could do to create a better relationship. We asked him to find a word that represented a new metaphor for his supervisor, and he chose "coach." He stopped interpreting her attempts to work with him as efforts to control his life. When he was able to uncover and acknowledge the hidden meaning of his relationship with his supervisor, and when he created a new metaphor that allowed him to think differently about the meaning of her behavior, the subconscious reasons for his resistance disappeared, and the rest of their agreements came easily. He shifted from metaphors of control to metaphors of learning.

Mediators can use metaphors to reveal misunderstandings that fuel conflict and to clarify emotional experiences on both sides. Questions—such as "What did that feel like?" or "What was that like for you?"—can elicit metaphorical responses that speak directly to a listener's subconscious mind and result in increased empathy for the speaker.

## Separating Fact from Interpretation

Every conflict story is organized around an event, which is presented by the speaker as made up of objective facts. The listener, it is assumed, will be forced by his or her acceptance of these facts to adopt the storyteller's interpretation of the event—including the speaker's attributions of meaning, which are based on those facts. Most external stories are built on facts that have been tailored to support a particular interpretation or point of view.

During the storytelling process, one way the mediator can interact creatively with parties in conflict is to encourage them to recognize the vast difference between facts and their interpretation. Every fact is simply that: a fact. Rarely, however, do facts get people into conflict, mostly because it is a waste of time to contest the uncontestable or rail against reality. What upsets the parties is the interpretation of fact.

Consider the words "You are lazy." That one person is working harder than another may be a fact. One way to interpret this fact is to say that the person described is lazy, but there are other possible interpretations. The speaker may have been tired, for example, and have asked the other party for help, politely, without getting any response. Or the speaker may expect work to be shared with the other party and may feel exploited. Or the speaker may be upset about the time it has taken the other person to get started on a task. Or the speaker may be using these words as a way to open a more authentic line of communication about his or her relationship with the listener, or simply may be feeling irritable because of lack of sleep, or may be in a foul mood or be joking. We could go on in an interminable process of interpretation that can be triggered for any set of facts in a conflict story. It is important for each party to understand that his or her meaning is not the only possible one, nor is it necessarily the correct one. An interpretation may reflect a listener's fear more than a speaker's aggression, a listener's irritability rather than a speaker's sleepless night.

At a deeper level, both the attribution of meaning and the selection of a single interpretation out of many possibilities are choices made by the listener. Again, an interpretation often reveals more about the listener's intentions and emotions than it does about the speaker's. Every interpretation tells the mediator something about the mental framework, expectations, and context of the one who is doing the interpreting. This information can be used in powerful ways to deepen the conversation. For example, employees who respond defensively to criticism by accusing their managers of harassment may be afraid of losing their jobs and unable to hear criticism until they have received positive feedback. Once they have received it, they become able to engage in deeper conversations with their managers about the responsibility they share for clarifying expectations, improving communication, and building better working relationships. It, then, becomes possible to probe deeply into the fear, defensiveness, harshness, and retaliation that have proved unsuccessful in past communications.

## Filters, Lenses, Mistaken Assumptions, and Unrealistic Expectations

The stories that parties tell about a conflict are partly efforts to reshape actions or events that they have experienced—to recreate them in the storyteller's image. In order to understand exactly how this is being done, mediators need to recognize the context, elicit the metaphors, and identify the interpretations that add meaning to the conflict. It is equally important for mediators to recognize the filters and lenses that parties use to *subtract* meaning from the events that shape their conflict stories. Even before it has been told, the conflict story has been patterned and fitted to a design: unwanted facts have been cut away, and those that remain are refinished and molded to achieve the effect that the story is intended to produce.

For example, a conflict we mediated between two sisters-in-law revealed the role that subjective lenses and filters can play in shaping a conflict story. Helen, whose marriage to Elaine's brother was disintegrating, told a story in which Elaine was described as trying to help her brother meet other women so he could betray Helen. The story was based on Helen's fears and on her interpretation of the fact that Elaine had invited her brother to travel to a business meeting that would be chaired by Cecelia, a strong, beautiful woman.

Elaine's story was equally colored by her own unrealistic expectations of her brother, her dislike of the way Helen picked fights with him, and her desire to encourage her brother to meet people who would support what she saw as his capacity for success. Helen had started with a set of preconceived ideas, colored by her poor self-esteem, about Elaine's history of lukewarm support for her marriage. To these negative feelings she added her fear that her husband did not love her and a recent history of emotionally unresolved marital arguments. These filters distorted the real purpose of Elaine's invitation to her brother and led Helen to invent a story of betrayal. The two women told conflicting stories about the same event because each of them had filtered it differently and was seeing it through a different set of lenses.

## Filters

A filter is like a sieve. It eliminates from the storyteller's account any information he considers potentially dangerous. It is difficult to identify a filter, however, because its presence in the story is not conspicuous; indeed, it can be detected only through the perceived absence of what it has removed. Identifying a filter is like noticing the missing pieces in a jigsaw puzzle, which become obvious only when all the other pieces have been inserted and connected. Therefore, the mediator needs to recognize what is required for a story to make sense, identify what makes a story unconvincing, unclear, or incomplete, and sense what has not been said. Once it is clear that both parties to a conflict have neglected to include certain pieces of information in their versions of the conflict, it becomes possible to consider why those particular pieces were left out.

It is also possible, although difficult in practice, for the mediator to extrapolate backwards from behavioral symptoms and pathologies that appear in a conflict to facts or issues that have been left out of a conflict story. As the mediator notices emotional dysfunctions or biases, she can assume that they operate as a filter, to block parts of the story from being told or heard. Freud commented, in a similar vein, that wherever there is a symptom, there is an amnesia.

## Lenses

In addition to filtering out unwanted particulars, the parties to a conflict view the facts through a variety of lenses, which subtly reshape whatever information remains after filtering, so that this information matches what the parties already know or want to be true. The information is refracted as it passes through a number of different focusing devices, including subjective perceptions, cultural assumptions, emotions, preexisting ideas, self-concepts, and personal or organizational paradigms, each of which both distorts and clarifies meaning. This process is illustrated by Figure 1.1. Words and actions, as they move through and are shaped by these lenses, become increasingly distorted and divergent from the original events or actions, to such an extent that the storyteller's descriptions of an event are often virtually unrecognizable, not only to his or her opponent but also to others who have witnessed the event in question. At the same time, however, the hidden, inner meaning of the story becomes clearer as the events described more truly reflect the storyteller's needs.

**Figure 1.1. Lenses That Shape Our Stories.**

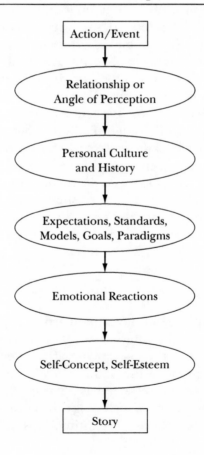

## Mistaken Assumptions and Unrealistic Expectations

As filters and lenses are identified and missing pieces are restored, a larger, more integrated story begins to emerge. Before this larger story can be understood, mediators need to carefully examine how filters and lenses are created by mistaken assumptions and unrealistic expectations.

Many conflict stories, for example, contain an assumption that people can and should be perfect. This assumption gives rise to an unrealistic expectation that one should behave with absolute correctness in all situations. To meet this expectation, people edit their conflict stories to omit everything that presents them in less than a perfect light.

Beneath this assumption is another, deeper assumption: that people are not good enough as they are and so require the approval of other people in order to feel right or okay. People expect to be able to earn the approval of others through actions, and they tell their stories in order to achieve this result. Whatever may incur disapproval is edited out or rationalized before the next telling.

There is also an assumption that if one has not been perfect, and if one's actions do not warrant the approval of others, then the cause of this failure is beyond one's control. This assumption leads to an expectation of helplessness, an irrational belief that one's whole life is determined by forces beyond one's control. As a result, people shape their stories to portray these forces (and their opponents) as larger than they really are, and they expect something terrible to happen if they do anything to address their conflicts.

As people become aware of these assumptions and expectations, they discover issues that have nothing to do with their opponents. They gain insights that open them to the possibility of resolving their disputes. As they go deeper and pull back the layers of their assumptions, they find yet another assumption, present in all conflict stories: that things *should be* the way they expect them to be. The expectation that things ought to be different than they are encourages people to adopt the position that it is the facts, rather than their interpretation, that is wrong. As a result, people make up stories to match the way they think things ought to be instead of describing the way things actually are.

Many people operate on the assumption that the more they want something, the less they deserve it or can get it or are entitled to ask for it. This assumption creates two expectations: that disguising one's emotional truth as a literal truth, or distorting it into the shape of a false absolute, increases the likelihood of getting what one wants, and that one suffers less when one's hidden desire is denied than if one had asked for it directly. Consequently, people fill their stories with words like *always* and *never,* which are always factually inaccurate and never literally correct. For example, consider what happens when someone makes an emotional request by saying to someone else, "You never do *x*" or "You always do *y*." The other person usually responds by saying, "I often do *x*" or "I don't always do *y*." But the first person's statement actually represents a request, as in: "I would like you to do more of *x*" or "I would like you to do less of *y*."

Beneath each of these assumptions and expectations lies still another assumption: that we must not become vulnerable or reveal to an opponent who we really are. This assumption is tied to expectations that becoming vulnerable will not help us get what we want, that we are not good enough, or that others will use our personal information in destructive ways.

Finally, there is what we call "the mother of all expectations"—that others will meet our needs and desires without being asked—that if we have to ask, it means that others do not love us enough. Most people, given the choice, would rather live with conflict than surrender the beauty of this expectation. As mediators peel back the layers of assumptions and expectations that the parties in conflict hold about themselves and each other, opportunities for strategic intervention automatically arise. Once we draw these hidden assumptions and expectations into the open and support or acknowledge the party who has revealed them, we can expand the opportunity for genuine self-reflection, and moments may appear in which it is possible for the parties to elicit positive feedback and empathy from their opponents.

For example, we mediated a dispute in which an employee referred several times to the "fact" that her manager thought she was incompetent. We asked why she made this assumption, and she said it was because he always criticized her work. We then asked her what she thought of her own work, and she said she knew she made mistakes but wanted to succeed and was trying hard. We asked what she thought her mistakes were, and she became extremely detailed and critical about her own performance. We asked if she assumed she was incompetent and was about to be fired, and she nodded and began to cry. Sensing a sympathetic response on the part of her manager based on her willingness to acknowledge her mistakes, we asked him to respond but did not cue him or point him in an empathetic direction. He said he thought she was actually quite competent but had such a poor self-image that he could not give her any feedback without getting a defensive response. We asked him to give some examples of things she had done competently, and as he listed several, she perked up and began listening in earnest. The manager's empathy and positive feedback allowed her to drop her twin assumptions—that she was a failure, and that he was out to get her—and together they were able to negotiate an improved relationship.

## Trading Power for Sympathy

The narrative structure of conflict stories is the framework on which storytellers hang their assumptions and expectations, arrange their metaphors, and set up their filters and lenses. The factual and interpretive content that makes up these conflict stories is expressed through and modified by their structure. As the mediator understands the narrative structure of a conflict story, its restructuring becomes possible, as do different outcomes. As mediators, we can learn a great deal by extrapolating from our own experiences. As we do so, we will stop thinking of ourselves as superior to people who are stuck in conflict and need our assistance, and we will improve our capacity for empathy.

To try this for yourself, stop and think of a story of your own and the way you usually tell it, a story about yourself and a conflict in which you were involved. Then ask yourself who in your story was the one who "did it" and who was the one "it" was "done to." If your conflict story is like most others, you were the innocent victim to whom "it" was done, and the other person was the evil or insensitive one who did "it" to you. If your story is typical, you probably constructed it in the form of a drama, casting yourself as powerless and depicting the other person as powerful. Whether or not you were actually powerless, consider what you gained by telling your story as if you were.

After years of listening to people tell stories about their conflicts, we have come to believe that this is one of the universal subtexts or metamessages: the storyteller is the recipient of unfair and unjust actions, more sinned against than sinning. In every conflict story we have heard, people position themselves as victims for one reason: to trade power for sympathy. Through their stories, they surrender their power in order to win a sympathetic response from their listener. They learn that the sympathy they receive increases in proportion to the other person's evil, which is measured partly by their own helplessness. Yet sympathy for them ebbs as their own responsibility for the conflict becomes more apparent, or as the story includes the other person's pain.

Thus people in conflict use stories to justify and defend themselves and to gain sympathy from others. As a result, they become locked in emotions that keep their conflicts going. They experience conflict as traumatic, shameful, anxiety producing, painful, and confusing, yet they are unable to tell stories that could heal their wounds. Instead, they nurture their negative emotions and remain locked in conflict. By positioning themselves as victims to whom the conflict is being "done," they reassure themselves that they are not as bad as they assume their opponents think they are. They tell themselves that all the nasty things the other party has said and done result from the other party's inherent callousness and cruelty, and the few nasty things that they themselves have said and done were only fair, given the cruel character and evil intentions of the other party. The more frequently they tell this story, the less they remember what actually happened. The less open they are to dialogue, the less able they are to empathize or communicate with the person on the other side. The less willing they are to take responsibility for what they themselves have contributed to the conflict, the less likely they are to find a way of successfully resolving it, and the more lost they are to the possibility of discovering something in their conflict that could release them from the impasse and from which they might learn something about themselves and others.

## The Princess, the Prince, and the Dragon

To understand the fundamental prototype of conflict stories more fully, we need to return to the fairy tales we learned when we were young in order to examine their narrative structure and the archetypes that reveal the hidden organization of conflict stories. Most often, these classic fairy tales have three main characters:

- The princess (as Snow White, Cinderella, Sleeping Beauty, an innocent child, a victim, a cute animal, or a damsel in distress)
- The dragon (as ogre, evildoer, perpetrator, demon, vicious animal, wicked stepmother, or degenerate witch)
- The prince (as hero, rescuer, knight in shining armor, fairy godmother, warrior, noble animal, leader, and all-around good guy)

Notice how these relationships interact, and that a triangle is formed by these roles. Notice also that this triangle perfectly describes the victim, the perpetrator, and the rescuer in every conflict

**Figure 1.2.  The Conflict Triangle.**

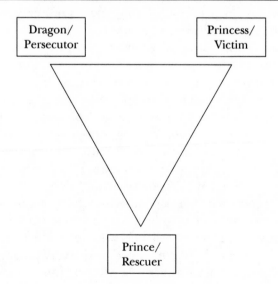

story. This triangle forms an extremely stable, self-perpetuating, self-fulfilling, logically unending, mutually satisfying story for all concerned, even the dragon. (This is shown in Figure 1.2.)

A fairy tale works only if all the roles are stereotyped—not so much in the familiar sense of gender, race, and class stereotyping (which are indeed present in these stories) but in the sense that stereotyping is a fundamental pattern in all conflict stories. In a fairy tale, the dragon personifies evil, the princess personifies beauty and helplessness in the presence of evil, and the prince personifies nobility and responsibility for solving problems. The only way a princess can meet her prince, or a prince his princess, is through the intervention of a powerful, evil, dangerous dragon. Not only must the dragon be powerful, the princess must be powerless by comparison. The only way the princess can attract the attention of the prince is by being helpless in the face of a peril that is beyond her capacity to handle by herself.

In all stereotyping, the essential pattern is the same: a single characteristic is selected, isolated, and exaggerated out of all proportion while other characteristics that reveal a complex nature are suppressed, as are individual variations. The whole is then collapsed and flattened into a one-dimensional representation of a complex person. A fraction of the person's nature becomes his or her sum total, and that is the purpose and goal of stereotyping: to make the Other both simple to understand and easy to fear and hate. Conflict stories have the same dual purpose: to make the other person simple and easy to understand while making them into the evildoer, the one who has "caused" the conflict and is, therefore, undeserving of sympathy or understanding.

It is extremely rare to hear people tell conflict stories in which they cast themselves as evil dragons. Most people play the role of prince only in stories that are no longer in progress. When people describe the events that have led to an active conflict, however, they immediately revert to the role of princess, in order to gain sympathy and justification for their own wrongdoing. For this reason, every conflict story is told by a princess. To gain sympathy from the listener, the storyteller has to become someone who is powerless and blameless in the face of evil, and who needs the listener's help in order to be rescued. This means that the very person who is a dragon in the first story turns into a princess in the second story, while the first princess turns into a dragon. Thus, princess and dragon are the flip sides of each other.

The dragon is simply an externalization of the power of the princess, a power she has to give up in order to find her prince. The dragon is also an externalization of all that is ignoble about the prince, an ignobility he must shed in order to attract the princess. In this way, the dragon is an elaborate masquerade, a conspiracy, a commonly told story agreed on by the prince and the princess. The more evil the dragon, the purer the princess and the nobler the prince. The impurity and evil of the dragon allow the prince and the princess to create themselves as pure and good and to make their relationship appear more romantic by raising the odds against it.

Who is really the dragon and who the princess is therefore a matter of perspective. It depends on who is telling the story and on each person's choice of roles. Each role summons forth its own form of audience approval: the princess is rewarded by the listener with sympathy and affection, the dragon with hostility and respectful fear, and the prince with fame and glory. As long as all three agree that they are different rather than one and the same, the princess will never be free of her inner dragon, which has been externalized to gain sympathy and throw the prince off the track. In fact, nearly all our dragons are internal. The ones that seem external are mostly imaginary, living only in stories told by princesses and princes. But the corollary is also true: the roles of princess and prince are also internal. In truth, all three roles are inside each of us.

## Freedom From Roles

Each of these characters performs a function and takes primary responsibility for it within the conflict. The princess is the one who is principally responsible for expressing feelings and being emotionally vulnerable. The prince is the one who is primarily responsible for coming up with solutions and overcoming evil. The dragon is the one who is fundamentally responsible for directing attention to problems that might otherwise remain unnoticed by two noble people who only want to live happily ever after.

What makes the dragon fierce, in this perspective, is the fact that the princess and the prince are living in denial. If the prince is the sole one responsible for discovering solutions, and if the princess is the only one responsible for expressing feelings, then the only option left for the dragon is to push the conflict into the open, where it can be resolved. The dragon is the one who makes change, learning, resolution, and transformation possible.

On this basis, we can draw a new, upside-down triangle to superimpose on the one shown in Figure 1.2. In this second triangle (see Figure 1.3), three lines separate the parties into their primary conflict-related responsibilities. This division allows us to substitute a positive, complex, internalized set of functions for the negative, stereotyped, externalized roles, shown in Figure 1.2.

Notice in passing that all the roles we traditionally consider positive conceal deep-seated weaknesses. The prince, in order to defend against and conquer the dragon, needs weaponry, armor, and a capacity for overcoming opposition. He cannot be vulnerable or express feelings. The princess needs purity and weakness, and she cannot express her strength or exercise responsibility for outcomes. These weaknesses will not serve either of them as they

## Figure 1.3. The Resolution Triangle.

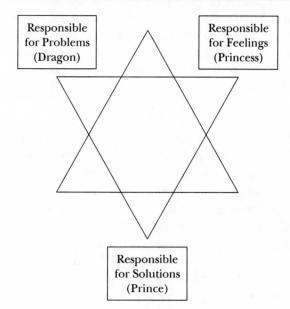

try to achieve familial bliss and live happily ever after. In fact, the sole binding element in their relationship is the dragon, who must continue breathing fire and creating mischief in order for their future happiness to be secure. All three need each other to play their respective roles so that they can find and hold on to their own, and this dynamic locks them in a perpetual cycle from which it is difficult to escape. They are unable to find their authentic selves, which lie beyond the roles they have assumed or have been forced to play. Each one becomes codependent and an enabler. Everyone is trapped.

To become free of her role, the princess must reclaim her power and become responsible for discovering solutions to her own problems. The prince, to become free, must express his feelings and accept that he is not perfect. And both must see the dragon as an expression of their own fear of transformation. The dragon must become open and vulnerable and also join in the search for solutions. All conflict stories, then, are incomplete because they do not acknowledge the pain and nobility of the dragon, the vulnerability and ignobility of the prince, or the responsibility and power of the princess.

Marina Warner writes in her brilliant study of fairy tales *From the Beast to the Blond* (p. 307):

> Beauty stands in need of the beast rather than vice versa. . . . Her need of him may be reprehensible, a moral flaw, or part of her carnal and materialistic nature; or, it can represent her understanding of love, her redemption. He . . . holds up a mirror to the forces of nature within her, which she is invited to accept and allows to grow.

To translate this idea into the idiom of conflict stories, the beast (dragon, opponent) is no longer seen as monstrous but as a reflection and a means of taming and transforming the monster within, the monster we all become when we are in conflict.

People in conflict need to recognize within themselves and to take responsibility for all three roles. They may slip back into these roles from time to time, but as they acknowledge their inner dragons, become aware that their inner princesses manipulate stories to gain sympathy, and recognize their inner princes' desire to rescue those who need to rescue themselves, they return to authenticity.

The three roles we have been describing, which appear in the guise of different people, are actually parts of ourselves that have been divided from our core selves, which are beyond roles. Across all cultures, the true story, as described by Joseph Campbell in *The Hero with a Thousand Faces,* is of conquering the dragon within, falling in love with the princess within, and becoming the hero within. This heroic journey is a metaphor for the journey we all take in discovering who we are. Each of us has the potential to play all three roles. We are all part princess, part prince, and part dragon. Real resolution comes when we reclaim all these roles and stories. Transformation comes when we transcend them.

## Reflections for Conflict Resolvers

One consequence of the division of conflict stories into these archetypal roles is that mediators can destabilize the story in three ways. First, we can refuse the role of prince, hero, or rescuer and ask the princess and the dragon to participate in a process that returns responsibility for solutions to them. Second, we can ask the princess how she thinks the dragon feels, what part of the conflict she is responsible for, or what options she can think of that could resolve the dispute. Third, we can ask the dragon to reveal itself as a princess or the princess to show her inner dragon. By encouraging each side to become vulnerable, we can move on to brainstorming options for resolving the dispute that allow all the parties to live happily ever after.

To move beyond the story, however, mediators also need to change. Many mediators enjoy playing the role of prince and hero—rescuing others, solving their problems, and helping them escape their conflicts—but in ways that can increase people's dependence on outside assistance and that do not make them independent or set them free. As long as there is conflict, princesses will appear who need to be rescued from evil dragons, making the role of prince or rescuer seductive for mediators. When we become the only ones in charge of saving people, we do them a disservice. The proper job of a prince is to convince the princess of her own strength, assist her in finding her own internal prince, and aid her in accepting the role of savior to herself.

By helping, we may assume that other people do not have the resources, skills, or inner personal strength to resolve their conflicts or to pull themselves out of quicksand. *Help* often implies that the one being helped is powerless or lacks something the helper has, making the one being helped needy and dependent. When this is the case, helpers easily become hinderers, reinforcing the parties' stories of victimization and demonization. We prefer the word *assist* because it includes the parties as active, responsible, engaged problem solvers, who can increase their skills and commitment to finding solutions aided by ideas and support from others.

As mediators, we can encourage the parties in a conflict to create a new story, one in which the prince is no longer a "helper" but instead becomes a teacher, coach, mentor, facilitator, empowering leader, and cheerleader, supporting both sides in learning about the conflict. When we make this shift, the princess is *automatically* encouraged to discover inner strength and power, and the dragon to discover feelings and inner beauty. Both are then able to own and correct their complementary dysfunctional behaviors.

As we increase our understanding of the hidden meanings of conflict stories, we can use this knowledge to alter the narrative structure of the stories we hear, in such a way as to encourage people to reach resolution of their conflicts. As we appreciate the context in which a story takes place, we can invent alternative contexts from which a different story can emerge. As we identify the metaphors of conflict, we can invert their meaning; for example, a metaphor of feeling trapped by a conflict can be neutralized if the mediator asks the parties whether they are willing to agree on solutions that free them from future problems.

We can separate facts from interpretations, and we can elicit alternative interpretations that do not rely for their meaning on other people's hostile intentions. We can observe the filters and lenses that people use to censor their stories or protect themselves against the stories of others, and we can create filters and lenses that increase their willingness to be deeply honest and empathic with each other.

We can distinguish the components and functions of stories, and we can use them to encourage the parties to accept responsibility for those parts of their stories that lead them into impasse. Finally, we can recognize in each story the archetypal roles of dragon, princess, and prince, and we can use our understanding of these roles to aid the parties in identifying and sharing responsibility for the conflict.

By using these analytical processes, instead of simply listening to stories as if they were straightforward factual accounts, we gain a much better understanding of what is being said and how it is being received. With this knowledge, we are better equipped to offer insights and ask revealing questions so that the parties can find their way to resolution and transformation. From simple understanding of stories, we can move beyond them, to transcendence.

# Chapter Two

# Transforming Stories to Resolve Conflict

*It was like that with stories: she could see beneath their surface, know the undercurrents, the whirlpools that could take you down, in a myriad of colors. Every time Trudi took a story and let it stream through her mind from beginning to end, it grew fuller, richer, feeding on her visions of those people the story belonged to until it left its bed like the river she loved. And it was then that she'd have to tell the story to someone.*

URSULA HEGI, *STONES FROM THE RIVER*

Stories are part of what make us uniquely human. We all tell stories, and we listen closely when they are told by others. In spite of stories' notorious lack of accuracy, the artistic flair with which they are shaped, and the subjective interests they serve, we are nearly always riveted, silenced, and transfixed by them.

People use conflict stories to justify their lives, rationalize their actions, convince themselves and others of the merits of their positions, and achieve victories over their opponents. As mediators, we have learned to appreciate the power of stories, their majesty and artistry, their enigmatic, paradoxical character, and their tendency to take on a life of their own. Our challenge is to find, create, and improve the tools, skills, methods, and strategies that help us use these stories to understand conflicts more deeply. As we do, we discover the hidden meanings and truths at the inner core of stories and conflicts alike. We encourage storytellers and listeners to reach beyond and beneath their stories to the living, authentic, core experiences that their external and internal conflict stories simultaneously recount and hide, diminish and magnify, alter and mimic.

## Stories and Transformation

In this chapter, we summarize our experience as mediators in using conflict stories to expose transformational possibilities, both for storytellers and for listeners. This process, to put it simply, consists of asking questions that probe beneath the external and internal stories, draw forth the core story, and reveal the authentic self.

When we speak of transformation, we are not referring to small incremental changes that unfold in a linear fashion, step by step, during the mediation process. Rather, we mean the sudden, dramatic, eye-opening, life-altering experiences people sometimes have when they come to grips with the real reasons for their conflict. Transformation, in our experience, means being led from the periphery to the center. It means returning people to the core of who they actually, authentically are.

Obviously, there are no magic wands or guarantees that what we do or say will produce a transformational change, nor should there be. Every decision regarding change belongs to the parties in conflict, not to mediators. Our role is to use honesty and empathy to show them the door, clarify what it could mean to walk through it, and support them in passing through it if they are ready.

We understand that there are risks for mediators in being deeply honest and empathetic, and in opening doors to transformational change. We know it is risky to approach the center of a dysfunctional system. Nevertheless, we urge you not to settle for settlement when transformation is possible.

## Truth and Falsity in Conflict Stories

In order to discover the transformational possibilities contained in conflict stories, we need to examine more closely the issue of their truth and falsity, which must be transcended for the parties to escape the hypnotic effect created by listening to their own stories. The classic fairy tale, described in the last chapter, begins with the words "Once upon a time . . ." and includes characters, times, and places that do not actually exist, and it is untrue. But because the morals, messages, and metaphors it communicates are accurate, even across countries, eons, cultures, generations, and personalities, it is also true. So are myths and fairy tales true or are they false?

The issue of truth or falsity takes on a different meaning in mediation. When people hear stories told about them by their opponents, they often respond, "That's not true!" And when their opponents hear stories told about them, they offer the same protest. Our experience is that no conflict story is either completely true or completely false. No one tells the truth, the whole truth, and nothing but the truth while embroiled in conflict. Indeed, it is impossible to do so, because no one is completely omniscient or empathic, and no one can come close to knowing the whole truth. The oath people take in court to tell the truth actually forces them to lie. Truth, in conflict, is always relative to one's role in it and to one's angle of perception. This does not mean objective truth does not exist, but that it cannot be determined by consensus. Moreover, mathematical and scientific truth rests on predictability, which requires uniformity, but no two conflicts or perceptions are sufficiently alike to allow for agreement, except in the most abstract terms.

As an aid in interpreting conflict stories, we offer the following ideas about truth and falsity, symbolism and meaning. These ideas, drawn from conflict stories to which we have listened, allow room for additional, even contradictory, truths, as well as for resolution and transformation. We hope these ideas will open a path for you to assist people in thinking about the veracity of their conflict stories and aid them in putting their individual truths in perspective.

- *It is impossible to tell a false lie.* Even a lie created from scratch has some truth to it because it was created by someone's subconscious mind, and nearly always for a reason. The symbolism of a story points us directly toward that reason. For example, if someone lies about how much money he has, he has told us the truth about his fear of losing it. He also may have told us the amount he actually does have, which has been reduced in direct proportion to the fear of its loss.

- *All stories and interpretations are symbolically or metaphorically true, and none is completely true in fact.* There are degrees and varieties of truth. All metaphors and symbols are true for the speaker, and sometimes for the listener as well, but in stories, as in life, two contradictory facts may both be true. Every observer experiences a different event relative to his or her angle of perception and may be unable to recognize a description based on someone else's experience. For half of the earth it is day while for the other half it is night. Which half is telling the truth?

- *If the meaning is believed, that belief makes it true, and the meaning is true to the extent that it is believed.* To put it another way, belief and truth, in a conflict story, are one and the same for both the storyteller and the listener. This does not mean that all stories of conflict are factually true, but that everyone tells their stories for reasons that are true for them.

- *The meaning of the story can be perceived and understood in the context of earlier, similar experiences that shaped it.* Childhood memories, expectations, and secrets powerfully shape the stories told in current conflicts. Often, unfortunately, the real truth of the story can be found only in incidents that are long past and forgotten.

- *A deeper level of meaning is revealed when the parties are asked, not whether a story is true, but what is true about it and why it is being told.* If we focus on what makes a story true for a particular person, we can discover her angle of perception. We can ask her to think about the story she is telling and why she is telling it. We can ask what she is trying to convince herself of by telling that particular story: her own innate goodness? Her lack of power or self-control? Her suffering? Her innocence? Her guilt? Why does she need this story? What role is it playing in her life?

- *The speaker may be telling the story to convince himself that it is true.* The storytelling process may satisfy his inner need to be convinced about a given configuration of events. The intensity, the passion, and the frequency with which he tells the story may reveal his internal questioning of the truth, and his need to state it over and over helps it take on the appearance of reality.

- *A deeper layer of meaning can be found when the storyteller is asked to whom the story is being told.* For example, if a parent tells a child a story about a princess who is put to sleep by an apple given to her by a wicked witch, the message may be "Obey the rules I have laid down about talking to strangers, or else you will be punished and lose my affection and protection." If the same story is told to a group of anthropologists, however, it may take on a cultural meaning that reflects the type of society that created the story.

- *It is possible to take two different stories about a conflict and create a synthesis, a third story, that is truer than either of the stories that led to it.* If we want to find ways of moving a conflict toward resolution, we can combine two people's stories into one, eliminating the parts of each story that demonize or make the other person wrong, as well as the parts that victimize the storyteller or strip the storyteller of all power to affect the outcome of events. The combined story will be truer than either of the original stories standing alone. We create a third story by turning judgments into curiosity and asking the listener why she acted as she did. In order to create this third story, we halt boundary violations, even subtle ones, and have the storyteller ask to be spoken to as a separate person, we help the storyteller describe defects as differences, and we build each party's capacity for empathy and compassion by asking questions that allow each one to reveal who he or she really is.

  All conflict stories come in pairs. We can think of each individual story as a search for its missing twin, and both stories as searches for the third story that will unite them. The story of the victim *requires* the story of the perpetrator in order to become whole. We need the stories that we dislike.

## From Stories to Authenticity

Stories play a dual role in conflict. On the one hand, they are the main method of attack used against a perceived adversary. On the other, they serve as a protective shield to justify and defend the speaker against counterattack. In their first role, they encourage insensitivity to others and disarm empathy and compassion in order to justify the attack. In their second role, they encourage defensiveness, prevarication, rationalization, and dishonesty, and they operate as a defense against authenticity and vulnerability.

Thus every conflict story is a weapon both of offense and of defense. It is a call to arms, a self-administered narcotic that numbs the speaker to the pain of potential counterattack. A story is a retreat from authenticity, yet it is a retreat that, in its structure, reveals deeper truths, provides access to vulnerable memories, and uncovers unconscious emotions, reactions, and needs.

We can look to other disciplines, such as psychotherapy and anthropology, for insights into the nature and uses of stories. Narrative therapy, for example, is an innovative and powerful form of psychotherapy in which the therapist works with the client's stories of past experiences. The therapist helps the client reconstruct his story in such a way as to solve the problems that brought him into therapy. Although the purposes and processes of mediation and conflict resolution are quite different from those of psychotherapy, there is no clear line that separates the two disciplines, and narrative therapy's approach to stories can be adapted, in some cases, for use in mediation. For example, consider narrative therapy's emphasis on helping clients tell stories about their present lives, stories that run counter to their stories about the past. Current stories of courage can reverse stories of cowardice based on past events, or stories about recent acts of independence may overcome older stories of dependence. Similarly, a mediator, by shifting attention from conflict stories about the past to concerns about the present, or to goals for the future, assists conflicting parties in overcoming the gravitational pull of the past and aids them in not being held hostage to their history. By bringing the parties' awareness into the present, the mediator expands their sense of what is possible and assists them in becoming more authentic to one another.

But there is a deeper problem. A story, by definition, is something that has been added to an experience; it is distinct from the experience itself. Stories are symbols, constructed in words, that represent real-life events and authentic experiences, but they can also be substituted for those events and experiences and may even, in a sense, become them. A conflict becomes confused, complicated, and intractable when a story about it is mistaken for the experience itself. In the language of Zen, "The sound of the rain needs no translation."

In our mediation practice, we have found, a conflict *invites* resolution once the people involved in it get in touch with deeper, more authentic truths about what actually happened and stop using stories to attack and defend one another. In this way, the parties take responsibility for their own experiences and come to see their stories as contrivances created to protect themselves from being vulnerable with one another. They can then recognize that in the process of creating their stories they have missed something valuable and unique. As they discover the real reasons for their stories, they learn how to resolve their disputes and transform their lives.

The challenge for the mediator is to assist the storyteller and the listener in recapturing the *actual* experience for which the story is a symbol. At our deepest, most authentic level, what we seek is not a story, or descriptions of battles and defenses, but rather the rage and fear that led to them. The deepest story is not one that recites the facts about a betrayal; it is one that expresses a desire for intimacy with the betrayer and reveals the love that fuels this desire. This core story may be a story about mistaken expectations on the part of the storyteller or about a series of minor, mutual betrayals that no one noticed. It may even be a story about an inner need to be betrayed, or about subconscious knowledge or intuitive recognition that there would one day be a story of betrayal.

A mediator can assist conflicted parties in returning to authenticity by asking questions about their stories that take them back to what happened before the story was created. The mediator may ask them to reflect on what they have learned as a result of what happened in the past, what their lives are like now, what price they are paying for their conflict, or what kind of relationship they would like to have in the future. The mediator may reframe the storytellers' projections and externalizations or encourage introspection and vulnerability. In short, the mediator can use stories without buying into them and can move the parties from stories about one another to authentic encounters with themselves.

It is crucial that the mediator begin by validating the stories as well as the storytellers. People who are stuck in adversarial stories benefit from delivering full and satisfying descriptions of what they have experienced, as well as from watching the mediator encourage and model a deeper level of listening than it is possible for them to give one another in the midst of their conflict. Only after a story has been fully told, heard, and acknowledged by the mediator (and, whenever possible, by the other side) does it become feasible for the parties to move beyond it. The mediator can then uncover the subtexts and hidden meanings contained in the story. In the process that follows, the mediator assists the parties in framing and telling their stories so as to encourage them to listen to one another. The mediator works with both sides to expand the range of possible outcomes imagined in their stories, to reveal their deeper interests, and to synthesize their different versions to include the essential elements of both.

## Altering the Narrative Structure of Conflict Stories

Turning stories of conflict into stories of transformation means altering the stories' narrative structure. This kind of alteration requires the mediator to perform an extremely delicate operation: one wrong step, and either party may assume that the mediator has taken sides. For this reason, it is useful for the mediator to begin by acknowledging and summarizing what is true in each party's story, leaving out the parts that, on the basis of empathy, might be objectionable to either side.

There are many techniques we can use to shift the narrative structure of a conflict story while not changing any of its essential facts or making it into our own story. For the most part, we elicit these alterations through questions, directed either to the storyteller or to the listener, that adduce information, which is then added to the story, or that alter the parties' perspectives in such a way as to compel the story's redesign.

We can indirectly and subtly encourage the parties to reconfigure the background elements that reflect the most intransigent, intolerant aspects of their tales, without changing any of the basic facts. For example, we can ask each party to write out his or her story of the conflict, without analysis, simply letting it flow, and after they do so, we can assist them in analyzing their stories, either in joint or separate sessions. We can ask the parties to try to tell their stories from the other person's point of view. Then we can pose a series of questions: Would the other party agree with this story? If not, why not? What story would the other party tell? What would the other party say had happened? What reasons would the other party give for what he or she did? What may have been the other party's motivation? We can ask each party what differences he or she sees between the two stories, and why these differences exist.

We can ask them what lenses may be distorting the meaning of their stories. We can request each of them, if possible, to tell his or her story again but combine it this time with the other story in such a way as to make both stories true, leaving out who is right and who is wrong and omitting any demonizations and victimizations that have been inserted to gain sympathy or support. We can ask the parties how their stories would change if they shared some common concern. We can ask how their stories would be different if they had been able to talk through their issues together from the beginning, and if it would be possible for them to tell a story in which their differences were fully resolved.

We can ask them to try to write an integrated story that ends in resolution, using the words "and they lived happily ever after," and we can ask them to read these stories to each other. We can ask them if there was ever a time when their relationship or communication worked, and, if so, to tell a story about that time. With divorcing couples, it is sometimes useful, and always highly risky, for a mediator to ask each of them to tell the story of how they met. As they tell their stories, they automatically return to a time when their relationship worked and begin to express grief at the loss they are experiencing. As they express their grief, they cease fighting and may realize they have kept the conflict alive as a way of holding on to their relationship, through a process we call *negative intimacy.*

We can encourage the parties to redefine the problem so that it shifts from being about "you" to being about "me" and then to being about "it." This redefinition can take place through reframing, by suggesting an alternative way of making a statement. For example, we can rephrase "You are harassing me" to "I feel harassed when you criticize me" or "When you criticize me without also mentioning what I am doing right, it makes me feel bad, and I respond defensively." The incident and the concern are the same, but the orientation and the speakers' responsibilities are entirely different.

We can ask the parties to repeat their stories after an interval of time and notice the subtle ways in which their stories have shifted in terms of facts, feelings, interpretation, and emphasis.

By charting these changes, we can monitor the barometric pressure of the story as it moves in the direction of resolution and transformation, or back toward impasse and escalation. As one set of interpretations changes, others become possible. This process may trigger a *repetitio ad absurdum,* in which the storyteller, exhausted by repeating the same old story, becomes ready to move on. We can even decide to take a big risk, and—carefully, politely, and privately—encourage them to cut the crap, drop the act, let go of the mask, lose the dramatics, and stop being so focused on playing the victim. Obviously, this approach requires a high degree of trust and empathy. We can facilitate this process by using a technique we call *overstating,* in which the effect described in the story, already heavily saturated with a certain meaning, becomes supersaturated and untenable as the mediator escalates the description, in search of a denial. For example, when people say, "You don't love me anymore," they are requesting a denial; if they tell a story in which they exaggerate being afraid, the mediator can ask if they were petrified or scared to death. This technique gives them permission to back away from an interpretation that is too dramatic to be real.

To uncover the hidden contexts that give a story its meaning and to reveal the implicit cultural assumptions that are constructing and sustaining the conflict, we can ask a different set of questions: "What was the context in which this happened?" "Why did you think or feel that way?" "What did you expect would happen?" "What would you have wanted him to do or say?" "What do people who belong to your culture usually do when this happens?" We can then ask the parties to compare their cultural experiences.

We can suggest what we call a *contrary interpretation* of a story. For example, when someone describes his or her pain, the mediator can respond, "You must care a lot to be in so much pain." Or when a storyteller says, "His anger scared me," we can respond, "It was very brave of you to stay with him when he was so angry." Bruce Rybarczyk, an assistant professor at Rush Medical College in Chicago, asked 226 patients undergoing major surgery or chemotherapy to tell him a heroic story about the challenges they had already faced in their lives that mirrored back their own heroism. He found that storytelling reduced these patients' anxiety and stress and increased their ability to cope. We can also respond with what we call a *coun-*

*terintuitive interpretation*—for example by saying "Good! What did you learn from being afraid?"

We can identify the moral structure of the story, the "should" and "should not" messages, and the judgments of self and others that are concealed in it. In mediation, every judgment is an externalization, a personalization of a problem, and a defense against empathy and compassion. Judgments give people permission to stop asking questions, to quit caring enough to become curious about what makes their opponents do the things that bother them.

We can map the evolution of the conflict by reconstructing in detail—perhaps on a flip chart, step by step—how the parties got into their current mess, and we can work with them to critique, improve, and simplify the steps, leading them toward resolution. Or again, in a process we call *correcting the conflict,* we can ask the parties to identify in detail where they went wrong, and jointly brainstorm detailed plans for how they will handle future disputes without conflict. This process creates a sense of awareness and optimism as the parties realize that there are other, more successful stories than the ones they have been telling.

We can contrast each conflict story with one told by the other side, to locate significant differences. Stories can be contrasted with the culture of an organization in which they are being told. Stories can also be contrasted with the parties' future goals for their relationship. These contrasts will encourage analysis, reveal small successes, and build an audience for a new story about their relationship.

We can ask the parties to actively investigate whether the assumptions on which their stories are based are true. Questioning their assumptions can assist them in reversing narratives of victimization and powerlessness and in creating a basis for future cooperative problem solving. We can ask each of them to conduct an investigation first on his or her own behalf and then on behalf of the other party. For example, each of them can find out from independent witnesses whether the other person actually said or did something he or she denies, or, during the mediation session, they can ask each other directly what their real motives are.

We can ask the parties what they think of their own stories. Can they identify the gaps? What did they leave out that the other party added? Why did they leave it out? Are they aware of the ways in which their stories disempower and isolate them or lock them into conflict? Are they able to see the hidden opposites in what they have described—the wish within the fear, the hope within the cynicism, the caring within the angry outburst?

We can reveal the assumptions about causation that are concealed in their stories. Every conflict story contains a set of built-in ideas about what or who has caused the problem. Parties often assume:

- The other person did it (and he or she is to blame).
- Some third person did it (and we can agree to blame him because he is not here to defend himself).
- Everyone is to blame.
- It was fate or karma or divine will (and the world or God is to blame).
- I did it to myself because I am a bad person (I am to blame).
- It just happened (and no one is to blame).

Once the parties have questioned these causal attributions, two transformational possibilities emerge:

- It is not about blame but about our need to improve our skills and take responsibility for what we have done, which I will begin doing immediately and will support you in doing as well.
- We have joint responsibility for correcting the systems and processes we have used to relate and communicate with one another.

We can encourage the parties to focus on the socially constructed meanings of their stories. We can encourage them to join forces in trying to change the systems, processes, and conditions that have triggered or fed their conflict, including hierarchical organizational cultures that pit them against each other; gender inequalities, which encourage incidents of sexual harassment; and the absence of social support for single parents, which fuels divorces. This means mediating along two tracks simultaneously. The first track requires us to address the individual human beings who are actually before us. The second track requires us to examine the *field* of their conflict by way of its components; much as an elementary particle, such as an electron, is a manifestation of an electromagnetic field.

Mediating a field means discovering what we call *ghost roles,* which are played by people and forces that have an impact on the conflict but are not explicit or visible in the mediation. These ghosts may include organizational policies or culture, socio-economic conditions, deceased relatives, or other people who have been damaged by the conflict. Switching roles, acting out, acknowledging, and mapping can be helpful in identifying the field that has influenced how the parties have behaved, and they can aid in releasing the parties from the grip of this field.

The object of these interventions is to support the parties in identifying for themselves the elements of their conflict stories that have kept their conflict firmly in place. Mediators can assist the parties in collaboratively unraveling and reweaving their stories. We, then, can *align* opposing conflict stories before moving on to create a third story, in which they are amalgamated and merged. In the process, we allow the parties to turn their stories into strategies for successful resolution and transformation.

## Subtexts and Metameanings

The narrative structure of every conflict story is replete with subtexts and metameanings, whose symbolic messages and unspoken contents are communicated along with the facts of the story. Each conflict story speaks to our nonrational, emotional, fantasy minds. If we want to go beyond its factual or explicit meaning to discover its metaphoric or implicit meaning, we need to pay careful attention to its subtexts and metameanings. Yet these are rarely apparent, either to the parties in conflict or to the mediator.

People in conflict hear the words of their opponents' stories but are defended against or oblivious to the deeper meanings. If we, as mediators, float on the surface of these stories, we may settle disputes but deny access to resolution and transformation. The deeper the parties can go in exploring the subtexts and metameanings of their stories, the greater their potential to shift both their conflict and their lives. As conflict resolvers, we can actively encourage them to read the subtexts of their stories and perceive their stories' metameanings.

The most important part of any communication lies not in what is said but in what is meant. The same communication may have different, even opposite, meanings for different people. Therefore, it is extremely important to discover what a storyteller actually means, her intention, and how her meaning has been heard and interpreted by the listener. Because the meaning of a conflict story evolves over time and is never completely frozen, it is useful to regard meaning as fluid rather than static.

Intention in a conflict story is communicated both actively, through choice of words and tone of voice, and passively, through unconscious body language and facial expressions. The form of a communication often produces meaning more accurately than the words that are being used. Consider yelling angrily at someone and pointing at her aggressively while saying, "I like you very much!" Which message is likely to be believed?

If there is ambiguity or inconsistency between text and subtext, surface meaning and metameaning, intention and impact, then there will be confusion and distrust on the part of the listener. The more room there is for interpretation, the greater the opportunity for a conflict to get blown out of proportion. When a story is incongruent because of a gap between the storyteller's meaning and the listener's interpretation, the story becomes a verbal expression of the deeper misunderstanding between the parties.

Recall that in Chapter One we distinguished external stories told for public consumption from internal stories told to protect the ego and core stories, which reflect the reasons why it was necessary to invent the first two stories. Although these stories are related, gaps and inconsistencies between and among them can make them appear incongruent to someone who is listening for their deeper meaning.

Each story reflects a different goal. The first goal of a storyteller is to establish a relationship with the listener based on the story's meaning. A second, less obvious goal is for the storyteller to maintain a self-image, a relationship with his or her ego, and a defense against guilt and shame. A third goal, deeper and almost beyond the realm of goals, is simply for the storyteller to be *authentic*—to manifest who he or she is, was before the story began, and will be after the conflict is over.

Together, the external, internal, and core stories form a system for the storyteller, one that defines the conflict story. The character of this system is both emotional and logical. The same story can be interpreted differently according to the emotional states of the storyteller and the listener, in response to different levels of feeling at the time the story is told or heard. The meaning of any conflict story is therefore relative and composite. It depends not only on the state of mind and emotions of the storyteller but on those of the listener as well.

In addition, as mediators, we have to analyze each story we encounter for its meaning in relation to the cultures of both speaker and listener. Every culture creates its own set of meanings, which are based on the unique metaphors, symbols, archetypes, myths, parables, and rituals that convey them. These meanings are most often communicated indirectly, without being spoken. Culture twists meaning and generates conflict even on a small scale, as we see in the very different meanings attributed to events by older and younger siblings in the same family. The same problems arise between urban and rural people, between men and women with different expectations, and between organizations that are more and less hierarchical. If we consider culture in its broadest sense, every conflict can be regarded as a clash between cultures based on uncommunicated meanings.

When we pay close attention to cultural metaphors, symbols, archetypes, myths, parables, and rituals in conflict stories, we see how they are used to invest ambiguity with meaning. The meanings they are assigned are clues to the storyteller's core story. They are secret markings, breadcrumbs along a trail leading into the labyrinth of the self. Many metaphors, symbols, archetypes, myths, parables, and rituals create possibilities of unity, even when their meanings diverge. Many are common across diverse cultures or have a common denominator in human experience. They can be interpreted to reveal a story's hidden, symbolic meaning.

Consider, for example, a typical petty domestic dispute over how important it is to be on time when meeting friends or whether it is acceptable to be fifteen minutes late. Major blowups occur over this issue, in spite of its apparent triviality, yet it is precisely the lack of congruence between apparent and real importance that tells us that something deeper is going on. If the argument remains at the level of who is right and who is wrong, then this deeper significance will be missed.

In mediation, we might ask each member of the couple to say what it feels like, or what it means, to be late or on time. We may be told that being late "feels like we are letting them down" or that it means "we are important enough to be able to arrive when we want to." Now we can start to see the deeper issues, which have nothing to do with the superficial ones. The deeper issues are connected to an internal need for approval and self-esteem, as well as to cultural patterns and expectations about time that originated in each party's family of origin. For resolution to take place, the parties not only have to pay attention to their surface conflict, which could be settled in a matter of moments, but also to the different cultural meanings that each of them brings to their communication. All words, especially metaphors and symbols, have profound emotional meanings. Because these become more powerful when they are not revealed, communication of metameanings becomes essential to the resolution of conflict.

An example of the layers of meaning that are hidden in every conflict story can be found by taking any insult or accusation and examining its external, internal, and core forms. The external form is an *accusation* or insult, but beneath that lies a *confession*, and beneath that lies a *request*. For example, if the issue is one of work ethics, the accusation is "You are lazy," the confession is "I am working hard and am jealous that you get to take time off," and the request is "Please give me a hand. I could use your help." Mediators can assist parties in turning their accusations into "I statements" or confessions or, more significantly, their "you statements" into "we statements" or requests. Doing so moves the parties from hostility to responsibility to relationship.

There is both benefit and danger in revealing the hidden meanings of a conflict story. The danger is that a person risks becoming vulnerable by revealing inner meanings to another; the benefit is that the other person may do the same in return. A transformation then becomes possible, both in the relationship, which may deepen and grow stronger, and in the parties themselves, who open up, reveal who they really are, and become more authentic. The true, hidden meaning of every conflict story is contained in this possibility of improved relationship and personal transformation. Here is where we find the real storybook ending, one that completes the conflict and leads the parties to a place of resolution. It is here that the meanings of events shift and that conflict disappears. When the parties learn how to bring this transformation about in all their conflicts, they actually begin to live, if not happily, at least *more* happily ever after.

## Putting the Story into Perspective

External stories are used by conflicting parties to *inflate* their conflicts and make them appear more significant, profound, sweeping, and dramatic than they actually are. Internal stories also inflate conflicts, thereby justifying avoidance, accommodation, and aggression as responses to perceived hostility. As a result, conflicts are blown out of proportion and appear harder to resolve than they really are, which inflates them even more.

Storytelling can also be used to *deflate* conflicts and to help people gain perspective on their problems and recognize the molehills they have disguised as mountains. Storytelling can be used to recalibrate problems so that the parties can focus not only on their disagreements but also on what they have in common.

Psychologist Ira Progoff tells a story about a rabbi talking with two families in conflict. The rabbi, after hearing each family describe the other in the worst possible terms, commented on how interesting he found their stories. As he was listening, he told them, he could not help thinking about the situation of the Children of Israel when they were in bondage in the land of Egypt. The rabbi described, in detail, their many conflicts with the pharaoh, their Egyptian taskmasters, and each other. When he finished, the families thanked him for having solved their problem, shook hands, wished each other well, and left, content with the way their dispute had been settled. What had happened? The rabbi, by describing far more serious conflicts faced by the parties' common ancestors, put their petty stories into a larger perspective. The two families realized that their disputes were minor by comparison with what they had in common.

All cultures contain a rich heritage of conflict stories, most of which involve the triumph of good over evil, but many of which also point to honest introspection, respect for differences, collaborative partnership, and mutual gain. Our dominant media culture, however, celebrates individual violence over dialogue and joint problem solving. Even our ideas of resolution are more solitary than collective, more competitive than cooperative, more about victory than about mutual gain. But the path we actually follow in conflict resolution and personal transformation rarely involves the clear-cut triumph of goodness and truth over evil and falsehood. Instead, conflict resolution and personal transformation require all parties to be willing to listen and respect their own and each other's integrity, ideas, perspectives, and experiences. The real victory over evil and falsehood takes place inside us. When we understand this, we can see that our refusal to dehumanize our enemies allows us to create a new story about our lives, a story based on a larger, truly heroic, transformational understanding. When we focus on our own internal struggles, we realize that we do not need someone else to lose or be bad in order for us to triumph and be good. A greater victory is achieved when it results in no one's defeat.

## Adam and Eve: A Story of Primal Conflict

Let's look more closely at a simple story of conflict, one seen by many as the first conflict: the story of Adam and Eve in the Garden of Eden. Because this powerful story is so widely known, we have taken the liberty of using it here to learn more about how conflict stories are experienced in our culture. As we hope you will see, the stories told by Adam and Eve are repeated in miniature every day in countless conflicts. Reflection on the story of Adam and Eve, with its strong associations, offers a unique opportunity to apply some of the methods for understanding the unspoken assumptions hidden in the conflict stories we hear as mediators.

In the standard King James version of Genesis, God asks Adam, "Hast thou eaten of the fruit of the tree whereof I told thee thou shouldst not eat?" Adam replies, "The woman You gave me, she tempted me and I did eat." God then propounds the same question to Eve, who answers, "The serpent, he beguiled me."

If Adam and Eve lived today, their ensuing dialogue might sound something like this:

*Adam:* This is all your fault, Eve. Why should I suffer for your mistakes? You're the one who's to blame, you and that damn snake. You tricked me.

*Eve:* There you go again, blaming someone else for your own mistakes. You chose, didn't you? I didn't force you to eat it. Besides, you never warned me about the snake.

*Adam:* You never think. You're too emotional and impulsive. And you're too gullible.

*Eve:* Well, you never pay any attention to me, and then, when something happens, you refuse to take responsibility for your own mistakes.

*Adam:* My biggest mistake was listening to you.

*Eve:* Go to hell.

The problem with each of these stories is that both sides are trying to blame the other for what happened instead of accepting responsibility for their own choices. At this moment, they have already departed from Eden: each of them knows once the apple has been eaten that the behavior of the other was either right or wrong, good or evil.

Yet, it is possible to read a number of different interpretations into this story. For example, it is possible to conclude that this story is as much about blaming others for our actions as it is about eating forbidden fruit. Adam tries to shift the blame both to Eve and to God when he states that the fault lies with the woman "God gave" him.

Another alternative would have been for either or both of them to take responsibility for their actions and say: "It was my temptation; I was the one who gave in. It was my choice, and I accept full responsibility for my actions." Along with knowledge and ignorance, however, comes cynicism, and with good and evil comes amorality. Denial of responsibility and blaming others go hand in hand. We can see that what characterizes the Fall is not merely eating the fruit but also the refusal to take responsibility and the casting of blame on one another.

It is also possible to conclude that Adam and Eve were set up. An omniscient, all-seeing Creator must have known in advance that the only prohibition in the Garden would certainly be violated. Why else have a "tree of knowledge," if the fruit was not to be ingested? Why create a being endowed with curiosity, if not to encourage discovery? Why forbid the eating of the fruit, if not to focus temptation in its direction?

Had Adam and Eve studied conflict resolution, either or both of them might have created an altogether different story, on which they both might have agreed. Either one might have said:

> God didn't warn us about the snake or about the desire He placed within us to taste forbidden fruit, but there's no sense in blaming God, the snake, each other, or ourselves for what happened. Instead of focusing on the past and blaming each other, we should concentrate on the future and how we can work in harmony to get what we both want. We can't make God responsible for our actions. We need to be responsible for ourselves. I apologize for trying to shift the blame onto you, and for being dishonest and feeling guilty about something that is not anyone's fault. A little knowledge can be a dangerous thing, and the more I learn about good and evil, the more I realize that they start with how we treat each other, and the kinder we are to each other, the closer we get to Eden. Want another bite of apple?

If we look beyond the text of this story to its subtext, and to the hidden metameanings it contains, several themes emerge. It is useful to reexamine these themes as a way of demonstrating that it is possible to create a number of very different conflict stories from the same set of facts.

In one interpretation, there is an abundance of sexual imagery and meaning, from the snake to the forbidden fruit to "temptation" and the symbolically incestuous brother-sister, husband-wife relationship between Eve and Adam. Translated into sexual terms, the story can be told as follows:

> Eve, unable to resist her attraction to the externalized symbol of Adam's sexuality (the snake), and beguiled by lust, tasted the forbidden fruit of incestuous desire, with which she tempted Adam, who also succumbed.

The story can also be read as a projection based on men's claim to objectivity, or as a response to their fear of women's sensuality. In these terms, the story has a different meaning:

> Adam, disturbed by his attraction to Eve and by his fear of her sensuality, divided the world into good and evil and created this story in order to blame her for his own contradictory feelings and justify assigning her unequal status in the world.

A third set of meanings can be seen in the story's symbolism of intellectual awakening, of discovery and knowledge of the world. It is less about knowledge of good and evil than about knowledge of the contradiction, polarity, and opposition between them, which symbolizes other oppositions (such as, between life and death, objective and subjective, rich and poor, powerful and powerless, true and false) and the rise of civilizations based on these divergent realities:

> The condition of Adam and Eve in the Garden of Eden is a symbol representing a unity that preceded the separation of polar opposites, a unity that is now lost or forgotten. Adam's response reflects his discovery of the difference between objective and subjective truth (a difference that forms the basis of science) and social inequality (a distinction that forms the basis of political and economic power).

A fourth set of meanings can be drawn from the punishment meted out to Adam and Eve: their expulsion from paradise. Their exile can be seen as symbolizing the rise of war, despotic governments, slavery, social regulation, and, with them, genocide, corruption, crime, the breaking of rules, and the social need for punishment:

> Expulsion from the garden symbolizes the fall of consensus and the rise of punitive, coercive, military governments, which supplanted a more egalitarian communal civil society. Adam's attempt to blame Eve is symbolic of the blaming of other peoples, civilizations, and cultures and the rise of patriarchy, slavery, and warfare.

As a fifth possibility, the story of the Fall can be seen as symbolizing the journey each child must make from accepting parental guidance and the inherent goodness of people to discovering the nature of good and evil and the limitations of human behavior:

> Eating the forbidden fruit from the tree of knowledge is a parable of lost innocence and individuation, in which Adam and Eve grow up and see each other as flawed.

Other interpretations have also been suggested: the fall from natural grace and abundance occasioned by the coming of the Ice Age, the beginnings of an adversarial rather than collaborative attitude toward nature, the rise of conflict as a result of tribal warfare, the fall of matriarchy, the economic divisions and separation into haves and have-nots that arose with private property, and a host of others.

For our purposes, it can be seen that every interpretation contains some truth and contributes some extra meaning that extends beyond the literal text. We could continue for some time to add meanings to those we have mentioned, without exhausting the possibilities. What is important for mediators to recognize is that every one of these interpretations is *metaphorically* true and cannot be conclusively proved or disproved, and that each possible story adds something to the richness of the original.

We can say the same about any conflict story. Each one carries the same multitude of possible interpretations; each interpretation adds to the difficulty of finding a single correct answer; and each version leads to the discovery of complex hidden meanings. In every story we encounter, our challenge and opportunity as conflict resolvers is to elicit multiple interpretations, a variety of formulations, and different sets of meanings.

Here is where we can use our capacity for creativity and our ability to see through literal definitions to symbolic meanings. We can separate facts from interpretations, brainstorm alternative interpretations for the same facts, and ask the parties to suggest contrasting or even contradictory interpretations. The storyteller, seeing that the same story can be interpreted in a number of different ways, can avoid getting locked into a specific meaning or stuck in rigid, isolating, superficial truths. Our role as mediators is to work with a story, poke it, get behind it and into it, find the truths buried inside it, and lead the parties to their third story.

## The Magic of the Third Story

When we encourage a deeper examination of the parties' stories, we spark both a sense of anticipation and momentum in the direction of resolution. The simple narration of events, without demonization or victimization, can alone generate a willingness to listen, a feeling of empathy or community with the storyteller, and a sense of participation in the events on the part of those who are merely listening.

Storytelling can also create an *expectation* of resolution, which takes place when each party discovers that their opponent is not evil, but is merely caught up in a story of good and evil. In fairy tales, as we have seen, resolution occurs when the dragon is finally vanquished. But it can also come about when the dragon is discovered to be, in reality, a princess or a prince. It can occur when the princess reclaims her dragonlike power, and it can come when the prince makes everyone into a prince, responsible for achieving resolution. It happens when Adam and Eve and the snake decide to stop blaming each other and return to the tree of knowledge for a few more bites of the apple.

The transformation story is one of awakening to the opportunity presented by the conflict. When the frog is changed into a prince, or the princess is awakened by a kiss, or the grandmother is discovered to be a wolf, or the child becomes a hero, we discover the presence of a secret within, the secret of the illusion of appearances, and the ever-present possibility of transformation.

The mediator, by drawing opposing conflict stories together and crafting a third, combined story that tells a deeper truth, *automatically* encourages the empathy and introspection that are elicited through storytelling and turns the conflict toward resolution and transformation. The third story can be found through the use of active and empathic listening skills; through summarizing, questioning, and reframing; and through the conscious use of parable, ritual, symbolism, metaphor, and ceremony. All of these methods merge the parties' stories into a single, agreed-on story that ends in resolution and transforms the parties' conflicted relationship.

Indeed, it is possible to define conflict resolution as the successful creation of a composite story, one that is made up of the essential elements contained in each party's version of what happened and is accepted by both sides. All demonization and victimization are excised from this third story, and a synthesis gradually emerges. This new story is richer, more detailed, fairer, and truer than either of the individual stories standing alone. Nevertheless, we need to be careful, as mediators, not to create the third story ourselves and impose it on the parties in order to force a resolution. The third story will emerge, as if by magic, from the process of taking apart and interpreting the original stories. We can clear the path and ask the right questions, but the parties need to discover and affirm the third story for themselves. They are the ones who have to recognize its greater truth.

Assisting conflicted parties in understanding each other's stories encourages them to accept the other's story as a *gift* that adds credence to their own story. Whenever we encourage honesty and empathic listening, find the deeper meaning of conflict, and develop ways of bonding or connecting people across the abyss created by their conflict, a unified version of what happened starts to appear. Our goal as conflict resolvers is to expand our capacity for honesty and empathy so that we can respond skillfully to the stories we are told. As we do so, we encourage the parties to listen to one another and to themselves and, in the process, reveal their own core stories. As they do, they may discover a shared understanding that allows them to end the conflict, achieve forgiveness, and experience a transformation in their lives. They will then begin to tell a different story—a story of how they overcame their difficulties and worked together to create a common story, and in the process began to live happily ever after.

# Chapter Three

# Stories Unheard and Untold

> Words do not label things already there.
> Words are like the knife of the carver.
> They free the idea, the thing, from the general
> formlessness of the outside.
> As a man speaks, not only is his language in a state of birth,
> but also the very thing about which he is talking.
> ANONYMOUS ESKIMO CARVER

As we recall the many individuals, couples, families, organizations, and communities we have seen over the years and assisted in freeing from conflict, it is not difficult to identify a cardinal element that kept them at impasse: in every conflict we have mediated, nearly everyone has felt unheard, that no one ever really listened.

Although people described what had happened to them, often telling their stories repeatedly and to everyone within hearing, almost none had told their stories to the people who most needed to hear them, the ones their stories were about, their opponents, adversaries, dragons, and snakes. In failing to do so, they unconsciously locked themselves in a *relational silence*. If they told their stories repeatedly yet remained unsatisfied, it was because they were speaking to the wrong listeners. In most cases, they were too frightened or anxious to share their stories with their antagonists or did not want to sully their beautiful stories by exposing them to the implicit criticism of different, possibly contradictory stories. As a result, they did not feel listened to by the right people, in the right way. The sympathy and support they received from friends for being the innocent victims of other people's cruelty was not enough. When people feel genuinely heard and deeply understood, they stop telling the same stories.

These relational silences always appear completely reasonable and justifiable. They are rationalized by the other person's history of cruel or insensitive behavior, which offers little reason for risking further cruelty. They also seem reasonable because both sides are at least subconsciously aware of their own failure to listen to the other side's story, and for this reason each party logically assumes that the other will not listen.

As a consequence, both parties bury their stories in secret places. They become unable or unwilling to reveal their inner truths to each other. They hide their truths deep inside and become unable to understand the core meaning of their conflict stories themselves. Most know intuitively that they will not feel satisfied or listened to until they sit down with the other person—not only to be listened to but also to listen empathetically themselves. They subconsciously know they will not reach true resolution until they become willing to accept and acknowledge the legitimacy of the inner meanings hidden in one another's stories. This implicit knowledge is what brings them to mediation.

As they begin telling their stories to each other, they mostly hear accusations, blaming, recriminations, censure, indictments, victimizations, and denunciations. These do little to encourage the listener to risk being deeply honest, empathetic, or vulnerable. Without a third-party conflict resolver to encourage them to get past superficial, external stories of demonization and victimization and internal stories of fear and reluctance, they can easily turn away from honesty, empathy, and vulnerability. They can retreat to the safety of their own external and internal dialogues and never reach their core stories.

Those who keep their core stories bottled up often do so out of fear of retribution, reprisal, or retaliation. They fear that their stories are too painful, either for themselves or their opponents. Each one is convinced that telling his or her story to the other person will be pointless or will only make the conflict worse. In this way, conflicting parties enter into subtle *conspiracies of silence* with one another. They reach unspoken agreements to keep their stories superficial so that they will not have to face their fear of being vulnerable or empathetic or honest.

Most often, their fear is a projection of their own feelings of rage or hostility toward their adversaries. Or they may reflect power imbalances, which mediators can work to correct. They may worry that if they tell the horrible tales they have been hiding, they will experience retaliation or hardship and pay a hefty price; what else can explain the price they have already paid by keeping their stories bottled up inside?

The true price of silence is isolation and stagnation. The price of suppression is the loss of democracy and the connection with the inner self. The price of not engaging in dialogue is the death of relationship. As Oscar Wilde said, "A man whose desire is to be something separate from himself . . . invariably succeeds in being what he wants to be. That is his punishment. Those who want a mask have to wear it."

## Authentic Communication

Conflicts are escalated and inflated not only by what is said but by what is buried in silence and is *not* said. Stories of conflict, told by adversaries to each other, not only create something new, they also reveal something that was already there. In our mediation practice, we often find that both parties know on some deep level what needs to be said and has not yet been spoken. When it is finally said, there is a profound feeling of relief, of being released from the conflict.

Yet the news is not always good, and the messages in conflict stories are rarely welcome. Our role as conflict resolvers is not merely to air these stories but also to design and facilitate a process that has the potential to free both the storyteller and the listener from the bonds that confine them and keep them trapped in the story. For many people in conflict, simply telling their stories to each other is not enough to bring about a resolution.

The purpose of storytelling is to jump-start the process of resolution by opening the dialogue, deepening the communication, and engaging the differences between their stories and self-interests. It is to increase the parties' empathy and vulnerability in each other's presence and encourage them to acknowledge the emotions and subjective perceptions that led to their conflict. We do this so that their stories can be forgotten and left behind. As long as their stories continue, it will be difficult for joint problem solving, collaborative negotiation, and mutual agreement to dismantle and rearrange the facts that have created them. Once the stories have been heard, acknowledged, analyzed, and reframed, new stories can be created, stories of resolution, forgiveness, healing, and transformation. These third stories are automatically substituted for the originals.

When conspiracies of silence are finally broken and the parties tell their stories to each other, they give themselves and each other permission to be who they authentically are, to speak their own truths. As they do so in each other's presence, a space of authentic communication gradually emerges, in which they discover a new sense of themselves and of one another. This invites a new level of intimacy into their relationship.

As each person's truth is told and dialogue ensues, both sides unmask parts of themselves they have kept hidden by their stories. They are liberated from a self-imposed relational silence and are suddenly able to communicate what really matters to them. They can acknowledge what they imagined, feared, guessed, hoped, and wondered. They can reveal secrets to one another, and the reasons why they have kept them. What is truly surprising is their discovery that what they thought were deep, dark secrets were actually known all along.

In *A Chorus of Stones,* a book about family, political, and social secrets, our friend Susan Griffin beautifully describes the extraordinary power and release that come from revealing secrets, both for individuals and for the larger society:

> I am beginning to believe that we know everything, that all history, including the history of each family, is part of us, such that, when we hear any secret revealed, a secret about a grandfather, or an uncle, or a secret about the battle of Dresden in 1945, our lives are made suddenly clearer to us, as the unnatural heaviness of unspoken truth is dispersed. For perhaps we are like stones; our own history and the history of the world embedded in us, we hold a sorrow deep within and cannot weep until that history is sung.

Social equality, political and economic democracy, organizational learning, and functional family life all require us to be open and honest, both internally with ourselves and externally with others. Just as in conflict resolution, we need to be aware of and move toward the hot spots and speak the unspeakable. We need to explore the edges, frontiers, and limits. We need to find the invisible meridians of energy, the acupuncture points, if you will, that reveal the source and flow of the issues. We need to expose the secret sorrows that simply allow us to be human. Only then can we create relationships that are based on authenticity.

The same sorrows are present in conflict. When secrets are revealed, even the listeners feel lighter and freer, as if the secrets also had been theirs. This freedom often comes painfully, with weeping and sadness, regrets and apologies, and recognition of the price both sides have paid for their silence. No one, when it is over, wants to go back to silence.

## A Place Safe for Truth

This is not an easy process, either for the parties involved or for the mediator. As conflict resolvers, our challenge is to be as fully empathetic and deeply honest as we can be. This does not mean being "neutral" in the conflict. Rather, it means being what we call *omnipartial*, or on both people's side at the same time. In doing so, we also are unavoidably moved by upsetting emotions, surprised by stories, and freed by the secrets each side exposes. As we listen in this way for the core stories, we need to be prepared for *anything* at *every* moment.

At the same time, we must remember that the conflict is not ours, no more than the stories or secrets or the decisions about whether or how to end it. Vulnerability, empathy, and honesty are *choices* that do not belong solely to us as mediators. We can ask vulnerable, empathetic, and honest questions, but if the parties are not ready to answer them, we need to acknowledge that the time is not right, or that we may not have the skills needed to overcome their resistance, and we must then retreat to a safer line of inquiry.

As you will see in the conflict narratives that follow, we often took several steps backward to reorient the process to a fresh reality. As we did so, we invariably respected what we perceived to be the limits of the parties' willingness to engage in more vulnerable dialogue. The crafting of an environment that makes it safe for whatever is to be revealed requires complete trust in the process and in the mediator's ability to be comfortable with whatever the parties might say.

When we encounter resistance in getting to the core story, we can do several things:

- Take a step back and request permission to ask a deeper question
- If permission is denied, respect the denial and find out, perhaps privately, why the invitation to go deeper was declined
- Breathe slowly and deeply and, if culturally appropriate, use intensity and body language to create a "tunnel" of unblinking, uninterrupted eye contact
- Lower the tone and slow the pace of our voice
- Use the resistance rather than the issues to reveal the core story
- Create a moment of silence, to allow the speaker's words to be heard and absorbed
- Offer reassuring comments and gestures
- Move closer physically and emotionally
- Ask the listener to acknowledge the courage and honesty of the speaker
- Be authentic and vulnerable ourselves, making it safe for the parties to be that way, too
- Open the door to deeper communication without trying to force anyone to walk through it
- Ask again later when defenses have relaxed

These techniques can help us create a safe environment in which deeper truths can be told.

In the following mediation narratives, high stakes were riding on our ability to open the conversation to stories that the parties felt were unheard or untold. Our approach may seem unappealing, and you may decide to create a different one. We welcome your critical assessment as you read each of these reports of our experiences.

In none of the mediations we describe did we have advance notice about the deeper issues, nor did we have an opportunity to plan what we were going to do. Like all mediators, we were compelled to shoot from the hip. We reveal exactly what we did, warts and all, as we labored to uncover the parties' core stories and reveal their deeper, more powerful, and authentic truths. We hope our examples will help you discover your own inner truths as you support others in discovering theirs.

# All in the Family

The elder sister finally couldn't stand it any more. She telephoned us, saying she was sick of the conflict, that her parents were in their eighties and not in good health, and that she had had a horrifying dream of fighting with her siblings over their parents' grave site.

As a result of their conflicts, it had been more than fifteen years since the siblings had all been together. All of them lived in the same city, and they were all adults in their late forties or fifties, but they would not see or speak to each other. Their dispute extended into the next generation as well: there were children who had never met (or refused to see) their aunts, uncles, and cousins.

The members of the immediate family were resistant at first to the idea of mediation. We had several conversations and some focused problem solving over the telephone, in an effort to get the two brothers and two sisters to agree that they would meet, along with both brothers' wives but without the siblings' parents.

As they walked into the room, they would not say hello to one another and avoided eye contact. The two brothers and their wives sat as far apart from each other as possible. The two sisters, who were unmarried, sat closer together in a more neutral space. We began the mediation process by welcoming them, thanking them for being willing to come together to talk about their problems, explaining the mediation process, and reviewing a number of common ground rules for the mediation process. We asked them to agree to be present in a spirit of honest dialogue and problem solving. Without comments or questions, they all agreed.

We then asked them to introduce themselves, and to tell us their names, their places in the family, one problem or issue they would like to have addressed during the mediation, and one wish they had for an outcome or for their relationship. We recorded their responses on flip-chart paper; their answers are shown in Table 3.1.

After the introductions were complete, we asked them to look back at the list we had made and see if they could find any commonalities. In our experience, when conflicting parties are asked to perform this exercise, they immediately slip out of their conflict roles and emotional processing and into a reflective space where they are able to actually see their conflict as an "it" rather than as a "you." They also gain a sense of process awareness and are better able to identify what they have in common without the mediators' needing to point it out.

Everyone agreed that all the problems had been accurately identified and that there seemed to be different ways of describing the same problem. We asked how they felt looking at this list of problems, and they said that the conflict among them made them feel superficial, dishonest, and like outsiders in their own family. They agreed that they were in complete unanimity about what they wanted, which was to be a family again. We reinforced their agreement and asked them to start being a family right now by being open, honest, and supportive of one another.

We then decided, given the tone of the conversation and the fact that we had only two hours to complete the mediation, to take a risk and move the conversation quickly to a deeper and potentially transformational level. Instead of inquiring about their issues in depth, we asked whether anyone had anything for which he or she wished to apologize, and we waited in silence for someone to answer.

After a few moments of nearly unbearable silence, the elder of the two brothers spoke. He apologized to his siblings for having stolen money from their parents several years earlier and for having lied about it. He said he felt horrible inside for having done this. He said he had apologized to their parents, offered to sell his house to pay them back, and had been paying them back each month for some time.

At this point, we could have thanked him for his apology and gone on, but it was clear from the intensity and quality of energy in the room that a major step had been taken, and we didn't want to leave the topic before opening the door a little wider so that

**Table 3.1. Problems and Wishes.**

| Family Member | Expressed Problems | Wishes for Family |
|---|---|---|
| Younger brother | "Ongoing conflicts back to when I was two years old; countless lies and untruths" | "That everyone live as a family" |
| Younger brother's wife | "The mother's habit of always looking the other way; the family is into avoidance" | "That all get along, tell the truth, and accept one another" |
| Elder sister | "Feeling like an outsider in my own family" | "That all the siblings be respectful, be involved in the same activities, and share in caring for our parents as they get older" |
| Elder brother | "Family's lack of sincerity and sensitivity; people being superficial." | "To make our relationship better" |
| Elder brother's wife | "We have never been open and are too much into competition" | "That all respect one another and put conflicts behind us" |
| Younger sister | "Our mother uses rivalry to divide the siblings" | "That everyone discuss issues respectfully and immediately and be happy as a family" |

family members could shift direction, open their hearts to one another, and begin a new family process based on honesty and acceptance. To amplify this opening, we asked the other members of the family to respond and give their reactions to what the elder brother had said.

The first to speak was the elder sister, who complimented her brother for his courage in making the apology. We asked the younger sister to speak, and she also thanked her brother and accepted his apology. Finally, the younger brother spoke. He said that he had doubted his brother's integrity since the age of two, and that this was the first time in his life he had seen his brother behave in a morally responsible way.

He then said, "I just have one question to ask you." We started to worry that he would raise some other issue before the resolution of this one had been completed. Instead, he asked, "If you were in so much trouble, why didn't you come to me for help? I'm your brother." At this point, it was clear that the conflict had been broken and that the transformation process had begun.

The elder sister also wanted to apologize. She was their stepsister and had come into the family when her father married their mother, within a year after each of their parents' former spouses had died. She said that at the time she joined the family, she was still mourning the death of her mother and did not feel she had really given the rest of them a chance. She had been deeply unhappy and felt she had not been a real sister to them.

Again, we asked the others to respond, but this time their response was one of disbelief. None of them had felt the way she thought they had felt. We turned to her and asked her to explain this discrepancy. When she couldn't, we asked, "Isn't there someone else you need to apologize to?" She said, "Do you mean me?" She and her siblings all agreed that she had been too hard on herself. They felt that if she had slighted them, it had been by not asking them for support when she needed it.

The younger sister also had a number of apologies to make. As she did, she was similarly accepted and welcomed with open arms by her brothers and sisters.

We turned next to the question of whether they were ready for resolution. We asked them whether there was anything holding them back from creating the family they had all said they wished to have. From the ensuing silence, we sensed that something was indeed holding them back. Because the younger brother had twice referred to his distrust of the elder brother and identified it as an issue that went back to the time he was two, we asked him to describe what had happened to him at that age.

The younger brother said that when he was two (although it is more likely that he was three or four) his brother had taken a pair of scissors and cut a pattern out of the drapes in the living room. Their mother was furious, and when they both denied having done it, she announced that no one would eat dinner until someone confessed. The elder brother threatened his younger sibling, telling him that if he did not confess, his kite would be broken. The younger brother confessed and saved his kite, but his respect for and trust in his brother were broken in its place.

We asked the elder brother to respond, and he apologized for what he had done. This time, his younger brother's response to his apology was incomplete; in his tone of voice we could hear the anger he still had over this betrayal. We asked him what it would take for him to let go of the anger he had been carrying for more than fifty years. He described the incident again, and after he had finished, we asked him again what it would take for him to let his anger go. Finally he said, "I want him to buy me a kite." It was clear that his response was exactly the right one because it came not from him on the day of the mediation but from the child of fifty years earlier. When his brother agreed to buy him a kite, he agreed to let go of his anger. To cement their agreement and the release of his anger, we suggested to the elder brother that he buy two kites and that they fly them together. They agreed, and for the first time during the session they smiled at each other.

We asked the siblings whether they felt, in retrospect, that their mother had known who had cut the drapes. They all said their mother must have known and should not have accepted the younger brother's confession. Her pattern had been to divide them against each other instead of uniting them. They agreed that they needed to develop a common strategy to use with her. They also needed a plan to include their father, who had basically bowed out of their conflicts and spent most of his time with them in silence.

After discussion, they came up with a common strategy, which was to go to their parents' house together and make the following statement: "We want to thank you for everything you have done for us. We have decided that what is most important to us right now is to have a family again, and we need your support to make it happen. We want to ask you to help us. You can do so by asking us, if we complain to you about each other, to go to the person with whom we have the problem, and you can also help us try to see the problem from the other person's point of view."

As we began to run out of time, we asked when they would go to see their parents and how they wanted to tell them what they had done. We urged them to do so as soon as possible. One of the brothers agreed to cancel a previous engagement, and they decided to go immediately to their parents' house, to tell them what they had decided and to plan their first family get-together in fifteen years.

We cautioned them that the change would not be total or immediate for everyone in the family. We urged them to be persistent and, if things got rough, to remember how much they had achieved in just a few hours. Finally, we returned to their list of wishes. We asked them how they felt about each other right now, and whether they thought their wishes had already come true, if only in the way they had already begun talking to each other.

They agreed, and as we ended, we reached over to hold hands with those who were next to us, and the circle of hands grew until it joined. The two brothers then got up and hugged and kissed each other for the first time in fifty years. Then they were all kissing and hugging and crying as they set off to tell their parents what they had done, and in that moment they were a family again.

Later, we received another telephone call from the elder sister. She thanked us for what we had done and told us that she and her siblings had experienced another breakthrough at their parents' house, where everyone had cried all over again. Their mother apologized for her behavior, and their father couldn't stop talking about how wonderful they all were.

## Observations

Family systems are fertile ground for unresolved issues from the past to fester. They are translated into stories of injury and betrayal that creep into current relationships and sour them. As mediators of family conflicts, we are often required to dredge up the past in order to discover the deeper stories of which the present dispute is only a single, yet representative, strand.

As can be seen, our method in this mediation was very different from the approach a therapist might have used to probe into the past and process the emotions connected with it. In this case, the younger brother's story about the drapes gave us an opportunity to symbolically resolve his deeper issues with his brother, to suggest that they go fly kites together, and to agree on a common approach in coping with their mother's pattern of dividing them.

Similarly, the elder brother's story about stealing money from his parents gave all the siblings an opportunity to change their stories about his cheating and lying into stories of ownership, acknowledgment, and forgiveness. Stories create families, and in this case it can be seen how different family realities emerge from different stories.

Finally, we made efforts not only to fix the problems revealed by their stories about the past but also to actively prevent those problems from being carried into the future. Not all mediations end this well, because not all parties are ready to let go of their old stories. But if a mediation can create a result like this even once, it is worth all the effort that goes into creating it.

# Date Rape: Getting to No

The legal officer at a large, prestigious university had been a personal friend of ours for many years. He was now facing a difficult case that he could see no possibility of concluding satisfactorily.

Two undergraduates had become embroiled in a widely publicized conflict. A young woman had accused a young man of date rape and had had him arrested. The young man claimed that they had been dating for months and had slept together many times, with the young woman's full cooperation and consent.

The district attorney had decided not to prosecute, and the woman had brought charges of date rape against the man for violating a campus code of conduct. The university's investigation had found truth on both sides, and our friend felt uncomfortable either prosecuting or dropping the case. He asked us if we would mediate the issue.

The two students agreed, and we met with them in mediation for nearly ten hours. The mediation was the first time that Carol and George had met or talked directly with each other since the incident that gave rise to the charges. When they entered the room, neither acknowledged the other's presence by word, glance, or gesture. They had no eye contact, and the hostility was palpable.

We began by indicating, with tone, words, eye contact, and posture, our awareness of the painful, embarrassing, sensitive nature of the topic. We shared our desire to help them come to some mutually acceptable understanding of what had taken place so that they could both learn from what had happened and not allow it to damage the rest of their lives. We encouraged their frank and honest participation in the process.

They agreed to a set of ground rules for the mediation, which included a rule that no outcome would be reached if it were not agreeable to both of them. They agreed to participate fully and in good faith in the mediation process, and they understood that afterward all charges would be dropped by the university.

We asked Carol to begin. Her opening statement was brief but rambling. She focused on the seriousness of the trauma she had suffered and on its reality for her. She said that she could not have made it up and that the experience had left her with a sense of vulnerability and lost self-esteem.

We then shifted our attention to George and asked questions about how the two of them had met and where they were from, to focus attention at the beginning on less contested and less sensitive issues. We wanted to provide ourselves with background information and a context for understanding their conflict. Gradually, through probing and active questioning of both of them, and by timing our questions, we progressively deepened the tone of their revelations and uncovered the following story.

George had met Carol at the university through mutual friends. He liked her sense of humor, her interesting friends, and her superior understanding of the problems he was facing in life. He was not ready for an intense relationship, however, and they remained acquaintances for several months. With a group of friends, they went to a dance. Carol fixed up her hair, wore contact lenses instead of glasses, and danced around the floor "like a wood-elf." Her extraordinary energy and vivaciousness attracted George, and they began to date.

Carol was a virgin. She had lived at home for several years before entering a college dorm, and she wanted to be a virgin when she married. Their dating became more and more physical, but they did not have sex because Carol did not want to. Nevertheless, they would go to George's room, lock the door, and do everything short of intercourse. George was not a virgin, and he always pulled back out of respect for Carol's wishes. They became boyfriend and girlfriend.

Carol began to assume a more and more deferential, passive role in relation to George. She was quiet with him and no longer projected her personality in the way that had attracted him at the dance. Meanwhile, George became interested in a girl who worked with him and asked her over to dinner.

George and Carol had arranged to go on a camping trip with several of their friends, but George now felt estranged and told Carol he wanted to break up. She asked him to continue to behave as though he were her boyfriend while they were on the trip, and he did. He tried to be supportive but firm in his decision. When they retired for the night, Carol, who had her period, removed her tampon, and that shocked George. They engaged in heavy petting, and he penetrated her by accident. He jumped away and apologized profusely. He asked if she wanted him to stop, and she said no. They made love, and she seemed pleased with the experience but shaky.

When they returned from the camping trip, they agreed that they would not make love again. Carol was upset at their breaking up, however, and George suggested that they meet to talk some more. After they had talked they began to hug, and then to pet, and they ended up making love again. This pattern repeated itself four more times. Each time, they would talk about breaking up, become upset, hold on to and comfort each other, and then make love. It felt to both of them like an addiction.

They were having mixed feelings and sending each other mixed messages. It was extremely important to George that he remain friends with Carol, and it was increasingly important to Carol that she put distance between herself and George. She asked him to stay away from dances at the dorm, but he came to one anyway. She felt that her wishes were not being considered. She then met another man and promised him she would not make love again with George.

Finally, Carol decided to end the relationship. She gave George a rose and spoke to him in her room about her problems with their relationship. He began crying. Carol's roommate came in, and so they moved to another room and began kissing and petting. They joked about having a final fling.

George said he wanted to make love to her, and he threw his glasses against the wall. Carol said there was an intense, angry look in his eyes, and she was startled. She shook her head no but continued to engage in heavy petting. She mentioned her promise, but George discounted it. He felt she always began by objecting and then ended up wanting to make love.

George told Carol that he had always felt responsible for holding back sexually but wasn't going to do that anymore, and that she would have to be equally responsible. She took off her panties, and they simulated sex, without penetration. He told her again he wanted to make love, and she said nothing. She relaxed, and he assumed this meant consent. Intercourse was unusually intense and brief as she shifted her body to a more receptive position.

From George's point of view, he had made love to Carol because he wanted to, because he thought she had agreed, and because he knew she would later change her mind, become angry, and create a clear break in their relationship. He hadn't wanted to make her angry; he just wanted to get her to want to end the relationship.

Carol, by contrast, felt she had been raped. She was surprised and shocked that George had used his sexual power over her. She said she had told him he would hate himself if he went through with it. Afterward, she said, she had asked him whether he regretted it. He had said yes and agreed that he had been trying to make her hate him so she would end the relationship.

George acknowledged much of what Carol said, and he agreed that he had been upset at the time, but he felt strongly that there had been no rape, and that intercourse had been consensual. He felt Carol had helped him by changing his attitude and helping him believe in himself. She had almost convinced him that people would like him just for himself, but now he was going to be denied access to the dorm, to dances, and to a circle of friends with whom he had become close. He was upset but not angry at Carol for her desire to end their relationship.

We occasionally held their emotions in check by asking detailed factual questions. At other times, we encouraged them to describe what they found attractive in each other, along with what they found problematic or repulsive. In this way, their emotional descriptions would not be one-sided or informed only by the quality of their last encounter. We stopped occasionally, but only briefly, to get confirmation or disagreement over feelings or events. We probed for a consistent thread of interpretation that would help us resolve the apparent discrepancies. We slowly but steadily encouraged them to talk directly to one another.

Gradually, we shifted the focus of discussion from the history and facts of the incident to a more detailed examination of their perceptions, intentions, and communication, as they had practiced it throughout their relationship. We commented on the differences between their respective memories and perceptions, pointing out how these were connected to the differences in their personalities.

George was visibly shaken and diminished as he gave a more detailed and precise account of the history of their relationship, whereas Carol seemed to speak more easily of its essential emotional character, and she became stronger as we worked our way deeper. George remembered events and ideas; Carol remembered conversations and feelings.

Both were honest, bright, and well meaning but sexually and romantically inexperienced. We asked them both what they thought about their past, where they were in the present, and what they wanted for their future. From Carol's perspective, the issues were simple: she had been raped, she was experiencing great pain and anguish, and she wanted George to suffer for it. She wanted to be certain he would never do it again.

George could not accept that what he had done could be called rape. He felt he had been the one who had held back throughout their relationship. Carol had wanted to make love the first time, after refusing to do so for months, and had repeated that pattern four or five times afterward. On each occasion she had resisted and then relented and chosen to make love with him.

Carol felt that things had been different between them the last time. She had broken up with George. He had become intense and impassioned and must have known she did not want to make love. She recalled that George had admitted, earlier in the mediation session, to having gone ahead and made love to her in part to make her angry so that they would finally break up.

George felt confused about this. He agreed, in response to our questioning, that some part of Carol had probably not wanted to make love, but he also felt that this had been true before. On the last occasion, she had consented to heavy petting and had voluntarily taken off her clothing. She had said no the first time he asked, but she said nothing the second time he tried. He had always respected her wishes before, and if she had said something, he would have stopped.

Carol said that George had been so intense on the last occasion that she had been afraid to say anything. When we asked, she agreed that she certainly could have stopped him if she had said something, but she had been too shocked and confused at the time and did not think of doing so.

We asked George if he would be willing to accept Carol's use of the word rape if it did not include the words force or violence, and he was not, but he did accept the fact that on some level she had not consented to make love to him. When we asked him if he felt it had been a mistake for him to continue, he said it had been. We asked if he would say that to Carol, and he apologized deeply and genuinely to her for his error.

We then asked Carol to respond to George's apology. She said she was willing to acknowledge that she had given him mixed signals, that she could have stopped him, and that he had held back many times before. We asked if she was willing to accept his apology, and she said she was. But she was unwilling to let him completely off the hook either by forgiving him or by taking back her allegation that what had happened had been a rape.

We asked Carol to describe directly to George, in some detail, how she had suffered. As deeply and genuinely as George had spoken, she told him about her now-found frigidity and fear of men.

We asked George if he was willing to acknowledge that Carol had suffered severely as a result of what had happened. He was. We then asked George to describe his suffering as a result of her allegations, and he spoke eloquently of his inability to date, his sexual abstinence, his confusion, his guilt, and his loss of self-esteem.

We pointed out that somehow each of them felt victimized and raped. Each had suffered from their inability to end the relationship, especially the sexual part of it. The incident that had traumatized them was one they were both responsible for creating. Neither of them had listened to what the other was saying, and neither of them had asked directly for what they really wanted.

With our prompting, they agreed to make an effort to let go of the experience and get on with their lives. They agreed that they had learned some difficult lessons from what had happened. Carol indicated that she had learned that she needed to be more assertive and clearer about what she wanted and did not want sexually in her future relationships. George said that he had learned to be more sensitive and careful, and he felt that he would go overboard in the future to acknowledge and respect rejection or lack of interest in the women he dated.

When we asked them what they wanted for the future, George said he wanted to continue being friends with Carol. Carol said she was not interested, and that she simply wanted George to leave her alone. George fully forgave Carol, but she was only partially willing to forgive him and was not willing to accept the idea that what had happened was not a rape, if it had been one in part.

Through this conversation, George and Carol moved toward a more cohesive and balanced appreciation of what had happened. They made small but significant progress in surrendering their self-definitions as victims. Each listened to and accepted a portion of the other's point of view. They both heard how they each had suffered, and they understood their own complicity in and responsibility for what had occurred. Neither was willing to completely give up his or her suffering, but each began to move in that direction.

Both of them felt listened to and supported. They felt that the process had been helpful because before mediation they had been unable to talk the problem through, confront each other over their different versions, or even meet in the same room. They felt they had been open and honest and had participated in good faith. They felt ready for the conflict to be over.

## Observations

At the end of the session, we complimented Carol and George on their honesty and openness and on their courage in being willing to talk to strangers about such sensitive and painful issues. We encouraged them to seek individual therapy so that they could carry the process of learning forward. We hoped they would continue to heal the scars that remained.

We commented that they had clearly had good times as well as bad times together and should work to understand what had happened in a way that was not blaming but instead balanced. We made it clear that they did not have to be friends or forgive each other, but we asked that they at least forgive themselves for what had happened and create new relationships based on what they had learned, on trust, honesty, and candor.

Given the nature of the issues and their past relationship, we wanted to avoid a yes-you-did, no-I-didn't shouting match, which would have yielded negative results. Our intention was for each of them to try to understand the other's core story, in circumstances that were filled with ambiguity.

The most desirable outcome for them was not a yes-or-no answer to the question of whether a rape had occurred. Rather, it was to reach an understanding of how this ambiguity in their relationship had developed, how they were each responsible for it, how it might be corrected in future relationships, and how they might begin to repair the damage to their psyches.

We provided a safe space in which they were able to actually communicate with each other at a deep yet protected level. In the mediation, they finally had a chance to listen empathetically, to speak vulnerably and say what they wanted to say. They both had their suffering heard, understood, and acknowledged and their apologies and refusals accepted.

As mediators in this highly sensitive drama, we had to deal directly with intense feelings resulting from a highly sensitive, potentially humiliating incident in their relationship. By creating a safe, empathetic space and asking questions that gave both of them permission to take the conversation deeper, we allowed their core stories to emerge.

Carol's external story of rape and George's external story of consent did not completely disappear during the mediation, probably for reasons beyond the scope of our mandate, but we helped to soften these stories, allowing the two parties to create a truer, composite, more integrated story of what had happened.

# The Fatherless Child

Lisa was in her early twenties. She had been married to Ramon for a little less than a year and a half and had a son, John, who was eleven months old. They had married when Lisa was three months pregnant.

Ramon was from Argentina, the only son of a large family. He had been married twice before but had not had any children, and John was the last male member of his family to carry the family name.

Their divorce seemed simple enough. There was no community property, and there were no significant debts. The marriage had been brief, both parties worked at relatively low-paying jobs, and there was a child who was loved by both parents. They each agreed to share in his financial and emotional support.

We started the mediation process and asked them to agree to a set of ground rules. One of the rules included the possibility that we might have separate meetings or caucuses with each side and would do so if we needed to confidentially explore any of the issues on which they were unable to agree, or that they might not wish to discuss in open session.

When we asked Lisa to start with an opening statement, she seemed unable to speak. We asked her what the problem was. She seemed in the grip of some powerful emotion. At last she asked if she could meet with us alone in caucus. Ordinarily, we prefer to hear from both sides before meeting in caucus, but because Lisa seemed unable to continue and gave every indication of some deep, dark secret that might compromise the mediation process, we decided to meet with her to uncover it.

We asked Ramon whether he minded if we met first with Lisa and then with him. He agreed and stepped outside. After he left, we told Lisa we would keep her communication confidential if she wished, but we encouraged her to speak openly to Ramon about whatever she wanted to tell us. Lisa immediately started to cry and told us she had a terrible problem. She wasn't sure what to do but felt that the truth had to come out because the lie was killing her. She said she had to tell Ramon that he was not the father of her child.

We asked what made her certain this was the case. She said she had been sleeping with Ramon at the time she became pregnant but had gone to a party and slept with another man during her ovulation. She had asked Ramon to take a blood test, ostensibly for insurance reasons, and Ramon was type AB, whereas the baby was type O, as was his father.

We asked her why she felt it was necessary to tell Ramon at this time. We pointed out that her revelation could result in John's losing the only father he would ever know and in her losing child support. She said that Ramon would insist on seeing John at all hours of the day and night. He would barge in, saying John was "the blood of my blood and the flesh of my flesh," and behave in a "macho" fashion toward her. Furthermore, she said, she could not stand the lying.

She was still ambivalent about her decision and expressed doubts that she was doing the right thing. She seemed paralyzed, unable to act, and tormented by her indecision. To catalyze her resolve, we asked whether she would like us to play the role of devil's advocate and ask her some of the hard, pointed questions she had probably been asking herself. She agreed with obvious relief and said she had not been able to discuss the situation with anyone. She also expressed a strong lack of interest in receiving counseling or therapy (as we proposed) before she decided.

As devil's advocates, we asked her a series of tough questions. The dialogue proceeded as follows:

*Mediators:* What gives you the right to deprive your son of a
loving father?

*Lisa:* He isn't really my son's father.

*Mediators:* Who says a father has to be biological?

     *Lisa:* That part would be okay, but I can't lie anymore.
*Mediators:* You lied to Ramon before. [*keeping the pressure on*] Why
            this great desire to tell the truth now? [*then following
            up*] Are you sure you aren't just doing this out of
            anger? Won't you regret this decision in ten or twenty
            years? Why not just wait and see whether a mediated
            visitation schedule and less angry communications
            temper your desire to tell him? How will you make
            ends meet without child support? You have to expect
            that Ramon will be furious and feel cheated and will
            have nothing further to do with either you or your
            son. What makes you expect that the natural father
            will decide to help you? What if he doesn't? Can you
            raise your son by yourself? Think of the pain you will
            be causing your son and Ramon and his family. Can
            you really hurt all these people so deeply? Is this really
            the best decision for your son, or are you in favor of it
            because it's best for you?

We asked these honest, hard-hitting questions to probe the limits of her resolve. In each case, her answer came back more clearly and strongly. She told us that she could not live with herself if she did not tell Ramon the truth, that the lie had been eating away at her, and that she, John, Ramon, and his family would all suffer as a result, but the truth had to come out. She said she knew she could expect nothing of Ramon or of John's natural father and that she was prepared to take responsibility for her decision and its consequences.

    We told her that she might be right or wrong in other people's eyes, but the decision was hers to make. We asked if she was sure she did not want to consult a therapist or think about it some more. She answered that she wanted to tell Ramon in the mediation session that night, and that she had already waited too long.

    We asked her how she planned to tell Ramon, and she said she did not know. We asked if she had any ideas, but she had none and asked for our help. We suggested that she meet with him alone, with us just outside the room in case he became violent, which seemed unlikely but possible. We felt a face-to-face private meeting with her would be more honest and ease his pain and embarrassment.

We asked her to tell him as if she were the one being told. When she seemed unable to come up with a specific opening, we offered one. We said that if we were the ones who were being told, this is how we would like her to begin: "Ramon, I'm deeply sorry to cause you this kind of pain. I know how much you love John and what a devoted father you've been to him. I've lied to you, Ramon, for which I apologize, and though I know I can expect nothing from you, I hope you will continue to love John and see him. My lie was wrong, and I have no excuse to offer you. I apologize deeply, and have suffered and will continue to suffer for it, but I have to tell you the truth. You are not John's father. I had a blood test done, and it confirms this result."

We suggested that, no matter what verbal abuse or anger he might display toward her, she remain with him and be as much a friend to him in this moment as she could, by letting him vent his anger toward her. We asked her to hear his anger as pain and understand the humiliation this news would cause him, in the hope that he would not later vent his anger in the direction of his son.

She thanked us for our support, and we left her to talk with Ramon, observing them from outside through a glass door. Ramon did not become violent, but he was deeply shaken and profoundly angered by the information, as any father might be who had lost his only child. They spoke for over an hour and came out together. Ramon thanked us formally for meeting with them and for our efforts to resolve the dispute. We asked to meet with him separately, to talk further about what he was going to do, but he refused.

We told him that we knew this was difficult for him and that if he wanted to talk to us later, we would be available, or if he would like to see a counselor or therapist to talk further about these issues, we could give him a referral. We appreciated his patience and his returning to thank us. He said he might call us afterward but was not interested in therapy or more conversation, and he left.

Lisa remained to tell us that she had taken all of our suggestions. Ramon had doubted her at first and then accepted the truth. He wanted to know who the real father was, but she had refused to tell him except to say that he did not know the man. She felt Ramon would refuse to see her or John again, and that she would have to raise John alone. She felt a tremendous sense of relief that she had finally told him the truth, and that a great weight had been lifted from her shoulders.

She thanked us profusely and told us repeatedly how grateful she was for our support and help. We told her that she had done a very difficult and courageous thing in telling the truth. We reassured her that we were sure she had done it in as sensitive and kind a way as she could. We expressed admiration for the way she had handled her complex feelings about Ramon. We knew that others might have decided to act differently, but that she had acted according to her own sense of what was right. The problem now was to help John. Even though he was very young, he would miss his father. If she needed help figuring out how to help John, we could indicate some resources that were available at low cost.

She thanked us again, and as she left, she reached over and hugged us tightly. We called Ramon the next day, to see if perhaps he had calmed down and would consider counseling or another mediation session to talk about John. He was unbending in his refusal and remained convinced that his course of action was correct.

When we called Lisa afterward, to tell her of Ramon's refusal and discuss her next steps, we asked whether she had considered contacting the biological father. She said she had, and she wanted to know what we thought about how she might arrange a meeting and tell him he was the father of a child, without scaring him away. We recommended that she send him a photo of his son, tell him she had no expectations of him and that he was under no obligation to her or to John, and ask him if he wanted to see his son. Two months later, she told us John's biological father had asked to help raise him and had offered, without being asked, to help them financially.

## Observations

It is difficult to understand or describe what kind of mediation this was. In a traditional mediation process, the parties are encouraged to negotiate agreements and resolve their differences. In this case, however, a revelation came at the outset and made it clear that there was nothing left for them to agree on. In our view, the problem became simply one of how to communicate the bad news. Our mandate was not to facilitate an agreement but to eliminate the need for one.

Nevertheless, we acted in several different and, we think, mediative capacities. We were confidential advisers, sounding boards, devil's advocates, confessors, protectors of the child's interests, financial advisers, and amateur therapists. We chose to continue using our skills to support the possibility of a different outcome, even after that possibility had all but disappeared. We believe that in so doing, and in modeling empathetic communication, we helped limit the damage and pain that might have been inflicted as a result of their anger.

It is possible that Lisa made the wrong decision and caused an unnecessary breach in a loving relationship that would have continued without her revelation. This is not the only possible outcome, however, and the decision was ultimately hers to make. The most we could do was ask the hard questions that would reveal any latent ambiguity or self-interest and support her decision by making its effects as gentle as possible.

With respect to Ramon, we did not have his permission to intervene or engage him in solving a problem he no longer recognized as his. Had he been willing to talk to us further, we might have explored, as we did later by telephone, why he could not continue to see John, or why anything had to change in his love for his son. Ramon was a proud man, and he felt betrayed. His family encouraged this feeling in him, and he subsequently obtained an annulment of the marriage and refused to see Lisa or John again.

The mediation process, although unable to produce an agreement, successfully supported the painful communication of a highly emotional but necessary truth. It resolved a deeper dispute by uncovering it and fashioning how it would be communicated to get what both parties wanted, with as little pain and anger as possible. In these terms, the mediation was a success.

# Chapter Four

# Stories That Sacrifice Life

*We have been silent witnesses of evil deeds; we have been drenched by many storms; we have learnt the arts of equivocation and pretense; experience has made us suspicious of others and kept us from being truthful and open; intolerable conflicts have worn us down and even made us cynical. Are we still of any use? What we shall need is not geniuses, or cynics, or misanthropes, or clever tacticians, but plain, honest, straightforward people. Will our inward power of resistance be strong enough, and our honesty with ourselves remorseless enough, for us to find our way back to simplicity and straightforwardness?*
GEFFREY B. KELLY AND F. BURTON NELSON,
*A TESTAMENT TO FREEDOM: THE ESSENTIAL WRITINGS OF DIETRICH BONHOEFFER*

There is a formidable danger for those who create conflict stories. It is that they will lose themselves in their stories—that they will sacrifice their lives or parts of themselves to defend their stories. Many people will sacrifice their authenticity for stories about who they are because who they really are has disappeared into their stories.

The cost of this sacrifice can be severe. It can damage the physical health as well as the peace of mind of the storyteller. It can make the mediation process more difficult and cause it to result in a stalemate or an impasse. For the storyteller, it can result in a permanent loss of perspective, impaired health, a weakened will, and an ego so crushed it cannot recover.

In our experience, many of these impasse producing stories concern people's intrinsic self-worth. They are triggered, for example, when an employee is terminated or fired from a job, an event that jeopardizes not only material livelihood but also ego and the sense of self-worth. A story as weighty as this is often based on an accumulation of insignificant, petty stories about minor conflicts in the workplace, often between employees and managers.

This kind of conflict story is usually designed, on the employee's side, to justify, rationalize, and defend poor performance, negative responses to authority, and chronic miscommunication—in short, to prop up the storyteller's shaky self image. On the manager's side, a different story is told, whose purpose is to justify causing terrible harm to another human being, to rationalize the organization's hierarchy, and to assert or defend the manager's personal power, authority, and right to "command and control" the employee.

Managers often focus, in employee performance review processes, on incidents or facts that demonstrate inappropriate or poor performance by employees, and these are cited as reasons supporting the employees' dismissal. The employees' focus is on incidents or facts that demonstrate the failure of the manager to communicate, or on personal harassment of the employees. In this way, both sides tell stories that justify, minimize, and defend whatever they have been accused of doing and, at the same time, accuse the other side of having caused the problem.

Mediation approaches the problem differently. Conflict resolution comes into play when employees and their union advocates, along with managers and their organizational advocates, recognize that neither of these attitudes will resolve their conflict or lead them to an understanding of what created it. Once both sides see that it is necessary to sit down together, jointly sort out what has happened, and understand what created the problem, they can begin working toward its resolution. They can then create a conversation that deflates and deescalates their stories and prevents these stories from controlling the lives of the people who are telling them and of the organization in which they are being told.

## Seduction and Hypnosis

The mediation process is rarely, in our experience, linear, straightforward, or simple. Using the example of the contradictory stories told by employees and managers, we are immediately presented with a dazzling array of detailed, intricate, circular, complex, and carefully selected tales that the parties have created to shore up their positions and defend their actions, and there is a tremendous temptation for conflict resolvers to be seduced and hypnotized by the drama of the stories.

In fact, we can easily be sucked into believing one party's story and its false characterizations of the other party that are based on unspoken assumptions of victimization or demonization. We then lose not just our objectivity but, more important, our capacity for empathy with the other side. In this way, stories of evil prepare the way for martyrdom and murder. They bring into existence the willingness to die for one's country or one's faith, and on a smaller scale to do harm to one's opponents. The stories people tell are dramatic and alluring. They appeal to the fairy tale sensibilities in all of us. Yet if we succumb to their seduction, we will never get past the superficial, external story to the deeper issues presented in the internal and core story—the path leading to resolution.

As mediators, we can easily become hypnotized by the story and get lost in a maze of allegations or we can watch the factual trees of the story and lose sight of the forest of meaning that appears when we see them in relation to each other. When we lose sight of the bigger picture, we tend to avoid, compromise, settle for settlement, and agree to disagree. In so doing, we forget the compensatory purposes of conflict stories—that they are designed to confuse and to explain why the storyteller has not done anything wrong. Stories are the only information we have to go on at the start of the mediation process, and many storytellers have worked long and hard to create a web of confusing justifications for unacceptable conduct.

An interesting dynamic develops as each story takes on a life of its own. As the story is told, the other side's disruptive, negative behavior is reinforced and strengthened by detailed justifications, defenses, and rationalizations. The storyteller's actions are—through justification—hemmed in, bolstered, protected, and given permission to continue; at the same time, the other side's dismissive, affrontive, defensive attitude, demeanor, and behavior lend detail and weight to the story. A spiral develops as the story reinforces the described behavior, and the response reinforces the story. An intertwining negative web is spun, one in which the individual's sense of self becomes trapped and cannot find a way out. In effect, people are forced to live their lives according to their stories.

The employees in the conflict narratives that follow have all broken the implicit or explicit rules of their workplaces. They all have told stories and have given reasons why they operated outside the framework of what was acceptable. As a result, they have become locked in patterns created by the stories themselves. Their managers have also become trapped in their stories about why their employees broke the rules, or why the rules were fair, or why they themselves were unable to make their employees successful.

All three of the employees portrayed in the narratives that follow created external stories about the misdeeds of their managers. They did so in order to prop up their internal stories, which excused them from living their lives and working responsibly. These stories also prevented them and others from discovering their core stories, which were grounded in a nearly perfect disbelief in themselves. By holding on to these stories, all three employees sacrificed important parts of their lives.

All three of the managers in these narratives also told stories about the innate incapacity of their employees and about their resistance, rage, and unwillingness to change. They used these stories to justify termination as a remedy so as to steel themselves against their own compassion and to rationalize the pain they had caused. They also used these stories to hide their own lack of skill and responsibility from their own supervisors and to justify their inability to risk deeply honest communication with less powerful but critical employees.

As conflict resolvers, our role is to get past these first-level stories, told for external and internal consumption, and penetrate the arguments about employees' misdeeds and managers' mistakes, in order to slowly and carefully approach each person's core stories. We encourage the storytellers to discover themselves and their own inner truths and to reveal what they discover to those on the other side. And in some cases, the parties resist and refuse to go along with these efforts.

Union representatives, direct supervisors, human resources personnel, and other organizational officials often participate in workplace mediations. We have heard their stories as well and have worked with them to move beyond superficial stories to directly engage the employees and managers at the center of the dispute.

Once we address the human side of both stories and locate the deeper issues, we return to allegations of inappropriate behavior. We translate these allegations into specific, concrete issues and focus on what each side could have done to prevent the dispute or end it sooner. We draft mediation agreements to address the specific details of what each party did, did not do, or wants to see done. In this way, we do not dismiss or ignore the details, and we have a direct impact on the daily lives of the parties. We avoid becoming hypnotized or getting stuck in the details; instead, we turn complaints into suggestions for improvement.

## Determining Who Is Responsible

There is an elegant, self-referential system operating in many work-related conflict stories. As is true of any other system, it is difficult to know where any part begins or ends. The driving force in the conflict is organized beneath the parties' external stories and is usually not immediately apparent to either side. The relational dynamic between the parties results in a dysfunctional dance that traps them in conflict.

The dance begins with small, subtle movements that trigger a response: an employee engages in some negative or unacceptable behavior that invites a managerial response, or a manager communicates in ways that encourage or reinforce negative, unacceptable behavior. Let's assume, for example, that an employee has made a mistake and performed unacceptable work. In the first place, the manager may have lacked the skills to hire someone who could do the work adequately. In the second place, the manager may not have communicated what is wrong with the work in a way that helps the employee improve: instead of offering constructive feedback, the manager may have criticized the employee harshly or insensitively, hurting the employee's feelings and triggering fears of termination. The employee may have responded defensively, with denial of having done anything wrong, or turned the criticism around and attacked the manager. At a loss, the manager may have blamed the employee and justified his or her own dysfunctional conduct with stories of the employee's misdeeds. The employee, whose poor self-esteem has been fed by constant criticism, may have blamed the manager and told stories of managerial harassment to justify his or her own lack of responsibility. Neither side may have been able to give or receive feedback or monitor and improve their working relationship.

In this system, each person triggers a negative reaction in the other, and neither can step out of the process to see the source of the problem or a path to its resolution. This system is not very different from the one that naughty children use to irritate, humiliate, and control their exhausted parents, and that parents use to suppress, humiliate, and control their naughty children.

The only ones in the workplace who recognize this dynamic or can find a way out of it are outside the conflict. These are the conflict resolvers. Unfortunately, however, as the parties' mutual distrust deepens, they become less and less willing to meet with each other or resolve their dispute, and the system gravitates toward bitterness, stress, recrimination, lost productivity, and termination.

A key to breaking this system is getting both parties to take responsibility for critiquing their own communications and dysfunctional behaviors and identifying what they have done or failed to do to make the conflict worse. The dance stops when one person admits having contributed to the conflict. When both can identify how they could have handled their relationship better, the old system is broken.

We begin breaking the system by asking each side responsibility-fixing questions, such as:

With 20/20 hindsight, how could you have handled the situation better?

How would you evaluate your responses so far?

What have you done that has been effective? What hasn't been effective?

What would you do differently?

Has your communication been effective in creating understanding in the other person? What could you do to improve it?

What have you learned from this conflict?

What have you contributed to making it worse?

What would it take for you to let go of it completely?

What skills could you develop to respond better to behaviors that you don't like?

As the parties reflect on their involvement in the conflict and the roles they have played, we ask them additional questions to evaluate what the conflict has cost them, such as:

What price have you paid for this conflict?

How have you suffered as a result of your own actions?

How have others suffered?

How has the organization suffered?

If you had it all to do over again, what would you do differently? Why?

When the parties on each side measure and acknowledge the real cost of their actions, a shift takes place. They usually recognize without much prompting that it hasn't been worth it, and that the stories they have told are no longer useful.

As we complete the process and both sides agree on terms for resolution, we endeavor to make the process a learning experience. One substantial benefit of the mediation process is that managers observe communication techniques that they can apply in supervising employees in the future, and that employees can use in relating to future managers.

Organizations also need to take responsibility for learning from conflicts and for developing systems and structures that prevent future conflicts, discourage employees' dysfunctional behaviors, and develop managers' skills. The resolution process ought to contribute to the organization as a whole. To this end, we often encourage organizational representatives to agree on plans for training managers, providing classes for employees, and designing systems for improving conflict-resolution and employee complaint procedures, so that everyone gains from the resolution of the conflict.

We also encourage conflicting parties to publicly tell stories of how they have resolved their disputes or stories of what they have learned about themselves by going through the mediation process or stories about what they are going to do differently from now on. Organizations can use storytelling to bridge the gaps between people and to mend their relationships. We once worked with a large motion picture company whose employees felt isolated and stereotyped by others. We asked each group to meet and prepare a presentation describing the stereotypes they thought other groups had of them, to tell the story of what they actually do in their jobs, and to answer all the questions other groups had but were afraid to ask them. The session was a resounding success. With other companies, we have worked to use stories as a way of describing company policies that no one ever read or to describe and transmit organizational culture to new employees.

We start with the assumption that conflict is systemic—that every disagreement captures, in some small way, the culture of the entire organization, just as every piece of a hologram expresses the whole. Each small problem in every system provides information about the weaknesses of the system as a whole.

Conflict provides feedback to a system, allowing the system to learn even from a single conflict how to improve the whole. Each person and each conflict are unique and at the same time each is inextricably connected with all the others. The lessons that people gain from the experience of conflict can transform their sense of themselves and change their lives. In the process, many people come to realize, with Eleanor Roosevelt, that "in the long run, we shape our lives and we shape ourselves. The process never ends until we die. And the choices we make are ultimately our responsibility."

# The Frightening Possibility of Success

Bob worked as a security guard at night at a downtown newspaper. His manager complained that he had become so abusive and angry that several women who worked at the paper at night preferred to walk to their cars alone rather than be in his company. He sexually teased the women in the office where he worked, told offensive sexual jokes, and repeatedly blew his top and screamed at people. Finally he was suspended, and we were asked to mediate, in the hope that Bob would learn enough to be able to keep his job.

The mediation was attended by Bob and by his immediate supervisor, Sid, who represented management at the newspaper and had full authority to reach whatever kind of agreement it might take to solve the problem. Both Bob and Sid agreed to accept a set of ground rules for the process and to talk honestly about the problems they were having with each other.

Because Sid had written a letter to Bob outlining the reasons for his impending termination, we began with Bob and asked him to tell us how he saw the situation. He said he had worked at the paper for more than seven years, always in some menial position. He felt that he had given the paper his loyalty, working extra hours without pay when he was needed and in emergencies. He felt angry and unacknowledged, particularly when a younger man with less seniority had received a promotion to a more creative position. Although Bob was ostensibly the head of security, he felt he had taken this job out of loyalty to the paper. He wanted an opportunity to use his intelligence and do more creative work.

From Sid's point of view, the sole problem was Bob's attitude. The managerial staff had been patient with Bob and overlooked several incidents involving him, but protests from other employees were increasing, and something had to be done. Bob had been suspended not just for the latest occurrence but for a string of incidents, and he would soon be fired if he did not improve his performance.

In mediation, whenever Sid went into detail about specific incidents, Bob responded defensively. He argued that others had provoked him or had made mistakes, and he denied having been as angry as other people had portrayed him to be.

We stopped Bob in the middle of one of his explanations and asked him whether he felt that his behavior and communications were having the effect he intended them to have on his listeners. He stopped being defensive and agreed that he was not having the desired effect. We asked whether he was willing to see his listeners' collective response as an indication that he was being perceived by others as violent and angry. He agreed that this must be how many people at the paper saw him. We asked if he realized that he was the only one who could correct this impression, if it was not true. Again, he agreed that he was. We then suggested that, if he just assumed for a moment that all the accusations were true and that he was in fact really angry about the way he had been treated, wouldn't it be better for him to admit his anger and talk directly about its origins?

With this invitation, Bob launched into an extended description of what he perceived as his unfair treatment by management. We asked questions designed to shift his focus from seeing others as the cause of his problem to seeing the effects his continued anger was having on the willingness of the management to promote him. As he began to take responsibility for what he had done and described how his repeated rejection made him feel, Sid began to soften.

We asked Sid whether it was true that Bob had been a loyal employee, had given a lot to the paper, had done extra work without pay, and had not been acknowledged or thanked for his efforts. Sid confessed that he had never acknowledged Bob for the good work he had done. He volunteered the information that Bob was bright and talented and had done all the things he claimed to have done. He agreed that the paper should have acknowledged Bob's contributions earlier, and that the failure to do so had been a mistake.

We asked Bob whether he thought his emotional outbursts and other expressions of anger were also a mistake. We wondered whether it might not have been better if Bob had gone to Sid directly and told him how he felt. Bob agreed that his acting out had been a mistake, but he felt that there had been no possibility of his going to Sid to complain, because there was "no way for employees to do that."

We asked Sid whether there was a procedure at the paper for employees to file grievances or complaints, and Sid replied that there was not. He agreed that this made it difficult for employees to feel safe in bringing grievances to management. He did say, however, that his door was always open and that any employee could come to see him about problems. We asked whether this meant that Bob could come to see him in the future if he felt something was not going right, or if he felt angry about some incident. Sid answered that he could.

We then asked Bob if he would be willing to try this procedure and agree to go and see Sid when he felt upset instead of taking his feelings out on others. Bob said he was willing to try. We asked Sid whether he would be willing to create an employee grievance system. At Sid's request, we gave him a set of guidelines on how such a system might be created. We asked for suggestions from Sid and Bob about how to make such a grievance system work, and together they came up with several valuable ideas, which Sid agreed to implement.

We then acknowledged what Bob and Sid had done, and we complimented them for being able to work together to come up with a number of creative solutions. We pointed out that they had just demonstrated their ability to collaborate successfully by identifying and solving a common problem, and that the new system they had designed would support them in continuing to improve their communication.

Flushed with this success, we brought their attention back to the underlying issues that had been uncovered but not yet addressed concerning Bob's anger over his lack of opportunity for career advancement, and his expressed willingness to improve his behavior and give up his anger.

We began by asking Bob and Sid what they wanted. Bob said he wanted to move into another job at the paper. Sid said he was willing to consider a transfer or promotion for Bob, but he wanted first to see proof that Bob could perform his job without incident. Each of them agreed with what the other wanted, and each was willing to recognize the validity of the other's point of view.

We then asked them to brainstorm all the alternatives for possible future jobs for Bob and encouraged them to suggest any idea that occurred to them, without censoring or predetermining its practicality or saying no to anything until all the ideas were on the table. Bob suggested that he could be personnel manager, which made us all laugh because he had more personnel problems than any other employee at the paper. He suggested a number of possible positions for himself in middle management. Sid suggested several midrange, nonmanagerial positions but balked because no positions were open and because Bob lacked several important job qualifications.

We then asked Sid to identify some of the tasks he needed to get done but had no time to complete. He listed several and agreed that Bob might be able to do some of them. He insisted, however, that before he would be willing to create a new position, Bob would have to prove that he could adequately perform his old one. Bob liked several of the tasks Sid had mentioned and felt he could do them well, but he did not like the idea of returning to his old job and waiting for Sid to decide whether he had proved himself. At this point, they seemed stuck.

We asked whether it would be possible, given Bob's schedule, for him to do two jobs at the same time. We proposed, as an example, that Bob work 50 percent of the time in his old job and 50 percent in the new one, and that he be moved into the new position at the end of three months if he had performed satisfactorily at both jobs.

Sid and Bob agreed that this proposal would work for both of them, and the mediation seemed to be nearing an end. We began writing up their agreement to give it concreteness and shape. While we were doing so, Bob began throwing obstacles in the way, wondering what guarantees there were that Sid would do what he said. He went back to venting his anger over how the paper had treated him and, in so doing, he insulted Sid's integrity.

We decided to take Bob on directly. We told him he had a choice to see the glass as half empty or half full. He could accept

Sid's offer of a promotion or he could continue to nurse his anger. But, we said, if he accepted Sid's offer, he would have to come to grips with the fact that he might actually succeed. He said, "You don't play games here, do you?" He then admitted that he was afraid of both succeeding and failing, just as his father, who was also a security guard, had been afraid. He said his father had once told him, "If you ever do better than me, I'll kill you."

We asked Bob whether he preferred thinking of himself as intelligent but underrated as a result of other people's harassment or taking a chance on success and giving up thinking of himself as a failure. He said he wanted to succeed but was frightened he would fail. We asked him whether he thought he could surrender his anger and try to succeed in the new position. He said quite honestly that he had always preferred blaming others to risking success and was not sure he would be able to give up his anger.

We thanked Bob for his sincerity and honesty in answering these questions. We also made it clear that he had a choice, and that this was the purpose of the transition period in which he would work two jobs and spend half his time in each. What he did not have a choice about was continuing to work at the paper and being angry with everyone. We asked if he would be willing to see a counselor or a therapist to talk about his anger and the proposed transition, and he readily agreed. Sid stepped in and agreed to pay for the counseling.

We complimented Bob again for his honesty and willingness to face up to an extremely difficult personal problem. We also expressed a high opinion of his intelligence and ability to succeed. We told him we felt he had already been successful in this mediation by telling the truth about his problems, and that we hoped he would use this chance to allow himself to become a success at work.

We complimented Sid for his flexibility and openness to creative solutions, for being willing to admit his mistakes, for working with Bob to design a new grievance procedure for the paper, and for volunteering to pay for Bob's therapy. Both men agreed to follow a set of rules we brainstormed for future respectful communication, including Bob's agreement to stop yelling at other employees.

We drafted a full agreement that incorporated everything they had agreed to, including the elements of the new grievance procedure and a pledge to use their best efforts to make the agreement work. They both agreed to continue communicating openly with each other and to return to mediation if they could not. They shook hands and left.

As a follow-up, we heard from Sid three months later that Bob was in therapy and was no longer yelling or acting out angrily and behaving aggressively toward women. Soon afterward, we learned that Bob had resigned from the paper to complete his therapy and had decided to go back to school to get a degree that would qualify him for a higher-level management position. Sid said he felt certain that Bob was now well along the road to success, and Sid had written Bob a highly complimentary letter of recommendation.

## Observations

We used a number of classic mediation methods in working toward a resolution of this conflict. We uncovered some of the underlying issues, brainstormed options, suggested alternative behaviors, acted as agents of reality, encouraged dialogue, acknowledged admissions of mistakes, refocused attention on goals, asked what the parties wanted, reframed issues, revealed internal blocks to success, improved existing grievance procedures, complimented both sides for engaging in constructive behavior, improved process awareness, wrote up agreements, encouraged agreement on ground rules for effective communication, and expressed optimism in the parties' ability to make their agreements work.

Each of these interventions was helpful in processing the conflict, but the key to resolution came when we unlocked the core story that was fueling the conflict and preventing resolution. Bob had a powerful stake in maintaining his story that he was a failure because other people did not appreciate his intelligence. This story helped him preserve his relationship with his father, allowed him to express his anger at himself for not trying to succeed, and blocked him from being responsible for his own disruptive and damaging behavior.

Our primary technique was simply to be curious about Bob's inner truth and follow the path he created for us through his story. It would have been possible to reach an agreement that Bob would suppress his anger in the future without touching the underlying issues. We also could have negotiated his departure from the paper with a monetary package, or we could have proceeded with the 50/50 work arrangement, ignoring the fact that it was doomed to fail. Only when we directly and openly pursued Bob's core story about fearing success and confronted his inability to surrender his anger were we able to get past his external story of managerial harassment and his internal story of unrecognized talent. Only then did he face a clear choice. He was given full latitude to make that choice and go in whichever direction he chose, with as much acknowledgment, support, and encouragement as possible.

The mediation process was successful in our minds because it revealed the actual underlying dynamic that created the problem. With Bob's commitment to failure on the table, he and Sid could come up with creative solutions. This left them free to decide whether they were in fact ready to resolve the conflict. They became involved in a partnership to come up with interim solutions and to make their relationship work.

Bob and Sid took an extraordinary journey together, from which they both learned a great deal. Sid changed his management style to include acknowledgment as a regular behavior that he was committed to practicing. Bob found new career possibilities by returning to college, and he was able to extricate himself from a story in which he had been trapped. They both used the opportunity presented by their conflict to grow personally, learn new ways of engaging with others, and improve their work lives. They both discovered truer and more authentic stories than the ones they had told when we started.

# Resigned to Being Different

Doreen was young and very attractive. She had worked for a local phone company for a year and a half, selling telephones, but had not seemed to enjoy it. She had been absent from work more than she should have been, and she had received a verbal and a written warning about her absenteeism and tardiness. At the time of the mediation, she was employed at another company in a different capacity.

After receiving the written warning, Doreen had decided she had had enough. She wrote a letter of resignation and handed it to Betty, her supervisor. Later, she began to reflect on what she had done, spoke with her union steward, and decided to withdraw her resignation and return to work.

She had spoken again with Betty, who said she would see what she could do. Several days later, Betty still had not responded, so Doreen approached her and asked again to have her resignation letter back. Betty said she would try and would get back to her. Betty called the human relations officer for the company and was told that she had an option: she could either return the letter of resignation or, if she felt that Doreen should not return to work, she could accept Doreen's resignation and force her to leave.

A week later, Betty met with Doreen and gave her the bad news: she was accepting the letter of resignation. Doreen complained to her union and filed a grievance. The issue went through all the steps of the grievance process without resolution. Just before the case was due to go to arbitration, the company and the union decided to try mediation.

As the mediation began, the company and union representatives wanted to be heard first on the issue of the effectiveness of the letter of resignation. The company representative said he felt that Doreen's letter of resignation had been effective, that she had quit, and that the company simply did not want her back. In addition, the company had uncovered evidence regarding an incident that had taken place after her resignation that supported her termination.

The union objected to the company's bringing this incident into the mediation, because it had occurred after what they referred to as Doreen's termination. The company representative countered that the incident had affected the company's belief that Doreen was a loyal, trustworthy employee. We encouraged the parties to proceed with the mediation, pointing out that solutions in mediation are voluntary and that if the union wanted to convince the company to reinstate Doreen, it needed to hear and respond to all the objections, even if they were not admissible in arbitration. Both sides agreed to proceed.

The union representative said that Doreen had been in a highly emotional state after receiving the disciplinary memorandum. When she calmed down, she had thought better about her letter of resignation and changed her mind. She had met with Betty and asked for the letter back, as had her union steward, on at least two occasions. One week after the second request, they were told for the first time that Doreen's resignation had been accepted. The union representative argued that an employee should have the right to change her mind any time before the company's acceptance of her resignation.

After the representatives finished their presentations, we asked Betty to speak. She described her contact with the human relations department and the advice that had been given to her. She told us that when she asked Doreen why she wanted to continue working at the company, Doreen said that her grandmother was upset about her letter of resignation, and that she had changed her mind about resigning.

At this point, we intervened and told the parties that there were really two sets of issues they had raised so far. First, there were a number of legal issues, including Doreen's right to withdraw her letter of resignation, which would be important if the grievance were to go to arbitration. But there was also a second set of issues that no one had addressed: Why had Doreen decided to resign in the first place? Why had she changed her mind? Why did the company decide to accept her resignation? Why wasn't the company willing to take her back? What had happened after Doreen's resignation that affected their willingness to think of her as a loyal and trustworthy employee? What was the company going to do as a result of that discovery? What were all the possible solutions? Finally, there was the larger question: Could all these issues be resolved to everyone's satisfaction?

As mediators, we asked these questions in the hope that they would take the process to a deeper level. We wanted to discover what was really going on in the dispute and thereby open up the possibility for resolution. Both sides agreed that it would be much more productive to concentrate on the second set of issues. Betty continued her narrative, no longer focusing on the letter of resignation but on Doreen's behavior, which had led to it. In doing so, she became less defensive and more open, balanced, and authentic.

The principal problem with Doreen, according to Betty, was her attitude. Betty's reasons for deciding to accept Doreen's resignation were based on Doreen's hostility toward the job. She said Doreen had often made statements to the effect that she hated her job and hated coming to work, and that she had made these statements more than once.

Doreen had continually violated the dress code by wearing sleeveless blouses and sometimes by not wearing nylons. Her job performance was poor, and she had to be prompted all the time to do her work. Betty felt that she had exhibited unprofessional conduct by talking loudly in front of customers, smacking her gum, taking off her stockings at work, and continuing to chew gum after she had been asked to stop.

Doreen's poor attendance and tardiness were also a problem, although Betty had worked hard with Doreen to improve this aspect of her behavior. She had even picked Doreen up at home occasionally and driven her to work. Under company policy, tardiness of even one minute counted as an absence, although the supervisor had discretion not to count it as an absence if the employee's reasons for being late were good enough.

Betty felt that Doreen had engaged in unethical conduct by using company telephones to call outside the area. She had been given a verbal warning for this behavior, but it had happened again just before Doreen had resigned. She had not been disciplined, however, because the telephone bill arrived only a few days before her last day at work.

Finally, Betty accused Doreen of fraudulent conduct, which had been uncovered after Doreen left the company. After her last day of work, Doreen had gone to a different store operated by the company and bought some expensive equipment, using a checking account that no longer existed. She then went to a second store in an effort to obtain cash by returning the equipment. When the store refused, she had a friend return the equipment to the store where she had worked, and she asked her union steward to help her obtain cash for it.

We asked Betty whether Doreen had any good points as an employee. At first Betty did not respond, but then she said that Doreen was able to do the work well if she wanted to, that she could be very professional, and that she had an ability to work well with the public. She said, in response to our question, that if Doreen had not quit she would not have been fired but would have been worked with in an effort to improve her performance. We asked Betty whether she would be willing to take Doreen back if she were convinced that Doreen had really changed her attitude and was willing to improve her performance in all the areas mentioned. Betty said she would.

Next it was Doreen's turn to speak. She began slowly but warmed to her subject in response to our questions. At first she spoke about minor details: her job title, the date when she had started working for the company, and what she did in her work role. She said she had been quite upset about the disciplinary memorandum and felt everyone at work was down on her.

She had had serious communication problems with Betty, who gave her the impression that she would be there for her but then wasn't. She had handed in her resignation and then spoken with her union steward and her grandmother and changed her mind. She had asked Betty twice to return her letter, and she had thought that Betty was going to return it. At the third request, Betty "blew up" at her and refused to give the letter back.

Doreen said that Betty used to tell other people, in Doreen's presence, that she "only had herself to blame" for hiring Doreen, and that she should have let her go after three months. This had hurt Doreen's feelings. She felt that sales work was hard for her to do successfully; there were four other salespeople and too few customers. Sales assistants received a pay incentive for sales, so they competed actively and sometimes took each other's customers, which also made it hard for her. She felt she had done well, though, and she had volunteered to help out in other areas.

At one point, a month before her resignation, she had worked as a customer service representative with no sales duties, and she had liked that much better than sales work. She had asked to transfer to this type of position but did not have enough seniority to qualify. At the company where Doreen was now employed, she worked as a customer service representative. She liked the job, but the benefits were not as good as at her former company.

In response to our questions, Doreen gave several reasons for resigning and then deciding to withdraw her letter of resignation. Her reasons for wanting to quit were based on her disappointment after being removed from work as a customer service representative. She also felt that she had too many conflicts with Betty, would never be able to meet her sales objectives, and would never be good enough for Betty. She had been twenty years old when she started working for the company and was the youngest person there. She dressed, thought, and spoke differently from the others. She thought of herself as "hipper" and "crazier" than they were, and she believed that they would never accept her for who she was.

Doreen was now working full-time and going to school at night, studying Spanish and typing. Her work hours were too long, she said, and too uncertain to permit her to attend school full-time, which she wanted to do. She liked working with her new company's equipment and with the computer, and she got along well with the customers. Initially, Doreen had not discussed her decision to resign with anyone. We asked if she had talked about it beforehand with her grandparents. She said that her grandfather was eighty-one and her grandmother was seventy-two and that they were not well. They had raised her from the time she was a child, after her mother died and her father moved away. Her father had suffered a heart attack and had died shortly after her resignation. She felt completely responsible for taking care of her aging grandparents, whom she saw more as parents, although they actually took care of her more than she did of them.

In response to several questions, Doreen reluctantly told us why she had changed her mind about resigning. She said she did not normally act that impulsively and was not as "bad" as the disciplinary memorandum made her look on paper. She had many abilities that Betty did not recognize. Her union steward had talked to her about her decision to resign and advised her against it. Doreen had liked working for the company, although she hated sales and the way it was structured. At the time she resigned, she was not thinking about the positive features of her job.

We asked Doreen to respond to the reasons that Betty had given for accepting her resignation, and Doreen gave the following explanations for each of the behaviors Betty had cited:

1. Betty had said that Doreen hated her job. Doreen remembered commenting that she did not like sales or the organization of sales work but got along well enough with the other salespeople and didn't dislike working for the company. She had never said she hated the company or all the work. In addition, she had been younger then and more immature, and she had said some things she hadn't meant.

2. Betty had cited Doreen's unprofessional conduct. Doreen said that the stockings she had taken off were knee-highs, not hose. She had been in a motorcycle accident and had received serious burns on her legs, and the stockings stuck painfully to her burns. The store had been closed at the time she took the knee-highs off, and she had been sitting behind the counter. She acknowledged that she had made mistakes, such as chewing gum, and had not taken full responsibility for herself.

3. Betty had cited her poor attendance and tardiness. Doreen felt that the attendance policy was unfair in counting tardiness of even one minute as an absence. She had not had a car at the time and had to take the bus more than forty miles to work. Her commute had sometimes taken her two or two and a half hours each way. Because she was only working part-time at that time, she would sometimes spend more time commuting than

at work. Her attendance was also affected by her father's heart attack. Now she lived closer to work, in her own apartment. She had a car, was older and more mature, and had no problems with tardiness in her new job.

4. Betty had pointed to Doreen's unethical conduct in using company phones for calls outside the local dialing area. Doreen said she had been unaware that the prefix she was dialing was out of the area. She had been calling a health care facility to check on her grandmother, but no one had told her not to, and no one had told her that it was a toll call. Also, she said, other employees, Betty among them, often called outside the immediate area. Doreen's understanding had been that the rule allowed employees to make calls on their breaks but did not allow them to make long distance calls, and she had thought that the phone she used was linked to a system that blocked toll calls.

5. Betty had labeled Doreen's behavior as fraudulent. Doreen agreed that she had gone to the store with "bad intentions" and knew that this was wrong. Afterward, she had called her union steward and asked for help. She was only trying to return the phone to the store where she worked; she had not been trying to get cash for it. We asked Doreen why she had tried to carry out this plan, and she could only say that she did not know why she had tried to do it, but she agreed that it was wrong. Further questions only produced the same answer.

Doreen felt that she had been able to get along well with Betty, who was not a bad person, and that they had been close, off and on. She was upset when Betty said it had been a mistake to hire her. She sometimes thought of Betty as a mother substitute or surrogate mother, and Betty had played that role with her, baking her a cake one year for her birthday and including her in her family holidays.

Doreen said that she felt much more secure and responsible today than she had before. Her parents' deaths and the age and health of her grandparents meant that she would soon be completely on her own and could not afford to be irresponsible any longer: the only one left to take care of her would be herself, and she had never realized this before. Having her own apartment and car also meant that she was now on her own and not dependent on anyone. She felt like a bird released from its cage.

We asked Betty if she felt she had been a mother substitute for Doreen, and she agreed that she had been. We asked if it made any sense to her to think of their dispute as a mother-daughter conflict and as a manifestation of adolescent rebellion. She laughed and said that she had never thought of it that way but agreed that this was what had really happened. She felt that she had made a mistake in getting too close to Doreen and that, by trying to mother her, may have triggered Doreen's anger at her real mother. We asked Doreen if this was true, and she said she thought it was.

We then asked Betty and Doreen what they wanted to do to resolve this dispute. Betty asked if she could meet with us separately to consider what she wanted to do, and we agreed that we would do so in a moment. First, however, we wanted to know what each one had learned from the conversation we had just had. We asked them, along with their representatives, to brainstorm what might have done to prevent this conflict and what they could do in the future to prevent similar conflicts.

They quickly agreed that the company needed to have clearer policies regarding letters of resignation and clearer rules for their withdrawal or acceptance, and that managers and staff needed to be aware of these policies and rules. They agreed that there needed to be a uniform time frame for acceptance or rejection of a resignation and clear rules for acceptance. They agreed that if there were problems in the future, there should be a mechanism for mediation or arbitration to resolve cases in which employees wished to withdraw their resignations. They also agreed that they should use standard legal rules to decide when a resignation has been accepted and can no longer be withdrawn and to communicate these recommendations to the company and the union.

Because they appeared unwilling to discuss in joint session what might be done in response to the deeper issues between them, and because they had asked to meet in confidential caucuses, we met with each side separately. Primarily, we wanted to talk privately with Doreen, to discover whether she was interested in returning to work for the company prior to exploring that option with Betty and the company representative. We agreed that we would keep confidential anything that they asked us not to divulge, and we thanked Betty and Doreen for their honest and thoughtful presentations.

In the first caucus, we asked Doreen what she wanted from the mediation. Her union representative responded by asking for her reinstatement with full back pay. We said we thought it was unlikely that the company would agree, and we suggested that they work together to create a list of all possible options, with that as their first choice. We asked them to suggest as many other possibilities as they could. The options they listed, with some help from us, were as follows:

1. Reinstatement of Doreen with full back pay
2. Reinstatement with partial back pay
3. Reinstatement with no back pay
4. Reinstatement to a new position
5. Reinstatement with expedited transfer to a new position
6. Cleaning up of Doreen's personnel record and permission for her to apply for a new job with the company
7. Rehiring of Doreen (as opposed to reinstatement) at a different location
8. Rehiring with a lateral transfer to a new position
9. No reinstatement or rehiring, but a cash buyout to compensate Doreen for dropping her grievance
10. No reinstatement, no buyout, and follow-through on the grievance
11. Reinstatement for six months and, if she received a satisfactory performance appraisal, rehiring as a customer representative, ahead of new hires

Some time was spent discussing the advantages and disadvantages of each option and the problem of Doreen's returning to a job that she really did not enjoy. We also looked at whether she wanted to work again for a supervisor with whom she had little trust or communication. We asked whether she wanted to return to the company in order to work out her relationship with her surrogate mother and whether this might cause her to slip back into her old resentments, or whether she genuinely wanted her old job back.

After a lengthy conversation, Doreen decided she was really ready to move on with her life, no longer needed a substitute mother, and did not care to return to a job that had no future. She said that the option she liked best was option 9, with option 11 a close second, but option 11 would have to be refined so that she would not be penalized for problems or circumstances beyond her control. Any rehire or reinstatement would have to begin as of the date of her termination, and the precise details would have to be fleshed out between management and her union representative. Doreen and her union representative gave us permission to use their list of options and reveal their preferences to the other side.

We then met in caucus with the company representative and Betty, to find out what they wanted and narrow the options. We presented them with the list of options developed by Doreen and the union representative and asked them to add to the list, if any other options occurred to them. The company representative and Betty expressed a preference for options 3, 6, 7, 10, and 11; option 9 was dismissed because the company had a policy against buyouts, so as to avoid the appearance of rewarding misbehavior.

Relying on our arbitration experience, we asked the company representative whether there was a chance the company would lose its case in arbitration. They agreed that working against them was the fact that the supervisor had not made the decision to accept the resignation until after Doreen had asked to withdraw it, and the supervisor had admitted that Doreen would not otherwise have been terminated at the time she asked for her letter back. The company representative felt that losing in arbitration would produce the worst possible result for the company.

We returned to caucus with Doreen and the union representative and revealed the company's preferences. Of these, the union representative preferred options 6, 7, and 11, but Doreen still preferred option 9. We agreed to return to the other side and try to reopen discussion of option 9, but with number 11 as a backup.

Betty and the company representative were still suspicious of Doreen's change of attitude and doubtful of her general trustworthiness, so when we suggested that a way might be found to keep the monetary results confidential, they agreed to consider option 9. We then asked them what they would need for a financial buyout to work.

They proposed that the entire agreement become null and void if anyone at work found out about it, that it be considered by the union to have no value as a precedent in future grievances, and that the money be repaid if Doreen disclosed the amount she had received. They were willing to offer $1,500—what her back pay would have been to the date of the mediation—if Doreen would drop her grievance and agree not to seek to be rehired by the company. They also suggested, in the event of problems in interpreting or enforcing the agreement, that they all return to mediation. Doreen and the union representative agreed to these terms.

We reviewed the agreement with both sides and asked what had led them to choose this option and how they felt about the mediation process. Betty and the company representative said they felt this was the best result they could achieve, given the chance that they might lose in arbitration, and given their lack of trust or confidence in Doreen's ability to change her attitude if she were reinstated or rehired. Her job would have required her to handle cash, and they still believed that she had done something dishonest, even if it had taken place after her resignation and might not have been admitted in evidence during arbitration. They were pleased with the mediation process and felt it had produced a solution that they could not have achieved through arbitration.

Doreen and her union representative also felt that this was the best result, but for very different reasons. They were influenced by the fact that Doreen really had not liked working as a sales representative and had found another job that she liked better. They recognized that there would have been a risk of future disciplinary actions if she had been reinstated or rehired, and that she now had a record of having quit without being fired. They were happy with the mediation process because they felt that they had received more of a day in court than they would have had by actually going to court.

Both sides felt that they had won something important that they wanted. Both felt that they had given something as well and that the result was fair and workable. Both sides agreed that they had communicated their deeper issues, and that a deeper truth had emerged through their discussions. Betty and Doreen ended the mediation with their self-esteem reinstated and were able to let their animosities go. They shook hands with smiles and pleased expressions on their faces.

We complimented both parties on their honesty and frankness in facing their past disagreements, on their willingness to compromise, on their ability to work together to come up with creative solutions to their problems, and on their willingness to participate in the mediation process. They all signed the agreement and complimented us on our work. Everyone left smiling and expressing satisfaction with the outcome and the process.

## Observations

Families of origin are the real training ground for conflicts at work and relationships in organizations. We learn in childhood how to respond to authority, how to get our needs met, and how to become responsible for our actions. Doreen's story revealed that she had not fully resolved these family issues and had been using Betty as a surrogate mother to work them out.

Although technically an adult, Doreen had behaved in juvenile ways in the workplace, just as a rebellious teenager might have behaved toward her mother. Her reactions to her father's illness and her grandparents' aging were those of a child just beginning to turn into an adult. Unfortunately, Betty had responded in kind. She had been drawn into a mother-daughter relationship that limited her ability to be Doreen's supervisor.

The mediation supported Doreen in recognizing that she had not behaved responsibly at work and in starting to understand why. It also encouraged her to become responsible for her choices and to end, as an adult might, her relationship with Betty. It clearly would have been difficult for her to return to work with Betty, and her preferred options for resolution reflected her awareness of this difficulty. We saw from her demeanor, tone of voice, and body language that she did not need to return to adolescence to resolve her youthful disputes. She was ready to transcend them and move on to fresh, age-appropriate disputes.

We could have probed deeper into these family-based issues, but we felt that neither of the parties wanted or needed to do so. We took a minimalist, intuitive approach that began with an exercise in empathy for ourselves. We asked ourselves whether if we were Betty or Doreen, would we want or need to go deeper in order to resolve this dispute and move on with our lives? In this case, our answer was no, in part because a series of real breaks had already occurred in their relationship, and there was no compelling reason to go back.

One of these breaks had been triggered by Doreen's actions following her termination. We have often found that people subconsciously engage in trust-breaking behavior in order to end a relationship when they do not have the courage or skill to end it through conversation. It may be that Doreen expressed through her actions her need to move on and chose consciously to move on only during the mediation.

Moreover, the legal issues regarding the letter of resignation had created a legalistic, abstract, superficial story that distracted the parties from the emotional, concrete, deeper story regarding the reasons that had led to the resignation. This does not mean, however, that the legal issues were unimportant; on the contrary, every organization can benefit from having clear policies on letters of resignation and on when they can be withdrawn.

Because Doreen and Betty decided to end their work relationship, it was unnecessary to work through all the details of these issues, including how they had become trapped and how they might free themselves from mother-daughter dynamics. The resignation and termination were strong, clear statements that the relationship was not working.

For these reasons, while the core story had emerged, it was not fully processed by the parties during the mediation. When, as mediators, we accept stories that lie at the periphery of the conflict, we can only work at the periphery. Superficial stories yield superficial results. When we discover the stories at the core, however, we can work at the core to discover what created the conflict in the first place and what the parties need to do to resolve it. In this case, the transformation had already begun, and neither side was interested in processing it together. Its time had come and gone.

# Addicted to Defeat

In November, Buddy had been fired by the company for which he had worked for more than sixteen years. The reason given was that his absenteeism had become chronic and apparently incurable. The company had tried using progressive discipline, including written warnings and unpaid suspensions, to give him time to think about how to correct the problem. Finally, he was suspended pending investigation and then terminated.

The union filed a grievance, and the case was proceeding to arbitration when the company and the union agreed to try mediation. They felt mediation might be able to resolve the dispute faster and more cheaply and might address not just the legal issues that would be present in arbitration but the underlying interpersonal issues as well.

After agreement was reached among all the parties regarding ground rules for the mediation process, a company representative began. He said that Buddy had a chronic problem with attendance and punctuality, which included tardiness in returning from lunch. During the past year he had been absent on numerous occasions. The company had tried progressive discipline, including counseling, warnings, and suspensions, but nothing had worked. The company believed that the only alternative left was to fire him.

The union representative said she did not dispute Buddy's extensive record of absences, but, given his long-term history of employment and competent work record, she felt he should not be fired. She thought the company had not dealt with the problem very well and might have done more.

We asked her why the absenteeism had continued for so long. She hesitated before answering, whispered for a moment to Buddy, and then said that he had experienced a serious drug problem for which he had sought help the year before. He had continued to struggle with the problem into the following year, when he finally admitted he had a problem and entered a local hospital for rehabilitation. While he was in the hospital getting treatment, the company had fired him.

The union representative went on to point out that Buddy was average or better in his work. During three of the last six years he had had acceptable attendance. Still, she admitted that denial regarding drug use was part of his problem. She claimed that he had successfully completed a substance abuse program, that he was now drug-free, and that the company's policy was that substance abuse was an illness and a disease that should be treated, not punished.

Buddy's direct supervisor, Jim, said that Buddy's drug problem had affected other employees on the job. We asked Jim what he had done in response to Buddy's drug problem. Jim said he felt he had no right to confront employees about their drug issues. Drug use was a delicate issue, he said, and he felt he could only make recommendations and refer employees to outside assistance. Since he was not a medical person, he could not say for sure if someone had a drug problem. He felt he could send an employee to see the company doctor but would not tell the doctor what he suspected. He had repeatedly offered Buddy a general form of "help," which Buddy had not taken.

According to the union representative, management had not informed the union of any offers of help to Buddy, even though a union representative had been present at all the meetings concerning progressive discipline. Buddy had been sent six times for medical evaluation, with no result. Jim had kept asking Buddy whether there was a problem, and Buddy had kept denying that he had one. The union had offered him counseling as well, but Buddy had not taken advantage of it.

Buddy's union steward had finally sent him for a company medical exam, but the treatment he had received was for alcoholism because that was the only program available at the hospital. His problem, however, was not alcohol but cocaine. When the company doctor examined him, he said that he saw nothing that would prevent Buddy from doing his job.

Management then decided to escalate disciplinary measures in order to get Buddy to change and to show him the seriousness of the situation. Buddy had been suspensed until further notice. He entered a twenty-eight-day rehabilitation program, and when he finished, the company converted his suspension into a termination.

The union felt that progressive discipline had not been adhered to. Buddy had been given a crisis suspension pending termination, a procedure that the company used when someone was dangerous to himself or to others. The union argued that this was not the case with Buddy. When the company had asked Buddy to return to his job after treatment, he had requested a transfer, to get out of the environment that encouraged his drug problem. His supervisor had talked him out of it, saying privately that he did not want to unload the problem of managing Buddy onto anyone else.

The company said its policy on employee drug use was to make it the employee's responsibility to change. The company had decided to fire Buddy primarily because it was not convinced he would change, given that he had done the same thing earlier and had refused help before. The company's policy was to encourage progressive discipline, but the employee had to be the one to change.

We had still not heard directly from Buddy, so we asked him whether he had any response to what had been said. He said he felt there were many inaccuracies in what had been said and that he could no longer believe the company because they did not understand his problem. He had discussed his problem with his supervisor. He felt that to solve the problems he was facing, the company needed to reduce the stress and "favoritism" toward others that had "made" him resort to drugs in the first place. He had talked to Jim about the stress and favoritism, but he felt that Jim had not really listened and did not like him personally. Jim had told him that lots of people in the company wanted to get rid of him.

We felt from these comments that Buddy had slipped back into denying he had a problem. To refocus his attention, we asked why he had started using drugs again after his first hospitalization. Buddy said he had been under a lot of stress. He felt Jim did a lot of things that made it hard to go to counseling, such as favoring other employees. He had called the therapist with the company's employee assistance program and told her he was so upset he couldn't work.

Because of his reference to favoritism, which in our experience often begins as a family issue, we asked Buddy whether members of his family had supported him in his substance abuse treatment. Buddy said they had not, and then his voice broke, his eyes began to tear up, and he paused to gain composure. He told us amid tears that his father was a popular pastor in the community church and still did not know about his treatment for substance abuse. He said he did not want to ruin his father's reputation, and he began to cry in earnest. He felt it was better to lie than to tell him the truth. He said his drug problem was "history" now, and that the company was "history," too.

We asked Buddy to explain why he felt his drug problem was history, and why he thought the company was history. He said it seemed as if he was always one step away from being suspended. Regarding the company, he said there wasn't much recognition for things he did that were positive, and he felt a lot of stress that encouraged him to use drugs. "You screw up once and it goes down in writing," he concluded, "but nothing good ever goes down in writing." The company responded that this was not true and that positive things were put in writing. Jim, for example, had made positive comments about Buddy, and these were in writing.

We asked Jim to repeat what he had said about Buddy that was positive, and, as he did so, to speak directly to Buddy. Jim complimented Buddy on his work record and skill and on his willingness to take on difficult assignments. As Jim was speaking, Buddy looked down and did not make eye contact, but he clearly was pleased with the acknowledgment.

The union asked if it could caucus with the mediators. We agreed, and the company representatives left the room. The union representative then reviewed the strengths and weaknesses of Buddy's case, as if they were going to arbitration, and mentioned that management had made a labeling mistake under its own rules by calling what they had done a crisis suspension instead of a suspension with pay pending investigation for dismissal. Also, there was no documentation of the investigation phase of the dismissal, and the company had fired Buddy while he was undergoing treatment.

We asked the union representatives whether they saw any difficulties with their case. They mentioned Buddy's chronic absenteeism and long-standing drug problem, the progressive discipline that had been administered by the company, and the fact that Buddy had been through the program once before and it had not worked.

We asked Buddy what he really wanted, but the union representative answered, saying that they wanted pay for one year, or $36,000. Buddy had found a new job and was no longer interested in returning to the company. We asked the union representative whether she thought the company would be willing to pay $36,000, given the weaknesses she had identified in Buddy's case. The union accepted the fact that the case was weak, and Buddy agreed. He just wanted "those guys up there" to understand that they had "mishandled the situation."

We asked them what could be done to prevent this type of problem from becoming so serious in the future. They felt the company should be more "up-front" and honest in its communications with the union and employees about drug problems. There could be a better training program for first-level supervisors in handling substance abuse problems. They felt the company should create an easier transfer policy in drug cases, to help workers get away from other drug users, and a clearer policy on confidentiality with respect to therapists in the company's employee assistance program. They said there should be a thirty-day suspension as an intermediate discipline before termination, as well as a policy allowing supervisors to confront employees whom they believe to have drug problems. We asked them if it would be acceptable for us to give this list to the company, and they agreed. We also asked how they would feel if some of the money they were requesting were used to fund a training program for managers and supervisors on how to respond to employees with substance abuse problems. Both the union representative and Buddy thought this was a good idea.

We next met in caucus with the company representatives, who said they wanted to offer a nuisance settlement at nowhere near Buddy's lost earnings. The company representatives understood that if they lost in arbitration, they might have to pay a year's salary, minus any wages Buddy had earned in the interim. To settle the case, however, they might be willing to pay something closer to $10,000.

We asked the company representatives what they saw as the strengths and weaknesses of their case going into arbitration. They thought the technical mislabeling of the suspension was a minor issue, but, in hindsight, they felt that a thirty-day suspension would have been more constructive. They agreed that discharging Buddy while he was undergoing treatment had been a mistake.

The company representatives agreed with all the points that had been suggested by Buddy and the union representative for how similar problems might be avoided in the future, and they thought it would be appropriate that we communicate these points as recommendations to the leadership of the company and the union. They suggested three additional points, with which the union readily agreed: the routine use of thirty-day suspensions before termination in all drug and alcohol cases, a requirement that employees attend meetings of Alcoholics Anonymous or similar self-help programs during this period, and a requirement that the union and the company work together to assist employees with chronic drug problems.

The company representatives liked the idea of putting some of the money available for settlement into a separate fund to train front-line managers and supervisors in how to help employees with substance abuse problems. They commented that this was something they could not have achieved through arbitration. We asked what the training would cost in ballpark terms, and they arrived at a figure of $15,000. The company representative said that they were also willing to give Buddy $7,000 as a cash settlement.

We returned to the union and Buddy to communicate this offer. We asked how they felt about the training part of the proposal, and they thought it was excellent, but Buddy said he found the offer of $7,000 unacceptable; he had $25,000 in mind. He said nothing could compensate him for what had happened to him and that he would rather go to arbitration and be vindicated.

We asked Buddy whether he understood that the company would probably not be willing to meet his demand and that he might lose in arbitration. We pointed out that if he did lose, his record of absences and tardiness, his drug problems on the job, and the company's record of progressive discipline could result in his walking away with nothing. Buddy said he had spoken to a lawyer and had high hopes.

We asked Buddy if he would accept any amount lower than $25,000, and he said he would not. We asked if he had ever been to arbitration before and if he understood how it worked. He said he had not but believed he was right and would take his chances. We asked what he thought would be the effect on the arbitrator of the fact that his record of absences was really quite long. He reiterated that he would take his chances.

The union representative asked if we could meet alone for a moment, and Buddy left the room. We said we felt Buddy was slipping into denial again or, at any rate, was being unrealistic about his chances for success. We wondered what she thought could be done. She agreed with our assessment and acknowledged, confidentially, that the company's offer was fair, but she had told Buddy he could say yes or no to the settlement offer.

We presented Buddy's counteroffer to the company representatives, who laughed. They said that if Buddy would not reconsider, they would go to arbitration. They agreed to raise their offer to $10,000 but would not increase the size of the pot any further. They were firm on that figure and would not go any higher.

We met again with the union and Buddy, to present the company's response. We reviewed again the strengths and weaknesses of the union's position, including the possibility of losing in arbitration. If Buddy went to arbitration, it could take six months to a year before he would receive an award. He would have to lose a day or two from his new job to attend the hearing and testify, and he would lose some after-work hours in helping the union prepare. Even then he might lose, as opposed to having $10,000 without delay and a management training program to prevent similar problems in the future.

Buddy was wavering but unwilling to agree, so we suggested that he take time to think about the company's offer and discuss it with his attorney, his wife, and other family members and friends. We also suggested that he discuss the proposal and his drug problem with his father. We felt it was important for his recovery that he stop denying that he had a problem, and telling his father would be a way of accepting responsibility. He agreed with us and began to cry again.

After a few moments of silence, Buddy said he realized that going forward with arbitration was not going to help him with his drug problem and that his father would learn about it anyway, and he agreed to accept the company's offer. He said he knew that to successfully change and give up his denial and drug habit, he had to confront his father and tell him the truth about what had happened and how he felt about him, but he was afraid of doing so.

We asked Buddy what he was afraid would happen if he told his father. Buddy said he was afraid his father would not approve of him. We asked him if his father approved of him now. Buddy cried again and said he felt his father had never understood who he was or ever said he loved him, and that he had never felt his father's approval. We suggested that Buddy start by telling his father how much he loved him and how much he wanted his approval. We suggested he tell his father about his pain, about how difficult it had been for him to get up the courage to reveal his drug problem, about how hard it had been to stop using drugs, and about how his father could support him in staying off drugs. Buddy looked relieved as he imagined this conversation, and he said he would try.

Buddy thanked us for our honesty and apologized for taking so long to agree to a fair settlement. We complimented him on his courage in facing his problems, on taking responsibility for his actions, and on being willing to face the future rather than continuing to focus on the past. We encouraged him again to speak to his father about his drug problems and to ask for his wife's advice and support.

We were later told by the union representative that Buddy had spoken with his father, had stopped using drugs, had been promoted at his new job, and was doing well.

## Observations

For many people in conflict, stories are better than any narcotic. Buddy certainly used his story about the company's "favoritism" toward others, which had "made" him resort to drugs, just as he had used cocaine: to ease his pain and divert attention from the truth. At the same time, the diversionary tactics that were revealed in his story indirectly told us the truth.

Buddy's story about Jim's lack of acknowledgment and disapproval exactly paralleled his story about his father's lack of understanding and disapproval. He referred during mediation to the lack of recognition for positive things he had done. He blamed management for the stress that had encouraged him to use drugs. He attacked management's attitude: "You screw up once and it goes down in writing, but nothing good ever goes down in writing." He may have accurately described his work environment, but he also depicted the history of his relationship with his father and his justification for continuing to use drugs.

In order to stop using one narcotic, Buddy also had to stop using the other. As long as he held on to a story that excused his addiction, it became integral to his addiction, and his inability to surrender his story was simply the siren song of the drug.

It was not our task to cure Buddy of his addiction. Our role was simpler: to find a way for him to conclude his relationship with the company on mutually acceptable terms. As a result, we did not probe any deeper into his story or his relationship with his father than we needed to do in order to resolve the immediate conflict. Yet, when he decided to tell his father about his drug problems, he simultaneously decided to accept the company's offer, and he revealed the interconnection between the two.

We encouraged Buddy to believe that he had the ability to open the one conversation that really mattered to him, the one that could actually end all the stories that he had used to sacrifice his life and justify his continued addiction: the conversation with his father. The real story of that conversation is one we wish we knew.

# Chapter Five

# Stories That Hold Organizations Hostage

*Because the ones I work for do not love me, because I have*
*said too much and I haven't been sure of what is right*
*and I've hated the people I've trusted, because I work in*
*an office and we are lost and when I come home I say their*
*lives are their's and they don't know what they apologize*
*for and none of it mended, because I let them beat me and*
*I remember something of mine which not everyone has,*
*and because I lie to keep my self and my hands my voice*
*on the phone because I swallow what hurts me, because I*
*hurt them I give them the hours I spend away from them*
*and carry them, even in my sleep, at least as the nag of a*
*misplaced shoe, for years after I have quit and gone on to*
*another job where I hesitate in telling and I remember and*
*I resent having had to spend more time with them than*
*with the ones I love.*
KILLARNEY CLARY, *WHO WHISPERED NEAR ME*

Organizations can be ground to a halt by conflicts or transformed
by them. Impending changes always announce themselves in the
form of increased conflict, including interpersonal conflict. It is
possible for us to learn to approach every organizational conflict
as an opportunity for improvement, an indication that something
needs to shift.

We can define organizational conflict, then, as the sound made
by the cracks in a system, the birth cry of a new paradigm, a call for
change in a culture or system that has outlived its usefulness. We

can see it as a space in which contradictory internal forces are manifested, a sign pointing to weakness in the organizational system.

Organizational conflicts are held in place by the stories people tell, stories that are often designed to justify the status quo, protect positions, rationalize actions, and retain power. If we define an organization as a complex arrangement of self-referential stories, we can find in these stories every important piece in the puzzle of what makes or prevents it from being successful.

One of the most important elements in organizational success is the capacity to learn from mistakes and to self-correct. To create a culture that encourages organizational learning, leaders need to recognize that conflict stories are opportunities that demand their focus and attention.

Conflicts can break apart a smoothly running structure. They can block organizational change, scuttle strategic planning, ruin morale, destroy productivity, and block future visions. At the same time, work life, morale, and productivity can be enormously enhanced, even transformed, when organizations decide to learn from their conflicts and resolve the underlying reasons that created them. In inquiry-based learning organizations, conflicts are not swept under the rug or ignored. If we want to encourage creativity, problem solving, testing of new ideas, and innovation, we need to engage our conflicts and learn from them.

## Creating Organizational Cultures That Support Resolution

Stories about conflict form a large part of every organization's culture. They tell us a great deal about the suppressed, unnoticed, and avoided issues that define its inner core and shape its values and beliefs. Conflicts mirror the personal expectations, patterns of interaction, modes of participation, styles of leadership, hierarchical relationships, and forms of communication that define organizational culture.

Most organizational cultures do not support employees or managers in adopting a learning orientation to conflict. More often, they avoid or suppress what they perceive as disorder. They circumvent open problem solving, minimize individual responsibility, ignore personal needs, distort communication, and discourage potentially cathartic showdowns. The damaging effects of these approaches to conflict extend far beyond the individuals who are embroiled in them; these effects can prevent the organization itself from being successful.

When we enter an organization that is embroiled in conflict, we canvass the cultural context in which the conflict is taking place. We analyze the invisible web of shared beliefs, attitudes, and customs that influence how the conflict is being fought. We explore the meaning within the culture of silence, public criticism, emotional expression, and direct confrontation. We discover how people negotiate, how aggressive or collaborative they feel they can be, how they communicate their personal bottom lines, how they compromise, and how they behave when they reach impasse. Here are some questions we ask to reveal an organization's conflict culture:

- What kinds of behavior do people exhibit when they are in conflict?
- How do others respond?
- Are conflicts swept under the rug or discussed openly?
- How do issues finally get resolved?
- How do people communicate when they are in conflict?
- What do people do when communication fails?
- How do people negotiate their differences?
- What happens when people reach impasse?
- Is resistance open or disguised?
- What are the openings for dialogue?
- Do people engage in "public compliance and private defiance"?
- Who are the internal conflict resolvers?
- What kinds of conflict behavior do the leaders model?
- How does organizational learning take place?

By focusing on understanding the culture of the organization, the parties can see their behavior as an expression of cultural norms for which alternatives can be found or created.

Taking even a single step in opposition to one's organizational culture can appear to call the system as a whole into question. It can trigger sanctions for violating the rules and isolate dissidents within the organization. Therefore, we support those who work inside the culture by taking risks, changing cultural norms, and trying out new strategies for resolution.

A dramatic example of a cultural shift occurred in an educational museum with which we consulted. The leaders and most members of the staff were committed to ending the petty squabbles that were dividing them and keeping them from transforming the organization. As they analyzed their culture, they discovered that the most damaging conflict stories took the form of gossip. These stories were secret, mean-spirited, disruptive, and cruel, yet engaging in gossip was, for many people, a way of being accepted, an opening to the inner circle. People were afraid to give it up and risk being on the outside. During a large-group mediation, we asked everyone to look at the price they were paying for communicating important information by indirect, covert means—through concealment and subterfuge. The entire staff agreed to start a no-gossip campaign. Everyone agreed to tell stories only to those who were directly involved in the problem or could do something about it. Buttons were passed around advocating: NO GOSSIP and GOSSIP-FREE ZONE. This single decision, taken unanimously, broke the conflict culture. It opened opportunities for a new culture based on acceptance rather than exclusion, and on internal collaboration rather than competition.

Culture matters. In order for an organizational culture to be understood and changed, it has to be revealed and its negative effects have to be exposed. Every conflict creates an opportunity to break old cultural patterns. In doing so, people contribute to making their organizational culture more conducive to effective communication, problem solving, and learning.

## Breaking the Logjam

Mediators who work inside an organization's culture face a difficult challenge: deciding who is actually a party to the conflict and who is not. Many conflicts that take place inside organizations reflect dysfunctional structures, systems, strategies, and behaviors. Many result more from an absence of shared values, teamwork, or leadership than from individual conflicts.

It is part of our role as mediators to create opportunities for people who are engaged in conflict to talk about what is not working and why and to trace the conflict to issues in the larger system. As we listen to people's stories, we often discover that what we thought was a purely personal dispute takes on an organizational character. All people in every organization have stories to tell about conflicts between others or about their own experiences. Often we find these stories are linked and reveal a common denominator.

For this reason, we often find it useful to broaden the story-telling process. We ask permission to interview a wide selection of managers or staff about their conflicts, to hear many different stories, and to assess the total impact of internal conflicts—not just on the immediate parties but on entire departments, work teams, and the organization as a whole. We create a safe environment so that interviewees will be frank and open, yet we make it clear that some of the information from their stories will be used, without attribution, to identify the sources of conflict. Through this larger organizational storytelling process, we amass a great deal of useful information that pinpoints dysfunctional aspects of organizational culture. Without permission to engage in a larger organizational approach, it is possible to reach resolution in a single conflict through interpersonal mediation but never to touch on the larger, systemic organizational issues that gave rise to it. We have seen interpersonal resolutions undermined or sabotaged by the larger organizational culture.

Once we break the logjam in an individual conflict, the parties require ongoing support to significantly change their behavior. Unfortunately, few organizations offer such support. For an organization to function well, the individuals who belong to it need to be supported in resolving their disputes and changing their behavior. To do so, the organization needs to create systems, structures, cultures, strategies, and shared values that do not reinforce conflict-promoting behavior.

## Leadership and Conflict Resolution

Organizational leaders at every level can be powerful advocates for conflict resolution through the telling of stories. In our experience, successful leaders are often skilled storytellers. They can also be good listeners, drawing illustrative stories from their colleagues to explain problems, reveal deeper issues, and encourage resolution.

There are also leaders who become personally involved and embroiled in conflicts. Unable to observe themselves, they become trapped in a downward spiral of misunderstanding and become imprisoned by their conflicts. Through negative modeling, they subtly encourage conflict in the organizational cultures that follow their example.

We can ask leaders to join us in analyzing conflict stories in their organizations, whether these are tales of success and promise or of impasse and retaliation. We can ask them to listen beneath the surface, to hear without censoring what is being said, to acknowledge every kind of communication, and to encourage people in taking responsibility for their stories and their impact on the organization. We see mediation as modeling the kind of leadership style described in the *Tao Te Ching* by the ancient Chinese scholar Lao-tzu:

> The best of all rulers is but a shadowy presence to his subjects.
>
> Next comes the ruler they love and praise;
>
> Next comes one they fear;
>
> Next comes one with whom they take liberties . . .
>
> Hesitant, he does not utter words lightly.
>
> When his task is accomplished and his work done
>
> The people all say, "It happened to us naturally."

# Conflict on Board

Karen was the executive director of a small nonprofit community service organization. For over a year, on numerous occasions, she had considered resigning because of constant conflicts with certain members of her board of directors, especially Larry, the board chair. The arguments had become so intense that mutually hostile camps had formed, and even day-to-day decisions had become fertile ground for disagreement and recrimination.

As the situation became more and more hostile, it became nearly impossible for the board and the director to meet or conduct business. Karen asked us to mediate between her and Larry, but he refused to meet with her unless the entire board were present. They both agreed that we could work with the entire board and try to uncover and resolve the underlying tensions in the organization.

## The First Meeting

At the first joint meeting with the board and the staff, we began by asking all the participants to introduce themselves, say why they had joined the board or staff, and say why they had wanted to work with this particular organization. We did so not merely to gather information about board and staff members but also to establish a common sense of purpose and remind them of the idealistic concerns that had brought them together.

As each person spoke, it became clear that although there were considerable differences, a common commitment to worthwhile purposes united the group. Everyone felt they were contributing to the betterment of the community in which they lived and made heartfelt, inspirational statements about their commitment to the organization.

After creating a context of positive common goals, we could begin to probe their problems and difficulties. To do so and at the same time provide each person with an opportunity to speak, we asked everyone to select a partner with whom he or she felt comfortable in discussing conflicts or problems in the organization. The board members had no problem finding sympathetic colleagues, and the staff members met with each other.

We placed flip-chart paper on all the walls in the meeting room and asked each pair to write down, on one of the sheets, the top three problems the organization faced. When the walls were covered and the listing process was complete, we called the group together to survey the results. There were many similarities and common problems listed on the charts (such as "miscommunication"), but everyone had skirted the deeper issues, and the underlying conflicts had not yet been revealed. Nevertheless, we congratulated the pairs on their work, noted the common issues for future dialogue, and said, optimistically, that they had made a good start and were in agreement on many of their perceptions.

We then indicated that we now had an opportunity to investigate the issues and problems more deeply and to identify the hot, top-priority items that had to be addressed quickly. We assigned everyone to one of four small groups of five members. We gave each group the task of reviewing all the conflicts and issues listed on the sheets on the wall, discussing and analyzing them in detail, calling problems by their real names, and creating a list of priorities that had to be tackled in order for the problem to be solved. We also told the groups that if they continued to identify a problem with a word like "miscommunication," no one could possibly know what to do to solve it. The groups had to go deeper and identify who, precisely, was miscommunicating with whom, and what the specific instances of miscommunication were. Each group was also asked to discuss and evaluate its group process.

In assigning the board members to small groups, we intentionally clustered the principal combatants (including Larry, his wife, and Karen) in the same group. We placed the other board members in groups containing people who were more compatible with each other. We did this because, in our experience, when small groups are assigned simple tasks, the groups with the most collaborative process usually complete their work first, whereas noncollaborative groups come to a grinding halt or reveal their dysfunctional process in their dialogue and in the inevitable comparisons with other groups. We wanted the protagonists in this conflict to actually experience their problems and see at first hand what was blocking their effectiveness and ability to work together. We wanted them to realize, immediately, directly, and experientially the price they were paying for the tensions and conflicts they were not addressing. Our plan bore predictable fruit: everyone in the first three groups completed their tasks with camaraderie and laughter while the last group bogged down and was unable to finish its tasks without assistance from us.

On returning to the large group, we asked the members of each small group to present their list and then to reveal their group process and how they had completed their task. We began with the three healthier groups, and by the time we came to the fourth, the contrast was clear. As each of the first three groups presented its top three priorities, there was considerable agreement among them on the issues requiring immediate attention. All three groups reported that the conflicts were being caused by negative relationships between individual board members, negative relationships between board members and staff, and lack of agreement on the purpose and direction of the organization.

The members of the fourth group reported that they had been unable to agree on how to set priorities for the identified issues and had not had time to evaluate or discuss their group process. We asked them if the problems they had experienced in their group were reflected in the top three issues that had been listed by the other three groups. They agreed that their problems were a function of these larger issues, and that conflicts in their small group had kept them from being effective as a group.

We then asked the members of the other three small groups to comment. They said the exercise had been an eye opener for them, and that the board and staff as a whole had to address the behavior that had triggered dysfunction in the fourth group. Several people spoke up and said that the real problem was the conflict between Larry and Karen. Others added that there were also conflicts that needed to be resolved between Larry and the rest of the board.

We congratulated the group on having honestly identified the real problems in the organization, and we told them they were exactly where they needed to be, which was where the conflicts were manifesting themselves. We asked them for permission to begin tackling the issue of the negative relationship between the board and the staff, and they unanimously agreed. We recommended this approach for three reasons. First, these conflicts were grinding the organization to a halt—fundraising, community development, and hiring of new staff were at a complete impasse. Second, we believed that if this conflict were resolved, the board might feel a greater sense of unity with the staff. Third, we thought that if there were greater unity between the board and the staff, there might be greater clarity about the purpose and direction of the organization.

We next divided those present into two small groups, separating the staff from the board. We asked each group to list its responsibilities, identify its expectations of the other group, and indicate its view of what each side was doing that was causing or contributing to the problem.

Both groups had lively and productive discussions. When we asked each group to present its results, the board began by listing what it thought its responsibilities were. We then asked the staff to present its expectations of the board, and a clear difference of opinion emerged. The same result occurred when the staff presented its list of responsibilities and the board indicated its expectations.

In the ensuing discussion, it emerged that although the board members saw themselves as primary decision makers and the staff as implementers, the staff members saw themselves as administrators and the board members as supporters or general policymakers. The board members expected the staff to keep them informed of everything that happened on a daily basis, whereas the staff expected board members not to second-guess staff decisions but instead to raise the money that made the staff's work possible.

The problems cited by each group, predictably, tracked this difference in perception. Because Larry and his wife had to leave early, we suggested that discussion of these differences be postponed to include these important players. We recommended that no decisions be made on how to resolve this problem without the full participation of both groups. In general, everyone felt good about the session as a first step, but it was clear that the underlying tension had not dissipated.

## The Second Meeting

Two weeks later, we met again, with everyone in attendance. The group decided that this session would be dedicated to a discussion of the negative relationship between the board and the staff. We decided to start, not with words or conversation, but with a graphic display of how each group felt about its relationship with the other.

We again separated board members from staff members, and we asked each group to design a "sculpture," using one another's bodies to create postures that expressed the group's view of the relationship between the board and the staff. This technique, developed by family therapists to support family members in communicating nonverbally how they feel about their family system and relationships, is one we have adapted for work in organizations. The instructions are simple. The participants create a frozen tableau reflecting the relationships among the parties. The tableau does not move, apart from simple mechanical motions, as in a kinetic sculpture. Team members in the sculpture hold the poses given to them by their team and display feelings, interconnections, patterns, and systems that are operating.

The results of this activity were dramatic and revealing, in terms of both process and content. In the sculpture created by the board, each group member had contributed at least one idea, and the result was chaotic. In their sculpture, some "board members" were standing impassively in the middle of the group, waiting for the "staff" to act. Another was standing on a chair, looking down judgmentally. A third whispered gossip in a "staff member's" ear. A fourth had taken a "staff member's" hand, as if to lead her forward, but at the same time was stepping on her foot and holding her in place. The staff sculpture, designed by consensus, presented a single picture, which was completely different. All the "staff members" were on their knees, with faces veiled, while "board members" in various postures argued with each other or turned their backs, completely ignoring the "staff" and revealing that they did not know or care who they were.

Afterward, we discussed the sculpture experience and talked about each group's differing perceptions. The participants described the similarity in how both sculptures had depicted the unknowing, uncaring, conflicted relationship between board and staff, and they felt that something needed to be done to correct this relationship. As a result of the sculpture experience, all present now had not only a phrase to describe the problem but also a clear, visceral sense of what it felt like to be in the other side's shoes. Again, Larry and his wife had to leave early, and full discussion of the problems was frustrated. We stopped the conversation to address the issue of their early departure for a previously scheduled engagement, as well as the difficulty the group faced in trying to solve the problem in their absence. Several members of the board said that this was becoming a pattern and that Larry and his wife were part of the problem. They asked Larry and his wife, before they left, if they would be willing to commit to staying for the full session at our next meeting, and they both agreed. All other group members agreed that they, too, would make the commitment to be present for the entire session. Before we adjourned, we described to those who remained a number of collaborative techniques for shared decision making that could be used by boards of directors and staff members.

## The Third Meeting

At our third meeting, there was no option but to plunge in head first and quickly place the conflict involving Larry and his wife on the table for discussion. At the same time, we wanted the group to identify the problem and knew that everyone would be reluctant to start the meeting by putting anyone on the spot. Therefore, we decided to use a written feedback technique to bring these issues to the surface. We handed out enough three-by-five cards so that everyone had a card for each person present. We asked everyone, without identifying themselves, to write one compliment and one request or suggestion to each person in the room. If they had nothing to say, they could leave the card blank.

Some people took a while to think of what they would say. After everyone had finished writing, we asked them to review what they had written before distributing their cards to their colleagues. We also asked them to consider whether the comments they had written were mostly complimentary or critical, and whether they had learned anything from reading what they had written. Several people had gained insights from the process and saw how hard it was for them to give their colleagues direct critical feedback. Most people felt that they had been excessively negative and were surprised at the anger they felt. Some said they had bottled up their feelings about some of the people in the group, feelings that they now felt a clear need to communicate. We talked about this exercise as a quick process that could not substitute for face-to-face feedback, which should be an ongoing part of their relationship.

They then handed their cards to us, and we gave them to the people to whom they were addressed. We allowed time for people to review the feedback they had received and to notice the feelings, insights, and questions triggered by each card. We then asked each person to reflect aloud about the messages he or she had received. And we said that after each person spoke, the rest of the group would have an opportunity to ask questions or comment.

Some people talked about their sadness or about the validity of the critical comments. Others were pleasantly surprised at receiving compliments. Whenever someone in the group focused only on the critical feedback and ignored the compliments, we asked about the positive comments they had received as well.

Some people spoke in support of others, to counter some of the critical comments they had received. The mood was largely positive, and there was little reaction until Larry spoke. He said he had received considerable negative feedback but saw these criticisms as an inevitable by-product of his intolerance of staff incompetence. He indicated no desire to change his behavior in response to the feedback he had received. He rationalized his current mode of operating and expressed a strong determination to continue raising criticisms of the staff. The rest of the group was stunned and silent.

Because no one responded, we intervened. We asked Larry if it was possible for him to communicate his criticisms respectfully. Through a series of questions to him, we tried to reveal the difference between style and content, between silencing him and making him *more* effective in getting his points across. Larry's wife came to his defense, wondering why we had commented only on Larry's reaction. Before we could answer, she tried to change the subject by shifting to a heated dialogue with another board member. We gently brought the topic back to Larry and invited other people to comment.

Other board members jumped in and spoke out strongly against Larry's aggressive, negative style. We kept the feedback process open for everyone who wanted to speak, and in one eloquent moment, a neutral board member told Larry that although she often agreed with his criticisms, she had had enough of his bickering, and she asked him to treat other board members and the staff with respect. Then other board members took their turns, and because there was no further discussion or comment by Larry, we returned to completion of the process that we had interrupted.

When Karen's turn came, she acknowledged the criticisms of her behavior and said they held important information for her. She was analytical but not apologetic about her mistakes. Other board members, including Larry and his wife, clearly wanted Karen to apologize and began pressuring her to do so. We asked Karen why it was difficult for her to apologize. Her response was painful to watch. She indicated that the idea of apologizing felt "heavy" and laden with blame. We tried to create a distinction between an apology that accepted responsibility for mistakes and their effects on others and an apology that expressed guilt for some failure.

Karen heard us, and her apology, although not perfect, was well received. We asked the rest of the group to give her feedback on her apology, and several people acknowledged her for her effort, but when we asked Karen's opponents if they had any comments or felt any different after hearing her apology, they said they did not. We asked what they needed to hear from Karen, and they said they needed a resolution of the issues regarding board and staff responsibilities. We thanked them for their suggestion and recommended that the group address those issues at the next meeting. We asked again whether Larry and Karen would meet to discuss their issues, but Larry was still unwilling to do so without the entire board present.

Because the time set aside for this meeting was coming to a close, we conducted a group assessment of the session, partly to normalize giving feedback and evaluating process and partly to let people know that everyone needed feedback, ourselves included.

The group felt that the evening had been a partial success in that we had exposed the conflict, modeled a process intervention, and used questions to probe into sensitive areas. Everyone also felt that although the air had been cleared to a great extent, neither Larry nor Karen had been able to completely let go of their conflicts in the group setting.

At the same time, they felt a breakthrough had taken place whereby board members had been able to speak openly about difficult personal behaviors and communication styles. Many now understood that between silence and hostility lay a number of intermediate steps, in which positive communication could be combined with disagreement, criticism, and apology.

Board and staff members alike felt that the purpose of the next meeting should be to create a positive pattern of social interaction between them, a pattern based on reaching consensus about their respective roles and the future direction of the organization. They wanted to practice respectful communication while expressing differences of opinion and clarifying responsibility for outcomes.

## The Fourth Meeting

We began the fourth meeting by saying that although the conflict-resolution process was not complete, it had been partially successful. From telephone calls with several board and staff members, we had learned that relationships and communications had improved tremendously since the previous meeting. In particular, we congratulated Karen and Larry on having had a successful, respectful communication regarding a problem that might have turned into a confrontation. We asked if our impression was correct, and Larry and Karen acknowledged each other for having communicated more effectively. The group expressed its support and complimented them on their success.

We indicated that it was now time for them to look at the positive results that might be generated from their commitment and to resolve one of the sources of conflict in their relationship: their lack of clarity about the organization's direction. We asked the participants to create a vision of what the organization would look like if they were able to work together as a team. We asked each person to start by expressing three wishes for what the organization might look like in five years' time. As people spoke, it became clear that the conflict between the board and the staff had enormously subsided and that there was almost complete unanimity on what the entire group wanted for the future. Four basic wishes emerged:

1. A sound financial footing for the organization
2. Greater outreach to the community and the public
3. Better use of the organization's resources through improved efficiency and administration
4. Better facilities for carrying out the organization's work

We then asked everyone to volunteer to serve on one of four board-staff teams, each of which would develop a single sentence describing its vision for one of these four wishes. Each of the four groups was asked to work on the basis of consensus and to select a facilitator, a recorder, and a process observer. We said the purpose of this exercise was both to develop a concrete statement of purpose that would define what the group had in common and to practice reaching consensus, improving collaboration, and resolving conflict.

After each board-staff team reported on the process it had used and read its vision sentence, the other teams were asked whether they had any clarifying questions or comments, disagreed with anything that had been said, or felt that something should be added. In the case of one team's sentence, there was a disagreement over language. Rather than proceed with the majority view, as several members wanted to do, we stopped to search for a mutually acceptable alternative, and consensus was quickly reached. We used this experience as an example of how similar disagreements might be dealt with in the future. We pointed out that when there were differences of opinion, the board and the staff could always stop the process, discuss the issue, and try to reach consensus on an alternative approach to the problem. Larry suggested that sometimes differences of opinion were valuable. We agreed and added that disagreement in the context of a broad consensus on goals was very different from disagreement in the absence of any sense of shared direction. The purpose of consensus, we said, was to create an environment in which dissent could be encouraged and not be seen as an attack.

The participants then returned to their teams to brainstorm goals, strategies, and action ideas that could make their visions real. Each team was given flip-chart paper and asked to brainstorm as many ideas as possible in the time allowed. As each team reported on its ideas, excitement intensified with the realization that visions could be turned from utopian dreams into concrete achievements.

We asked each of the teams to meet again to prioritize their ideas, discuss the factors that could either hinder or help their realization, and prepare an action plan that included a list of the tasks to be completed, who would perform them, the resources required, and the dates by which these tasks would be completed. As the teams reported on their results, they saw that their commitment, which had brought them into the organization in the first place, was still there and that their goals could be achieved.

In the final discussion of that session, the teams made a commitment to continue working together to achieve the goals they had selected. We asked everyone to reflect on the differences between this meeting and the previous three. People said that when it came to identifying visions or goals for the future, or discussing how they could be brought about, they had been able to reach agreements with a minimum of dissent and had actually enjoyed themselves. They felt good about reaching consensus and working together on common goals. They saw that it was not necessary for people to feel bad in order for the organization to make progress.

We said that conflicts and problems would certainly continue, but that we hoped they would remember what they all had in common and how much better it felt to work as team members than as hostile board members and harried staff members. Conflicts could become opportunities for learning, communication, and change, rather than threats to continuity or collaboration. The group asked us to conduct a final meeting, to bring home these lessons and firmly establish the new common ground.

## The Fifth Meeting

At the fifth and last meeting, one month later, we asked the group to think of an event during the intervening month that had revealed how collaboration and communication had been or could be improved. We suggested this exercise in order to support the participants in their new behaviors and give them feedback on how they could improve their problem-solving skills.

The group immediately focused on an incident involving a fundraising idea. The idea had been developed by a board member and sent to the finance committee, which recommended a number of major changes without the board member's knowledge or involvement. The new plan was then sent to the board, where, after debate, it was promptly rejected by a majority, although a strong minority continued to support it.

After the vote, some new facts were brought to light, and Larry, as chair, called all the members of the board to see if they would reconsider their votes. He asked for a two-thirds majority, and he excluded anyone who had not been present during the debate from the voting. It became clear from the discussion of this incident that the role of board committees and their relationship to the board and to individual members still had not been defined, that there were overlaps and uncertainties regarding the jurisdiction of the committees, and that the conflict between Larry and Karen was not over.

We asked other members of the group to comment, and some people questioned the way democracy was working in the organization. Some wondered why Larry had decided to exclude board members from the vote if they had not been part of the debate: Shouldn't all members be entitled to vote? Others questioned whether the board should have considered new information or revised votes that had been taken in committee. Some people were upset about the lack of trust: How were they supposed to encourage individual initiative if they could not trust each other, and how could committees do their work if their decisions were not taken seriously? Finally, Larry was criticized for how he had communicated concerning the committee's decision and the voting process. These comments revealed a residue of anger and distrust. The stories being told were obscuring the core story of the organization, and we saw that we had not gone deeply enough into the causes of the problem.

After this discussion, we asked each person in the room to comment on the real causes of this incident, and on why it had stirred so much acrimony. This question assisted the group in gaining perspective and examining the conflict as though from the outside.

One person thought the cause of the conflict was different people's personalities. Others cited a history of adversarial relationships among board members. Some felt there was anger because people had not been treated with respect, or because their expertise had not been appreciated. Some felt the issue was hard-nosed, hard-money people on one side, focused on cutting costs, and kindhearted, soft-money people on the other, focused on outreach. Some felt the problem was that they had not worked for consensus and that the issues had not been fully aired, or that the swiftness of the decision had caused a failure of trust. Still others felt there was an attitude of "if you're not with us, you're against us."

We asked the participants if they wanted some feedback, and they said they did. We told them we thought all the causes they cited were correct, and that simple, practical solutions were available for each cause. We said that if they defined the problem as one of personalities, there was little they could do, but if they thought of the problem as an "it" rather than a "you" or a "them," there was a lot that could be done to solve it. We said that anyone, when it became clear that the process was not working, could have stopped it and suggested fixing the problem before it went any farther. In this sense, everyone bore some responsibility for the incident. We also said that Larry and Karen bore particular responsibility for the incident because they had been unwilling to meet and work out their issues with each other.

We recommended again that Larry and Karen meet, either with our assistance or without, to work through their issues. We asked Larry directly what it would take for him to do this. Larry said he would be willing to meet alone with Karen to discuss their issues if she was willing, and she said she would love to meet with him. We recommended that, after their meeting, they report to the board on what they were each willing to do to improve their relationship and communication, and they agreed.

We then suggested that the group start trying to fix the problems that had been identified, and we asked which issue the participants wanted to address first. They quickly agreed to establish three ad hoc board-staff committees to revise and clarify the committee structure, redesign the budgeting process, and improve internal communication. The participants broke into these committees and came up with a number of excellent interim recommendations.

At the end of this session, several people spoke strongly in favor of improving interpersonal relationships as a priority for each of them, and they agreed to immediately implement several of the proposed solutions. The tenor of this discussion was very positive, with both sides referring to their problem in terms of "it" rather than in terms of "you."

## The Denouement

The three ad hoc board-staff committees continued to meet for some time afterward. They proposed several important changes in board process and clarified board and staff responsibilities in ways that helped the organization become much more effective.

Karen and Larry had their meeting and later told us that their relationship had improved substantially afterward. Their personal acrimony had decreased, their communication had become more respectful, and they had begun to see their conflicts as opportunities to improve their process rather than reasons for resignation, blaming, or unpleasantness.

The organization was able to improve its fundraising results, bring in new board members, and find ways to build a more collegial relationship between Larry and Karen. Within a year, Larry stepped down as board chair. He and his wife remained active board members, but Larry said he was under too much stress to give Karen the support she needed from the board chair.

## Observations

The ability of nonprofit organizations to contribute to their clients and communities is enhanced by the volunteers who serve on their boards of directors and give freely of their time and expertise. It is not uncommon, however, for volunteer boards to get into conflicts with their staffs and executive directors over unclear roles and responsibilities, or over lines of authority and control.

Nonprofit staff members often get stuck trying to meet conflicting board priorities and expectations or satisfy their own unmet needs and interests. Board members and staff members all have their own stories about who is responsible for problems and misunderstandings. As their conflicts escalate, they all wonder why they are working so hard for an organization where they will never be paid enough or thanked enough for what they have done.

In these cases, we try to reach beyond the individual parties in conflict and extend the resolution process to the organization as a whole. In this way, we can address larger communication issues, structural problems, and the dissonance created by conflicting expectations and roles.

In this mediation, we uncovered Larry's abrasive style as board chair and involved the board and staff in giving him the feedback he needed in order to acknowledge his contribution to the conflict. His initial unwillingness to meet separately with Karen to work through their issues made the process more difficult. We considered his reluctance a place to start in our effort to encourage and empower the group to solve its own problems.

Mediators walk a fine line when key organizational leaders not only have to agree to fund and participate in the conflict-resolution process but are also the people most involved in the conflict. Every effort to uncover their behavior or allow the group to comment on it can be seen as a personal attack on their leadership and as an excuse for stopping the process. It can also be frightening to those who have not dared to do so, for fear of what might happen. When we move beyond stories of who is at fault or whose difficult personality is getting in the way, groups can see their problems as issues that can be resolved through collaborative dialogue.

In this case, as long as the parties' stories defined the problem as Larry's personality or Karen's unwillingness to apologize, the board and the staff could not see that they had the capacity to tell entirely different stories. They used the mediation process to create a new story, one about vision, dialogue, and working through difficult issues, about brainstorming and communicating honestly how they felt, about the power of their commitment. This story augmented and enhanced their ability to change the way they worked together. Their subsequent success and expansion told this story loud and clear.

# School for Scandal

Tiny Tots was a cooperative nursery school that relied heavily on parents for administration, fundraising, and teacher assistance. The parents were upper-middle-class professionals who sent their children to Tiny Tots because of its reputation for excellence and the professional skill of its director, Alice.

Alice had been the director of the school for more than twelve years and seen conflicts before. She was in her mid-sixties and was capable, intelligent, and resourceful, yet somehow everything seemed to be going wrong. The parents had split into pro-Alice and anti-Alice factions. Mothers were yelling at each other in front of the children and running in tears from the playground. Fathers were loyally supporting their wives or entering the fray on their own and raising angry voices at parents' meetings. Allegations of manipulation and unprofessional conduct were being hurled back and forth, and the anti-Alice faction was demanding that Alice resign.

Alice fought back, and several parents had now left. The school was deeply in debt and continuing to lose money rapidly. A teacher had been fired, without full disclosure to the parents of the reasons for her discharge, and rumors were rife. Fundraising was going slowly, negotiations were pending in a labor-management negotiation between the director and the teaching staff and their union, the by-laws were unworkable, the president of the parents' association had resigned, every meeting had become a confrontation, and the school seemed ready to go under. Alice decided to try mediation, and she convinced the main representatives of both factions in the parents' association to attend.

The meeting started with our acknowledging the high level of feelings on both sides of the dispute. We asked each person to indicate one goal, wish, or hope they had for the school. This exercise reminded them of what they had in common: their desire to provide the best education they possibly could for their children, the wish that their school would run smoothly and efficiently, the hope that the conflict would be resolved satisfactorily for all, and the need to raise funds to improve the school.

We then asked each of the people present to identify what they thought the problems were and indicate where they thought the possible solutions might lie. Alice was asked to start because she had convened the mediation. She described, without going into great detail or citing examples, the increased tension between parents and staff, the "poisoned atmosphere," the lack of cooperation at the school, the mounting debts, and the inability to control the expenditure of money.

One of the fathers went next, describing how a popular teacher had been fired over Christmas break and how the parents had not been informed of the reasons for this drastic action. He felt the main problem was Alice's poor leadership. Alice, meanwhile, had asked for a raise in her contract. Tuition was being raised by fifty dollars a month, but that was not going to solve the problem.

One of the mothers spoke about how great the school was, but she felt it needed clearer direction and more leadership from Alice. There needed to be more control over the number of children admitted to the school and greater continuity in the school program. She felt the school had changed radically every year.

Another mother felt the parents ran the school, and that Alice also ran the school, and that in between there was a vacuum in which no one ran the school. Yet another mother had set up a system for the school office, and it had been ignored. Alice had the titled leadership position in the school, but she was too busy defending herself to exercise any leadership. There was a complete breakdown in communication, everyone had polarized and formed factions, and the whole atmosphere and energy were unpleasant.

Nancy had been president of the school until two weeks before, when she had resigned. She was furious about the financial state of the school, the increasing debts, and the pay raises. She felt that Alice had manipulated the situation to pay herself the highest salary in the business. There was also a great deal of confusion about Alice's status. The school was a union school, and Alice was an employee covered by the union contract, but she was also the director and had the power to hire and fire employees. She said that the teacher who had been fired had been accused of engaging in inappropriate sex play with the children but had been allowed to resign "for personal reasons." Another mother, who also worked afternoons as a teacher, said she could not afford a tuition increase. The teachers were on twelve-month contracts, but the parents had to pay on a nine-month basis, which made it difficult for those who were less wealthy. The school also desperately needed administrative help and financial restructuring.

A mother who had been active in the leadership of the school said the paramount problems were overbudgeting, a lack of clarity about leadership, and the conflict between Alice and the teachers. She believed that the teacher who left had resigned over money issues and personal issues with Alice, not over any incident involving inappropriate sex play with the children.

Other parents spoke similarly. We asked Alice if she wanted to respond to these comments, given that a number of personal comments had been made about her since she had first spoken. Alice spoke extremely defensively, was surprised that some of the parents seemed to have joined the "attack force" against her, and said provocative, mean things about those parents. She believed there had been secret meetings between the parents and there was a conspiracy among them to get rid of her.

In response to several immediate objections to her comments by the parents who were present, she allowed that it was legitimate for them to criticize her defensiveness. She said, however, that she was not an office administrator, and, again defensively, that her primary concerns were first the children, then the teachers, and then the parents. Several parents said she was not the only one whose first priority was the children.

We said that because everyone's expressed priority was the children, they were in agreement over something. We offered that it would be possible, instead of trying to figure out who was right and who was wrong, to see whether we could come up with solutions to the problems that had been identified. We asked whether the group felt ready to do that, or whether they would rather continue focusing on their disagreements. The group indicated it wanted to try the first approach and see if solutions were possible.

We tried to summarize the points that had been made, broke them down into three groups of issues or problems, and reframed the issues so that they no longer focused on people or personalities but on concerns about behavior and on the organizational systems, structures, and strategies. On the basis of the parties' comments, we judged the main issues to be:

- The structure, organization, and handling of administrative tasks
- Leadership and communication, handling of criticism, and relationships involving collective bargaining
- Financial restructuring and fundraising

The group agreed with our list. We suggested that the group now shift its attention away from fixing blame and venting anger about past problems and try instead to come up with practical solutions for the future. We recommended that the group make this shift collectively, in small groups and by consensus. The parents at the meeting said they felt that all they could do was report back to the parents' association on the ideas that were agreed to in the meeting; they were only representatives, they said, and as such lacked the authority to resolve these issues by themselves. Teams were then formed to come up with concrete proposals for solving three problems: the administrative structure of the school, by-laws and collective bargaining, and fundraising. Each team was composed of parents and staff members who were present and had an interest in solving the particular problem the team was being formed to address.

There were several parents who had a great deal of expertise or interest in serving on such teams, but they either had not been invited to the mediation or were unable to attend. Therefore, each team was asked to meet briefly in order to pick a facilitator and a recorder and to set a time when its members could meet before our next session. Each facilitator was asked to make sure that every interested parent and staff member was informed of the dates and locations of each meeting.

We then asked the participants to engage in a general brain-storming session and, using one of the issues that had been identified, to come up with general suggestions for improvement. We made this request so they would leave the meeting with a sense of optimism and a feeling that it was possible for them to find practical solutions to their problems.

The problem they chose was the firing of the teacher over the Christmas break. The group brainstormed a number of possible solutions, and reached the following points of consensus. They agreed that any proposals for action with regard to future personnel issues should be communicated to the parents before final action is taken. They agreed that a clause should be inserted in all employee contracts, requiring mediation in cases that involve the discharging or disciplining of an employee. They agreed that a full investigation should take place before personnel decisions are made, and that a committee on policies and procedures should be established, to promote uniformity in such decisions. Everyone made a commitment to honor these agreements, and the meeting adjourned.

As agreed, the three teams met before our second session, to come up with solutions to problems in their designated areas. At the second session, the teams reported back to the whole group on their work. We complimented and acknowledged each team for its efforts, ideas, and suggestions. The principal suggestion that emerged from all the problem-solving teams was that an administrative assistant be hired to serve the following functions:

- Free up more teaching time for Alice (all the parents agreed that Alice was an excellent teacher)
- Establish continuity and clarity in administration
- Maintain school files
- Focus on parents' responsibilities
- Be a liaison with parents
- Assist in fundraising

Several parents felt the issues were not really pro-Alice or anti-Alice but were based on confusion and disagreement over facts, finances, roles, and responsibilities. The group discussed how it was going to tackle difficult issues, such as paying the school's debts, deciding on the director's salary increase, reducing the atmosphere of hostility in the school, improving communication, clarifying responsibilities, elaborating school policies, and filling the leadership vacuum in the school.

During a lengthy discussion of these issues, it was suggested that the participants could approach these problems more effectively by dividing them into four categories.

1. Organizational structure (as addressed in the bylaws)
2. Finances (as addressed in the budget)
3. The director's responsibilities (as addressed in the director's job description)
4. Communication

Issues in the first three categories could be addressed by revising three major documents, and issues in the fourth category could be addressed in a mediation agreement.

The first three categories were easily agreed to, and the group began to turn its attention to how it could resolve the problem of communication. As the discussion proceeded, communication began to break down. There was increasing criticism of Alice and increasing defensiveness on her part, which she directed at the parents opposing her. It became clear to us that neither side was listening to what the other was saying, and that the time was right to get beneath the surface to identify the source of the problem.

We stopped the meeting and indicated our sense that neither side appeared to understand what the other side was saying. We asked the parents if they would state, as best they could, what they understood Alice's position to be. One of the parents did so. Alice, according to this mother, felt that in a cooperative nursery school it was the parents' job, not the director's, to define responsibilities, and that she was being blamed for things that were not her fault. We asked Alice if this was correct, and Alice said it was, with a few minor changes.

We then asked Alice to restate, as best she could, what she thought the parents' point of view was. Alice said she had no idea what their position was. We asked her if she could mention some of the criticisms that the parents had leveled at her, thinking that she would be able to reason backwards from the criticisms to the points the parents were making. Alice said she was unable to say what their criticisms were. We rephrased the question a third time, to make it completely clear that we were only asking her to give her understanding of what some of the parents' issues were, and again Alice was unable to respond. It suddenly became clear to everyone that Alice had not heard anything the parents had said, and that her inability to listen was the cause of many of their problems. Because we had reached a point where inquiring any further could only result in humiliation to Alice, we decided that it was time to caucus. We announced that we wanted now to meet separately with each side—first with Alice, and then with the parents.

In our meeting with Alice, we asked her directly why she had so much difficulty answering our questions. Alice said that she was so defensive, she really did not hear the parents or know how to respond. We asked her if she felt her defensiveness was a part of the problem, and she said she knew it was. We asked her if she would be willing to say this to the parents, and she said she would.

We then decided to give her some coaching and get her to focus on developing her skills. We asked whether she wanted to learn some new ways of responding that were not defensive, and she said she did. We suggested that whenever she heard a criticism or felt herself becoming defensive, she ask a question to find out more about what the other person was really saying. We recommended that in the beginning she not respond with statements but only with questions. We suggested simple questions, such as "Is this what you are saying?" and "What do you think happened?" and "What do you think went wrong?" We suggested that she ask these questions both to clear her mind of defensive responses and to gather information. We suggested that her next statement be "If I understand you correctly, you feel . . . . Is that right?" If the answer was yes, she could then go on to explain what had happened from her point of view, but not until then. We tried this with her in the caucus, and although she found it difficult, with practice she was able to get the basic idea.

We asked her if she was willing to practice this exercise during the following week, and especially at our next session. She thought this might work, agreed to try, and thanked us for our suggestions. We asked if she was willing for us to coach her as she spoke during the session, and she said she was. We also recommended that she consider counseling or therapy to gain more insight into the pattern of her defensive responses. She said she would consider it, but it did not seem as if she really meant it.

We next met in caucus with the parents and asked what they thought had happened in the interaction with Alice immediately before we caucused. They felt that she had clearly revealed her defensiveness and inability to listen. We said that Alice knew she had a problem with her defensive reactions and needed their help in breaking her automatic defensive responses. We asked if, during the next week, they would try to bring matters to her attention that they would naturally discuss with her. If she started to become defensive, they should ask her to tell them what they had just said and repeat the gist of their remarks. Whenever possible, they should help her state the issue neutrally, as a problem that had an existence independent of her and did not represent an attack on her. We suggested that they give her feedback on where she was accurate and where she had not been listening, and they all agreed to do so.

When Alice rejoined the group, we asked her whether she had anything to say. She told the parents that she knew she had not been listening. She apologized and said she would try to listen better in the future. We acknowledged her for her willingness to try to change her communication patterns. We also said the parents needed to improve their listening as well, so as to be able to know in the future when Alice was having difficulty listening to them.

As the session came to a close, the discussion returned to the idea of hiring an administrative assistant and what needed to be done for this to happen. The teams that had formed in the first session were given additional homework. They were asked to continue their deliberations, identify strategies and action plans for implementing their ideas, and investigate the feasibility of hiring an administrative assistant.

At our next session, one week later, we asked whether anything had changed since the previous meeting. Everyone said that communication with Alice had improved remarkably during the week. It was agreed that having an administrative assistant was feasible, and there was a qualified applicant who was available. During the session and throughout the discussion of each team's proposals, Alice was cooperative and nondefensive, and the parents concentrated on solutions rather than problems. A number of changes were suggested in the bylaws and in Alice's job description, and these were agreed to by consensus. Several creative fundraising proposals were agreed to, and everything looked favorable.

At the end of this session, we complimented the participants for their hard work and for their efforts to solve their problems by working through them together. We said their problems were not resolved yet but that partial solutions had been found or were being considered for every one of them. We indicated that if these solutions did not work, they should try to continue this process on their own. We told them they still had to pay attention to their communication patterns because these would not disappear overnight. Alice expressed a resolve to improve her listening and leadership, and the parents agreed to support her in doing so. Everyone left in high spirits,with great hopes that their children would have a richer experience as a result of their efforts.

## Observations

Three months after our final session, we spoke to Alice, who told us that the agreement had broken down. Half the parents had left the school, and a new, more pro-Alice group had entered. Alice felt that the whole atmosphere was much improved, but others thought the school was worse than ever. What had happened?

The relationship between Alice and the parents was one that we thought had been moving toward a favorable resolution, with agreements and solutions leading to a final meeting that seemed a model of collaboration. Yet the real sources of Alice's difficult behavior—her core story—remained beneath the surface. It had not been resolved, only scratched and somewhat patched over. The mediation process that had held her accountable was now over, and there was no recourse now for those who wanted to challenge her.

Once the pressure of organized opposition and the mediation process were over, Alice did not go into therapy or have the will to continue improving her communication skills or make her relationship with the parents work. We had pushed her as far as she was willing to go, and even though she had been successful, supported, and acknowledged in using her new skills, her underlying belief system was based in a me-versus-them story. Moreover, we had ended the mediation near the close of the school term, when many of the most vociferous parents were leaving. Over the summer, it became easy for Alice to force her remaining opponents out of the parents' leadership. Had timing and finances permitted, the mediation process might have continued for two or three more sessions and produced a greater chance of lasting success. The energy the parents were willing to invest in resolving this conflict was limited, however, and they were exhausted by years of bickering. Their children were graduating and moving on, and they could easily justify leaving the problem for future parents to face.

For Alice, the problem lay deeper and had its roots in her past, her ego needs, age-related issues, and emotional vulnerability. These existed independently of the school and were reinforced in ways that made her small steps forward more temporary than long-lasting. Alice needed counseling, and although the mediation was able to lead her to her own issues, the decision to go deeper and search for more lasting change was ultimately hers. Alice indicated to us that she had learned her lesson and would not act defensively with the new parents, but neither she nor the parents had developed skills much beyond those of the school's children when it came to the ability to handle emotional conflicts with peers.

In this case, we also still had plenty to learn. We resolved every major issue, but the conflict that had created the issues was not over. We learned that when we work with someone like Alice, who relies on defensive behavior, we need to do more. We need to provide greater follow-through, offer more meticulous ongoing coaching, and set clearer limits. In this case, we also needed to encourage the parties as a whole to take collective responsibility for continued improvement, set up mechanisms for revisiting issues, and provide training that could assist them in giving up comfortable yet dysfunctional patterns.

Moreover, the conflict reflected not only disagreements between Alice and the parents but also deeper problems that were systemic and organizational. Alice's multiple roles created pressures on her that she could not successfully balance. She simultaneously acted as an employee and as a leader of the parents, as director of the school and as lead teacher, as the main spender of money and as lead fundraiser, as chief union spokesperson and as chief school administrator in charge of implementing management policies and hiring and firing employees. The school was organized both as a democracy and an autocracy, and the two structures did not mix.

Alice was fine with having the parents clean up and raise money for the school. She often stated her belief in parental involvement and parent-staff teamwork. But underneath her rhetoric, she wanted to be in control. She was unwilling to surrender or authentically share her authority or power with people who had the ability to deny her a raise or fire her.

We did create joint parent-staff problem-solving teams that continued working, but we did not go far enough in clarifying the role of each group in the daily operation of the school. The fundamental philosophy of a cooperative nursery school involves parents intimately in every aspect of creating and operating the learning environment, and yet there was no real consensus between the parents' group and the director about what would happen if they disagreed or even about how noneducational, purely administrative programs ought to be run.

We learned that an organization can be held hostage by conflict stories if it does not build internal support structures to maintain and encourage changes in people's behavior. A team of coaches for Alice, to whom she would be continuously accountable, or who would have the right to raise her salary or offer a bonus if she changed, might have provided the guidance, framework, and clout needed in evaluating her progress and helping her make the changes she so desperately needed to make. This was truly a school where everyone learned some of life's most difficult lessons.

# Communication Down the Drain

We were approached by the manager of plant facilities for a large unionized company, who asked us to help him resolve a difficult issue that had arisen between the plumbers and their supervisors. We were told that the conflict had reached a point where communication had completely broken down, and that there was considerable bitterness and anger among the plumbers.

These problems were continually cropping up, requiring extra time from supervisors and contributing to poor work performance and unnecessary costs. As a result, the company was considering laying off all the plumbers and outsourcing the work, contracting it out to an independent, nonunion shop. We were asked to conduct a mediation between the plumbers and their supervisors, to see if we could resolve these conflicts and create a smoother working relationship.

We began by introducing ourselves and explaining the mediation process. We immediately met resistance from some of the plumbers, who were unwilling to proceed with the mediation without the presence of their union representative. They said there were outstanding grievances that had been filed, and they were unwilling to discuss settling those without the union's participation. We indicated we had no problem including their union representative in the process, although the conversation we wanted to have with them lay outside the traditional process for resolving grievances, and our focus was not on trying to settle the grievances.

In spite of our guarantees that mediation was nondisciplinary and nonbinding and would focus only on management issues that lay outside the union's jurisdiction, one of the plumbers was unwilling to proceed. It became immediately clear in the discussion between the plumbers that there was extensive distrust of supervisors, overt hostility toward the foreman, or "leadman," and considerable antipathy among the plumbers as a group.

We took a break to call and invite their union representative to the session, but he was out of town and would be unavailable for at least a month. In light of the plumbers' refusal to continue without him, we agreed not to proceed with the mediation as a group. We did not want the process to die, however, and the supervisors said their decision about outsourcing could not wait a month. Therefore, we came up with a counterproposal: we suggested that we meet with each person individually, and everyone agreed that we could conduct a series of private interviews, in order to discover the sources of the conflict, assess what might be done to resolve it, and act as agents of communication between the opposing sides.

We then met privately with each person, saving for last those who had the greatest apparent hostility. Our goal was to gather background information to assess the whole situation. We asked all the people we interviewed what they thought the problems were, what they thought had caused or aggravated the problems, and whether they could think of any solutions. The answers they gave were long on problems and causes but short on solutions.

After the interviews, we brought the plumbers together again to report on what we had found and keep the conflict-resolution process moving. In this session, we focused on describing the problems they had raised in our interviews, using their words. In the process, we validated their concerns and normalized open communication about problems. We helped them translate their angry statements into words their supervisors could hear, facilitated direct communication between people who had been unable to speak directly to each other, and reframed their problems to more easily allow them to come up with solutions. This process encouraged them to see their points of agreement, helped us legitimize their concerns by restating them, and gave us a chance to model a more positive attitude toward their conflicts and encourage them to return to the mediation process.

In a joint session with the plumbers and their supervisors, we handed out a written summary of the plumbers' gripes and concerns, without censoring or toning down their comments. The effect was dramatic and eye-opening on all sides. In the discussion that followed, the supervisors recognized that they had not fully understood the extent of the plumbers' problems or the focus of their concerns. The plumbers commented that they had not fully realized the level of agreement among themselves or the extent to which their concerns were shared. Both groups felt they had not recognized the extent to which their conflicts were potentially resolvable, and everyone felt encouraged to continue talking.

We met afterward with the supervisors, to contextualize the summary we had made and make sure that they were able to see the plumbers' hard-hitting criticisms in a positive light. We also met with staff members from the human resources department, to let them know that some progress was being made and to ask for their continued support. We encouraged the supervisors to start implementing some of the plumbers' suggested solutions immediately, as a way of building trust and supporting the resolution process. The supervisors began to sound more cooperative, and we encouraged them to become creative themselves and come up with ideas for possible solutions, even if that meant backing down from previously held positions. They agreed to do so.

We met again with the plumbers as a group and asked them what it would take to solve their problems. We indicated that we had now uncovered the main problems and issues between them and their supervisors, and we told them it was time to start generating solutions. We said that management was willing to go a long way toward solving the problems that had been identified. We asked the plumbers how they felt about coming up with their own proposals for solutions.

Again, we met with resistance, but there was less this time. After some discussion, the plumbers agreed to discuss their problems, as long as their supervisors and the leadman were not present, and to proceed with the session. We asked them if they would be willing to go through their list of problems and come up with possible solutions for each problem. They agreed, if they could have time off from work to do so. We agreed to ask on their behalf.

When we asked the plumbers when and where we might meet with them, several people referred to one of the most common and repeatedly mentioned issues we had summarized: the plant management's lack of respect for their work. This issue was symbolically represented for them by the lack of a plumbing workshop—a place where they could all gather and talk or hold meetings. All the other trades represented at the company had their own workshops, and the plumbers felt considerable resentment over the fact that they were the only group that did not.

We met again with the supervisors and asked if the plumbers could have time off with pay to come up with ideas for solutions to their problems. This was readily granted. We told them about the plumbers' strong feelings regarding the lack of a workshop, and we asked whether it would not be possible to find them a space. The supervisors said there was a space that the plumbers could use, and it was agreed in principle that the plumbers could fix up a workshop for themselves.

We relayed this information to the plumbers at our next meeting. We wanted to let them feel they were being empowered and could take positive steps on their own to solve their problems. They were excited and encouraged that their requests had been granted. Now we wanted them to take the next step and propose solutions for their other problems. Moreover, we did not want them to become dependent on our intervention, so we asked them to meet on their own, to come up with recommended solutions to their problems. They made plans to fix up a workshop for themselves, set a date for their meeting, and agreed to produce a list of proposed solutions. The mood was positive and excited.

The list of solutions they came up with was thoughtful, detailed, creative, and positive. One of the central problems for the plumbers was their relationship with their leadman, and many of the summarized problems and proposed solutions had to do with the way he was interacting and relating to them.

After receiving their list, we decided to conduct a separate meeting with the leadman. In this meeting, we tried to explain the plumbers' anger and concerns in a way he could understand. We encouraged him to act more as a leader by working with them to resolve conflicts instead of arguing with them as a protagonist. We asked him to understand that he could not continue to be respected as their leader if he was unwilling to meet their legitimate expectations. He agreed to try to change his behavior and leadership style and to speak and act more respectfully. We gave him several practical suggestions on how he might do this.

At our next meeting, all the parties were present, but the plumbers said they would not proceed unless the supervisors and the leadman agreed that the session would be confidential. They also wanted reassurance that there would be no retaliation for anything they said. Both sides discussed these issues and agreed to a precisely worded confidentiality agreement. We wrote up their agreement in a document that we asked everyone to sign. Afterward, we talked about how they had reached consensus, and we used it as a model for how they could learn to trust and respect each other through open communication and collaborative dialogue.

Before the plumbers presented their proposed solutions, we asked the supervisors and the leadman if they would respond separately to each proposed solution, and they agreed to do so. We encouraged them to respond positively and not to look only for reasons why they could not do what the plumbers suggested. We asked that they search instead for ways of satisfying the interests that underlay each proposed solution. We challenged them to come up with alternative suggestions if the ideas proposed were impossible to implement.

The supervisors and leadman said they would try, and they asked for time, after the plumbers had presented their ideas, to meet and consider their responses. The plumbers agreed to this request and presented their proposed solutions, which they described in detail, together with the reasons for each proposed solution.

Afterward, we met separately with the supervisors to discuss their responses, advocate for the plumbers' ideas, suggest some possible alternative solutions, think about how to address the plumbers' relationship with the leadman, and address how the supervisors might encourage the leadman to change and improve his relationship with the plumbers. We also met with the leadman, to encourage him to demonstrate his leadership by responding respectfully to the plumbers' ideas.

The supervisors and leadman came up with responses to the plumbers' suggestions, and we all met again as a group to discuss them. We asked first whether anything had changed or shifted since the last meeting, and everyone agreed that relationships and communication had changed significantly for the better. Everyone felt optimistic, and the plumbers openly acknowledged their supervisors for having agreed to the proposal for a plumbers' workshop.

Everything appeared to be going well, but we nearly came to impasse over an issue that had not been raised before, an issue that involved the plumbers' use of ladders in their work. The conversation began to bog down, so we stopped the discussion and pointed out that the communication had gone awry. We asked the parties to recall what had happened. They remembered that one of the plumbers had mentioned a problem, another had made a suggestion, the leadman had said the suggestion wouldn't work, a supervisor had said the problem was the plumbers' responsibility, and they had all gone right back to their old patterns.

Several plumbers said the attitude being displayed was not one of working together as a team but of passing the buck. The parties were not discussing the problem or brainstorming solutions or trying to reach consensus on how to solve it; instead, they were attributing blame for not solving it. After recommitting themselves to changing the way they addressed their problems, the entire group turned again to discussing the problem involving the use of ladders, and they quickly reached consensus on a solution. We indicated that they could do the same thing with all their problems.

The parties then reviewed the supervisors' list of responses to the plumbers' proposed solutions and reached agreement on every point, sometimes negotiating, brainstorming, and modifying as they went. We withdrew increasingly from the discussion, letting them carry the ball so they would understand that they could continue successfully negotiating solutions to their problems without our being present to facilitate their conversation. The meeting ended on a positive note.

Only two problems remained: first, the relationship between the leadman and the plumbers, which had improved, but not enough for the plumbers to feel he was capable of providing the kind of leadership they needed; and, second, the grievances that were still outstanding and proceeding to arbitration. Future disputes with the leadman could easily poison the constructive atmosphere that had been growing in the group, and adversarial grievance proceedings might undo much of the positive work that had been done.

On the issue of the leadman, the plumbers met on their own and voted unanimously that there needed to be a new leadman, who should be chosen by them. They said this procedure was one that the company had agreed to and that was reflected in their collective bargaining agreement. We met with the plumbing supervisors, who agreed that this was the plumbers' right. They had discussed the problem earlier and agreed that they needed to create a new position for the current leadman.

We then met with the leadman, to ask whether he would have any objections to such a move. We told him that although he had made significant progress in improving his relationship with the plumbers, everyone would probably be happier if the plumbers could choose their own leadman. We told him that the plant management had considerable confidence in his abilities. We also suggested that he continue trying to understand what had gone wrong in his relationship with the plumbers, in order to learn how to communicate and lead more effectively. He agreed that he had made considerable progress but that this was a good idea for the group as a whole. He indicated that he would do his best to improve his relationship with the plumbers until his new assignment became available.

As for the outstanding grievances, there was a disagreement among the plant's managers over whether to settle them, and on what basis. We asked the union representative by telephone what he wanted to do, and he agreed to unilaterally withdraw the grievances, given the changes he had seen in the plant management's attitude toward the plumbers.

In the final session, both sides agreed to start with a clean slate so that they could try to rebuild trust. The plumber who had filed the grievances and resisted the process in the beginning said he would continue to monitor the plumbers' progress and would let go of his anger about what had happened with the leadman in the past. All the parties agreed to do their best to make the new relationship work, and that new grievances could always be filed if the new relationship was not working.

We raised the possibility with both sides of organizing the plumbers into self-managing teams capable of taking responsibility for their own work assignments. They might also make other key decisions, such as who would be the new leadman, how to choose him, how to keep up the stockroom, how to manage job rotations, how to determine procedures for use of the new shop, and other issues. Both sides became enthusiastic about these new possibilities and agreed to meet to discuss implementation.

We reminded both sides of the progress they had made. We contrasted the negative mood when they started the mediation process with the positive mood they were feeling at that moment. We acknowledged that their job was not simple, that it is easy to destroy trust but difficult to re-create it, and we recounted the many efforts each side had made to demonstrate their genuine goodwill and desire to make the relationship work. We congratulated them on their willingness to back off from their hardened positions, to come up with creative solutions, and to drop their anger and distrust as changes were actually made. The session ended with everyone applauding.

## Observations

In working with organizational disputes, there is a great temptation for mediators to settle for small improvements in communication or relationships between the parties, rather than trying to revise the roles, structures, systems, cultures, and strategies that chronically produce the conflict stories that bring the parties to mediation. In this case, we were able to use conflict as a platform for long-term change. We encouraged the creation of a new team structure that would empower the plumbers to fix their internal problems in the same way they fixed plumbing problems in the company: with skill, dedication, and hard work. We were able to support the plumbers in creating a workshop, which expressed their new role in the company and continually reminded them of what they had achieved. We also made significant progress in changing the relationship between the leadman and the plumbers. But the selection of a new leadman was a better long-term solution for the plumbers, because they were not interested in changing the attitude and behavior of someone who had forfeited their trust and who did not, in their eyes, deserve the mantle of leadership.

Although problems with the plumbers certainly continued after the mediation, these problems no longer resulted in dysfunctional outbursts. A great deal had been learned by everyone about how to convert anger and frustration into dialogue and joint problem solving. Strong and potentially abrasive personalities existed on both sides of the conflict, but so did compromise, collaboration, and leadership, often in the same individuals.

Afterward, we met separately with each side to emphasize what each could do to continue making the relationship work. We also met with staff from the human resources department to report on what had been accomplished. In addition to those that had already been made, we recommended the following changes, to ensure long-term success:

- Regular, more frequent staff meetings between the plumbers and their supervisors, where gripes could be aired openly, without fear of retaliation
- Periodic social occasions for plumbers and their supervisors so they could get to know one another better
- Increased opportunities for career and pay advancement among the plumbers, including internal promotions
- Increased pay allowances for professional development and education
- A yearly facilitated retreat, to possibly include the other trades as well
- Throughout the company, expression of respect for the positive work done by the plumbers
- More intertrade meetings, where problems and common concerns could be discussed
- The design of conflict resolution systems to encourage early-intervention, grievance mediation, and complaint mediation for all employees
- Increased involvement and use of human resources personnel in informal problem solving and conflict prevention before disputes got out of hand
- More responsibility for self-management for the plumbers and their leadman
- Periodic 360-degree performance evaluations (upward, downward, client, self, and team) in the plumbers' unit
- Positive reinforcement by upper management for the outstanding work done by the parties in turning this dispute around

With these changes in the organization, the plumbers were able to improve their performance and avoid the outsourcing of their jobs. In a follow-up companywide morale survey, the plumbers' attitudes were better, and they had greater job satisfaction than any other group in the company.

# Chapter Six

# Stories of Boundary Violations

> *Like a standup comedian, the tale must sense the*
> *aspirations and prejudices, the fears and hunger of its*
> *audience; like seaside pier palm readers, [storytellers]*
> *know that a tale, if it is to enthrall, must move the*
> *listeners to pleasure, laughter or tears; if they fail in this,*
> *nobody will want to hear their stories any more. The*
> *genre's need of an audience forces the teller to enter that*
> *audience's economy of beliefs; the memory of its oral origin*
> *makes a fairy tale long to please. The sultan is always*
> *there, half asleep, but quite awake enough to rouse himself*
> *and remember that death sentence he threatened. In the*
> *kingdom of fiction, the tension between speaking out and*
> *staying silent never eases.*
> MARINA WARNER, *FROM THE BEAST TO THE BLOND*

We rarely take time to celebrate our connections with others except at occasional ceremonies, such as weddings, births, and anniversaries, or occasionally at family holidays. When our relationships with others are smooth and even, our connections become transparent, and we barely notice them.

We are forcefully reminded of our connections and the importance of our relationships at death and during serious illnesses or unexpected catastrophes. Each of these events marks the fleeting, fragile nature of our associations by threatening or cutting them off.

One of the other times we become most aware of our relationships is, ironically, when we are in conflict. Conflict is a painful reminder of how difficult it is to recall our interrelatedness and live together in peace. Indeed, every conflict we experience reminds us of our isolation and lack of connection with others. In this way, conflict is a kind of death, and so we avoid, deny, bargain, and become angry with it, just as we do with death.

Conflict is also a kind of illness, a sort of catastrophe that threatens our relationships and connections. Indeed, one way of defining conflict is to see it as reflecting a lack of awareness of our essential interrelatedness, or of the immanence of death, illness, and sudden catastrophe. Conflicts arise whenever there is a failure of connection, collaboration, and community, and, paradoxically, whenever these connections go too far, do not recognize our individuality, and result in boundary violations.

## Conflict, Connections, and Boundaries

Every conflict we experience represents both a loss of connection and a boundary violation—a failure to value, respect, or acknowledge our integrity, principles, and borders or those of others. As we recognize and respect our own and each other's boundaries, we experience fewer conflicts and are able to form closer relationships. Thus, although conflict reflects our interrelatedness, it also reflects our separation and need for clearly defined boundaries.

The main purpose of fairy tales and conflict stories is to teach us where the boundaries and interconnections are located, and for this reason, conflict presents us with unique opportunities to learn about both. It turns out that the more we are aware of our essential interrelatedness, the more we respect our own and other people's boundaries, and the fewer conflicts we experience. The more we share responsibilities, and the more we work together to solve life's problems, the more our own needs get met.

Our friend and mentor Heinz von Foerster, one of the founders of the field of cybernetics, uses recursive mathematical logic to demonstrate that interactions between people become communicative if and only if people are able to see themselves through each other's eyes. "Consciousness," he writes, "is thus attained through conscience"—that is, through identifying oneself with the other; in this way, "communication, ethics and love converge into the same domain."

Conflict can also be understood as a loss of perspective regarding our ability to work together in solving our common problems. Conflict is the creation of unnecessary boundaries that obstruct our cooperation, communication, ethics, and love. When we talk and act together, our conflicts turn into disagreements, but when we yell and hurt each other, our disagreements metamorphose into conflicts.

Our colleague Peggy Dulany, founder of the Synergos Institute, has reached out for many years to people in other countries, to build grassroots leadership that can create and support interconnections. In a recent speech, she called on leaders to "build bridges that transcend the boundaries of sector, ethnicity, thinking style, or whatever other definitions set us apart from each other. One of the key characteristics for bridging is the importance of trust, and of creating chains of trust as essential prerequisites to solving the complex, multifaceted problems of our time."

Yet the boundary violations that take place in every conflict destroy trust. The power of mediation is that it can aid parties in becoming aware at a deep level of their interrelatedness and in finding paths to reconciliation and resolution. It can help them see, feel, and know directly that their destinies are tied to those of others, to realize that they are not alone. As mediators, we are often privileged to witness this transformation in awareness taking place.

## Perceiving the Other Through Empathy

Mediation is a complex process of encouraging people in conflict to perceive and accept their commonalities and at the same time to acknowledge their differences and see themselves as separate from their opponents, with clear boundaries, identities, interests, and rights. Robert Frost's idea that "Good fences make good neighbors" has become a cliché in our culture, yet its essential wisdom can be found in many conflicts.

In the stories people tell about their conflicts, the lines between the players are often either blurred or too precise. Boundaries, identities, interests, and rights are both defined by and subordinate to other people's encroachments, intrusions, positions, and violations. Conflict stories replicate these boundary violations, merging the parties into a single intertwined, falsely differentiated system.

Indeed, that is often their purpose. In this way, conflict stories both create and dissolve the ego; they define and disregard the self.

We see mediation as a method of rebuilding boundaries and reestablishing true connections. We start out by assisting each party individually in using their stories to define their separate identities and prerogatives, establish their limits, and deny others permission to intrude. We support each person in creating a sense of self that is separate from the conflict. This may mean fully communicating stories about boundary violations or expressing strong emotions. It may mean going deeply into detail. It may mean affirming or acknowledging boundaries or asking others to agree to respect them.

A system is always created between those who invade other's boundaries and those whose boundaries are invaded. In this system and the story that encodes it, the ones invaded feel shame, humiliation, anger, and distrust. They suffer when others fail to recognize their existence as separate human beings. Yet the invaded have often failed to stand up for themselves or have been unclear about where their boundaries, identities, interests, and rights lie. As a result of having been invaded, they may refuse to recognize the invaders' existence as separate human beings, or they themselves may embark on a course of boundary-violating revenge.

The invaders, in turn, often try to defend or justify boundary violations by telling stories that cite some important, overriding goal, or that blame those whose boundaries they have invaded for standing in the way or provoking a defensive attack. The invaders may believe strongly in something, or they may want to make important points or express emotions that have not been heard. Their rationalizations, however, are all forms of not listening to or respecting another person as a separate, unique individual. These rationalizations conceal a desire for what we call *negative intimacy* and become a way for invaders to feel better about the boundary violations they themselves have experienced. This is true because whenever anyone experiences a boundary violation, three primary emotional responses are possible:

- Anger or rage, followed by counterattack, which passes the violation on to someone else and turns the person invaded into an invader of others

- Self-blame, shame, and pain, which the person invaded holds inward or sinks into, becoming a victim or an invader of himself or herself
- Confrontation of the invader without either rage or shame, denial of permission for the invader to enter, and simultaneous expression of empathy and compassion for the invader that ends the violation by replacing it with positive connection

Notice that these three possibilities correspond to the external, internal, and core stories described in earlier chapters. In order to achieve the third possible outcome and reach the core story, mediators must accomplish three reconstructive tasks:

- Supporting those who feel invaded in setting limits, saying no, and clearly asking for what they want
- Assisting those who have been invaders in turning into listeners who are capable of hearing the word "no" and respecting the wishes of others
- Working with both parties to discover and reveal their inner selves and, as they do, develop the ability to feel empathy for others

If we do not assist those who feel invaded in reestablishing their boundaries, then their existence as separate beings will not be recognized, and the violation may happen again. If we do not also help them retain their ability to be vulnerable and open, even in the face of brutality, then invasion and violation will win. If we do not support them in developing a sense of empathy and compassion for their invaders, the truth of their interrelatedness will be lost. If we do not encourage those who have been invaders in empathizing with and understanding the people whose boundaries they have transgressed, then we will not be able to lead them to uncover boundary violations they themselves have experienced and help them to stop violating other people's boundaries. They may then realize that they can create new patterns of behavior, and the violations can stop with them.

Having stated this, we need to acknowledge that the violated and the violator are archetypes or models that possess elaborate subconscious meanings. These meanings rarely reflect the truth when matched with real human beings. There are many archetypes that fill peoples' conflict stories, including the *anima* and *animus* of Carl Jung's collective unconscious. There is the archetype of the tyrannical boss, matched with the archetype of the irresponsible employee. There are numerous archetypes in families, from the punishing father and the child who is never good enough to the favorite sibling or the smart one and the pretty one.

As mediators, we reveal these archetypes as patterns, scripts, and expectations, and we defeat them by making the people they characterize too complex, subtle, and human to match their image in the other person's mind. Every conflict story uses archetypes as easy identification points for the listener who is searching for a way of deciding what the story means. And many archetypes in a conflict story describe a violated person and a violator.

## Forgiveness Within Recognition of Boundaries

In the rough-and-tumble of conflict, as emotions build and rational dialogue fades, the parties often lose sight of who they are and of where they begin and end. Whenever people become clearer about their own boundaries and the boundaries of others, the possibility of resolution and interconnection grows stronger.

The mediator's role in these moments is to help the parties set boundaries, perhaps in the form of ground rules, and to ask questions that make it possible to distinguish "me" from "you." There are many questions mediators can ask to separate the external and internal elements in conflict stories and assist people in recognizing the distinctions between them. In effect, when we clarify these distinctions in a conflict story, we establish boundaries within the conflict. Through analysis, the storyteller can see the story as distinct from the self. This helps prevent the story from undermining the storyteller's self-image. It also helps the storyteller understand the conflict as a discrete entity that can be managed and addressed.

As the parties discover their core stories and reveal them to each other, and as they clarify what they do and do not want, they are better able to separate those elements of the conflict that have kept them locked together. They learn to see each other as distinct and separate from the problem, their interests as different from their positions, the future as dissimilar to the past, and empathy as the opposite of judgment.

By creating boundaries and making distinctions within their stories, the parties can see their conflict as separate from themselves and who they are, and they can distance themselves from it. They can then consider taking responsibility for their unique roles in the conflict, and even forgive themselves and the other person for what has happened.

Forgiveness also is a kind of boundary. It means giving up all hope of having a better past. It means releasing oneself from the conflict and letting the other person go. It means surrendering one's false expectations for how the other person ought to have behaved, releasing the other person to his or her own fate, and taking responsibility for clarifying the boundaries in one's own life. Forgiveness is always a choice. This act of forgiveness is described by Walter Kerr, onetime drama critic for the *New York Times,* in a review of Eugene O'Neill's play *Long Day's Journey into Night:*

> I think he wrote it as an act of forgiveness. Not as a pontifical forgiveness, mind you, not as an absolution from the harm that had been done to him. That he was damaged by his family is only a fact now, a piece of truth to be put down out of respect for the whole truth; there is no residual rancor. He seems to be asking forgiveness for his own failure to know his father, mother, and brother well enough at a time when the need for understanding was like an upstairs cry in the night; and to be reassuring their ghosts, wherever they may be, that he knows everything awful they have done, and loves them.

The eternal possibility of love arises when we rebuild people's boundaries and support them, if they choose, in forgiving—but never forgetting—the violations they have experienced or perpetrated. This love is simply a reflection of our innate interconnectedness. It is what finally makes the struggle to tell and hear conflict stories worthwhile.

# Sex, Lies, and Mediation

We were asked to mediate a complex, multiparty sexual harassment dispute in which the real issues lay far beneath the surface. The attorneys on both sides had little interest in bringing these issues out into the open. For this reason, the mediation took place entirely in caucus; the attorneys all agreed beforehand that the principal parties should not meet together face to face.

Ordinarily, we bring the principal parties together so that they can hear each other's pain, communicate their emotions, come to grips with each other's stories, work through their disagreements, negotiate collaboratively, and start the healing process. Instead, we were asked to settle a lawsuit that would have cost both sides a great deal in time, money, emotion, and energy. What follows are the stories we were told separately by each side.

## Sybil's Story

Sybil was a highly competent administrative assistant to Harry, the CEO of a large nonprofit public service organization. She had gone to an executive retreat, had too much to drink, and decided to go to her room. She became ill, lay down for a few minutes, and then woke up and noticed Harry was in her room.

According to Sybil, Harry told her he just wanted to make sure she was all right, but then he started to kiss and fondle her. She was very drunk and told him this was not right and that she didn't feel comfortable. She didn't scream or fight back, and they ended up having intercourse. Harry didn't spend the night. Sybil thought she had lost her job, but Harry never mentioned anything about it again. She didn't tell anyone, and he never tried anything again. She continued to work for him without incident for several years, but she told us she felt as though she had been raped.

Sybil thought Harry had probably slept with other women at work. She had heard of other incidents through the grapevine—that he had had sex in his office with a secretary; that he had touched, groped, kissed, and propositioned another employee and asked her in a meeting whether a client had gotten "in her pants" yet.

Sybil thought Harry disrespected women, mostly because of his constant sexual banter and the way he talked about women's bodies. She had been the subject of numerous crude jokes by Harry regarding the size of her breasts. She tried to ignore these jokes, but they became more and more common. On one occasion, he came into her office, closed the door, and in a joking way told her to take her clothes off.

Later, Sybil began to think Harry was engaging in financial improprieties and felt she had a responsibility to tell Ted, the chairman of the board, about her perception of Harry's financial misdeeds. She told and, after conferring with him, decided Harry had done nothing wrong, but Harry learned from Ted that Sybil had gone behind his back, and he accused her of violating his trust.

Their relationship began to deteriorate rapidly, and it became obvious that things were not working out. Sybil began crying at work and getting upset over small setbacks. She overheard Harry talking angrily on the telephone about her, saying he would make her life so miserable that she would either leave or he would fire her. In May, Sybil noticed that Harry had stopped talking to her and was confiding in others instead.

Sybil knew she was in trouble, but Ted told her not to worry about her job and that everything would be all right. Still, the tensions continued. She met Harry once in an elevator, and he looked right through her. One employee informed Sybil that Harry had told him he should not talk to her any more. That was when she knew it was over. The next day, she was told she was being moved to a new office. Harry wasn't speaking to her at all. He communicated only by memo.

Sybil had come in on a Monday and found her office was being moved. She was told not to touch anything or take any files with her. It felt to her as if she were being court-martialed, as if her work were being taken away from her. Sybil called the department of human resources, to find out what was happening. Unfortunately, however, no one was in the office. She went out on stress leave. A week later, she resigned. Two months after that, she filed a lawsuit, accusing Harry of sexual harassment.

## Harry's Story

Harry vehemently denied ever having had any sexual relationship with Sybil, at a company retreat or anywhere else. He could not fathom why Sybil would make false accusations against him. He liked Sybil, although he was upset and angry at what she had done to him. He could not understand why she had decided to do it, other than for monetary reward.

When Harry was going through his divorce, Sybil had been very much a friend to him, and he believed she might even have been in love with him. Once when a woman had come to the office to see him, Sybil had kept her away from him and appeared intensely jealous. Several years before, he had invited Sybil to join him and his second wife at dinner, but Sybil had seemed jealous of his wife and became hostile and angry.

Also, Sybil herself had once been sued for sexual harassment, wrongful termination, and financial impropriety, and the company had settled the lawsuit; Harry thought that Sybil might have decided to use the same tactic herself. She had also made a number of bigoted remarks, telling prejudicial jokes about Jews, African Americans, Poles, and so forth. Harry thought Sybil's biases, which were a kind of distorted view of others, could have fed her ability to create a stereotype of him.

Harry admitted that he had engaged in a lot of sexual bantering, jokes, and innuendo at the office. He also said that Sybil had clearly initiated, consented to, actively participated in, and welcomed it. Sybil had not complained to anyone about any of what she later called sexual harassment until after she had been transferred and resigned. Harry had never slept with or made sexual overtures to any of the women at work, as Sybil had alleged, and had only engaged in harmless and consensual sexual joking.

Shortly after his second marriage, Harry had discovered that all the expenditures he authorized were being sent to Sybil for her approval, at her request. He became furious and asked her not to second-guess his decisions but to come to him if she had a problem with an expenditure, because they had worked together for a long time. At first Sybil had denied having countermanded Harry's authorizations, but then she admitted it. She said she had felt some of them were illegal and had sent them to the chairman of the board. Harry felt this had been the first sign that Sybil no longer considered herself a member of his team and was going behind his back in a secret power play.

Harry felt he needed to be able to trust his administrative assistant not to attack him behind his back, and that check approvals were not a part of Sybil's job description. The office became a war zone. Communication and teamwork deteriorated, and their earlier partnership unraveled. Harry felt he eventually had no choice but to reassign her to a different office. He said he had not transferred her in retaliation and was not directly involved in any of the decisions regarding her move to the new office.

Before the conflict, while things were still going well, Harry had felt there was a spirit of fun and camaraderie about the banter and jokes in the organization. He maintained that Sybil could have stopped them easily with a simple rebuff. He felt the allegations of sexual harassment were a way for her to reclaim some of her lost power. He saw it as her revenge, which she had directed against him after he won the power contest with the board, when she accused him of financial wrongdoing.

Sybil had become a powerful person in the organization because Harry had extended his power to her. He reflected that it had been a lot of fun working with her as long as she had seen him as being on her side. But Sybil had also angered a lot of people. Some employees called her "the axe woman" or "the ice woman." She used her power to punish people she didn't like but would bestow valuable favors on those she appreciated. She had received stellar reviews and generous salary increases from Harry, which she used as a form of power over others. Harry felt that her use of power had corrupted and confused her sense of what was right.

Harry felt his life had been ruined by her false accusations and that the damage to him had been enormous. There was continuing suspicion of him on the part of board members, who had told him, "Where there's smoke, there must be fire." The accusations had destroyed his closest friendships and work relationships and placed his career in jeopardy. He felt that the board members needed to find a way to put this crisis behind them, and that healing was desperately needed. He said that if the accusations and assumptions of his being a sexual harasser did not stop, he would resign as CEO.

## Who Is Telling the Truth?

When people tell stories about past events, it is never easy for outsiders to know what the truth is, who is telling it, or what actually took place. It becomes even more difficult to know what happened when the stories concern sexual harassment. These stories are filled with faulty recollections, distorted perceptions, conflicting prior expectations, fantasies, moods, disappointments, rationalizations, and emotional fragility. Accusations like the ones in this conflict are often more a matter of distorted perceptions than of one person's telling the truth and the other's engaging in intentional misrepresentation.

The effort to reconstruct what actually happened becomes even more difficult when the stories involve sexual communication, nearly all of which depends on the invisible intentions of the parties and an assessment of nonverbal cues and contexts. For the most part, the information is private in nature and no longer available to examine except through the eyes and words of already prejudiced second- or thirdhand observers.

It is difficult, in the best of circumstances, to prove the nonexistence of a fact, or that nothing happened. It is far easier to make sweeping allegations than to defend oneself against them. No matter that a story may be wildly untrue; if it is internally consistent, then at least part of it will be believed. Allegations of sexual misconduct and sexual harassment are even more difficult to deny, in part because sexual intention is formed in secret and in part because we sense that whatever deeply shocks us may actually be true.

It is equally important for us to recognize that absence of evidence is not evidence that a thing is absent, and that an event may take place yet leave no sign that it ever occurred. Sexual acts are clearly of this character, and it is impossible for anyone other than the parties involved to say conclusively whether or not sexual intimacy actually took place. Sometimes when there is smoke, there is only smoke, and sometimes there is fire, and for anyone who was not present, it is difficult to know for certain which is the truth. Because the parties in this case emphatically disagreed about what had happened, it was impossible for anyone to reach any conclusion without facing a 50 percent chance of error.

Yet it was clear that someone had lied, for Sybil was alleging that Harry had had sex with her, and Harry emphatically denied having done so. Everyone in the organization had personal convictions about who was telling the truth, but these remained unprovable. A number of people who worked for the organization spoke in support of Harry's denial that he had engaged in sexual harassment. This group included several women Sybil had identified as having been objects of Harry's sexual interest. They did confirm that a great number of sexual jokes and a lot of sexual banter had taken place, but most people described this behavior as simply playful, saying that Harry had a good sense of humor and was trying to reduce the stress of work through jokes and repartee.

It was important, in coming to closure, for each side to acknowledge that there would never be a final decision about who was telling the truth. Both parties also needed to see that whoever was lying about the facts was not doing so out of evil intent but out of defensiveness and a sense that the story he or she was telling was metaphorically and emotionally true. We wanted them both to recognize that there might be falsehoods in each of their stories, falsehoods that they felt fully justified in asserting, given the way they were being treated by the other side. This does not mean that we justified lying, but that we recognized the deeper reasons for lying.

## Truth in Mediation

Our intent in mediating this incident was not to assess anyone's guilt or innocence but to exchange stories so that those involved could learn and come to terms with what had happened. We also wanted to assist them in beginning to heal and in reaching closure so that they could move on with their lives. This usually does not happen unless the parties are willing to meet face to face, which allows us to help each of them hear the other person's story without rancor or defensiveness and become less concerned with vindication than with learning.

Our object in this mediation was to assist the parties individually in understanding what had gone wrong, what they might have done better, what warning signs they had ignored, and what they might do in the future to make certain that whatever had happened would not happen again. It also was to encourage organizational learning and focus the board on making needed changes. We wanted to use the mediation to come up with practical suggestions for how the organization could encourage greater respect between co-workers, greater willingness on the part of aggrieved employees to speak out when they felt sexually harassed or treated unfairly, and greater sensitivity to relationships between people when there were inequalities of power or position.

## What Was Clarified

It became clear early on that this conflict represented a loss for everyone. Sybil resigned before filing her lawsuit, and Harry resigned after it was settled. We helped Sybil settle her claim for hundreds of thousands of dollars, but a huge portion of it went to her attorneys and to taxes, and her life was never the same afterward. Harry left with his career and his self-confidence destroyed, and he went into early retirement. The organization lost two excellent staff members and was disrupted for months by wild rumors and angry feelings on the part of supporters of both Harry and Sybil, some of whom also left the organization. There was great uncertainty and debate among staff members about who had told the truth and who had lied.

Some things clearly had happened, although they were not stated as openly or honestly by the organization as they needed to be for the issues to be resolved. For example, there were no clear facts that could have proved convincingly that Harry had slept with employees, but it was clear that a number of people thought he had, given the sexual nature of his jokes and banter. An enormous amount of staff time had been devoted to discussing these issues, with additional time spent in preparation for trial. The total paid out in attorneys' fees was more than the combined annual salaries of the organization's top officers.

As mediators, we were unable to bring the parties together to exchange their stories and process their differing versions of what had happened. We did successfully settle the lawsuit, however, and reduce the costs and emotional damage brought about by the failure to resolve the dispute at an earlier stage. We also encouraged the parties to recognize and agree on a number of general points regarding what had taken place.

We were able, in caucus, to get each side to accept large parts of what the other had asserted, once we had reframed their original stories and omitted the demonizing characterizations. Some things were clear in both stories of what had happened. For example, it was clear that an atmosphere of sexual joking, banter, and play had been present, that it had been fueled and condoned by Harry, and that it had been joined in and consented to by Sybil. The number and frequency of these sexual exchanges gave force and fuel to Sybil's allegations of sexual harassment and to a feeling that women in the organization were not being treated professionally.

It was also clear that Harry, as the leader of the organization and the one who had the most power in it, was seen as a model for how others should behave. In this respect, what he modeled, the direction in which he led, and the standards he set were not of the highest order, nor were they congruent with the values inherent in the organization's purpose. If Harry's behavior was judged, not by its intention, but by its effects on the women who worked with him, Harry clearly had not communicated strongly enough that the culture of the organization would not permit disrespect toward women or their sexual objectification, which some saw as an undercurrent of his sexual banter. The rumors about Harry's having had affairs with several different employees were only rumors, yet their very existence reflected an assumption that such things could happen, and so there was an implied need for communication to the effect that such things should not happen.

It was clear that Sybil's transfer and subsequent departure could have been avoided had either side been willing to enter into dialogue over her allegations of Harry's financial wrongdoing, allegations that had led Harry to believe Sybil was disloyal to him. Sybil had known he would see her accusations as disloyalty, just as Harry had known she would see his response as retaliation. Loyalty to an institution does not mean loyalty to all the actions engaged in by those who lead it, nor does financial irregularity necessarily mean financial impropriety. There were numerous methods Sybil and Harry could have used to resolve their differences, short of bringing accusations to the board or transferring Sybil to a different workplace. There were also methods that the board president could have used to bring about dialogue and reconciliation, but none of these methods were ever implemented, for reasons that were psychological, political, and emotional rather than legal.

It was clear that Sybil's and Harry's mutually supported self-fulfilling prophecy was fulfilled: Harry became increasingly retaliatory, and Sybil became increasingly disloyal. Ultimately the organization lost two very capable employees and incurred enormous expenses. This outcome was primarily a result of the organization's insensitivity to their predicament, its intolerance of their confusion, and its lack of open, direct, and honest communication. It was also due to a number of mixed signals, to bad timing, and to human error, which turned a simple problem into a catastrophe. Anyone in the organization could have seen this coming and intervened in time to reduce the loss.

It was clear that Sybil felt humiliated and retaliated against, yet she had not complained initially about sexual harassment but about the way her move to a new workplace had been orchestrated. She interpreted these events and the failure of the institution to treat her honorably as evidence that the sexual banter she had engaged in was, in retrospect, evidence of sexual harassment. She did not report the harassment when it occurred because at that time she had felt respected, and the joking had not felt like harassment. Once she had experienced herself as powerless, however, her very participation in the repartee became a form of harassment.

It is clear that these errors resulted less from hostile intent on the part of Sybil or Harry than from negligence and insensitivity. These errors reveal the background of subconscious disrespect that is common in many large, aggressive organizations where great sacrifices are called for and where goals have become so important that they overshadow the way the organization goes about reaching them. This disrespect was felt more strongly by the women in the organization than by the men, who constituted an "old boys' club" at the top, a club that excluded women from higher positions. It was less important for us as mediators to discover whether the organization's disrespect of women was "the Truth" than to see that there were employees who believed it was and acted accordingly.

It was clear that employees' participation in telling jokes and bantering became a kind of consent, which vitiated claims of sexual harassment, and that Sybil was an active participant and initiator. It was also important to recognize that her consent was irrelevant from a personal or organizational perspective. The question we found most useful was not whether the employees had participated in prohibited activity but whether the leaders of the organization had initiated, participated, modeled, and condoned it—in other words, whether they had met their obligation as leaders to set a higher standard.

It was clear in this case that neither Harry nor Sybil refused to participate in the banter and thereby condoned it, not only for themselves but also for others, through the subliminal messages sent by their behavior. When they later tried to decide who was to blame, they failed to accept responsibility for the modeling behavior they had engaged in. Sexual banter can be a perfectly innocent and harmless form of fun, or it can be a way of disempowering and harassing women. The difference lies not in the particular joke or comment but in the intent and the context. A sexual joke can be merely a joke if its intention and context communicate respect, acknowledgment, and acceptance of women, who are seen and treated as professionals. But if the intention and context communicate disrespect or disempowerment of women, then the joke ceases to be funny. Harry's jokes and comments revealed an underlying disrespect and hostility toward women, but they were also a form of innocent fun. How his jokes were interpreted was personal to each employee based on whether she felt respected and acknowledged. It is clear that Harry was not sensitive enough to his listeners to know what they were feeling.

The organizational issues in this dispute concerned not only how to respond to people who tell sexual jokes at work and pass along rumors of managers having sex with employees but also the use of transfers and retaliation as a substitute for honest communication and conflict resolution. Also revealed were the inadequate support for employees with problems and an organizational culture that was perceived as lacking respect for women as professionals and for employees as critics.

Sybil could have acted more openly, honestly, and skillfully in telling Harry what was bothering her, and she could have done so much earlier, but the burden of communication, problem solving, and conflict resolution cannot be placed solely on her shoulders. Harry also knew that there was a problem, and he did not act soon enough or clearly and energetically enough to solve it. He gave the impression of having wanted to produce the effects that Sybil had experienced. A communication can be judged only by its effectiveness, and primary responsibility for achieving effective results lies with the speaker, who was also the most powerful leader of the organization and the person who set the standards for others.

It is clear that Sybil, whom most people in the organization considered a competent and loyal employee, did not become incompetent and disloyal overnight. Rather, communication had failed at a deep level over a long period, and the parties involved on both sides of the dispute lacked the willingness or skill to bridge the gaps and repair the damage.

Although the mediation process was unable to bring Sybil and Harry together to discuss their issues directly, we communicated messages to both sides, and we helped each side learn from their experiences. It became clear to us that they would not easily or readily repeat their mistakes. At the end of the process, they understood that either of them could have reduced the damage by acting earlier, more collaboratively, and more skillfully.

## Observations

Personal and organizational learning take place only when the individuals in an organization are able to meet and discuss their experiences openly, honestly, and empathetically. The parties in this case were unable to do so because of restrictions placed on the process by their attorneys. Harry and Sybil were prevented from telling and hearing their own and each other's stories, probing beneath the surface of their conflict, learning from each other, coming to the truth of their relationship, and possibly reaching closure and forgiveness. They were unable to release themselves from their stories, which insisted on the other's guilt, proclaimed their own innocence and virtue, and reinforced the status quo. Because they were prevented from addressing their issues in direct dialogue, the only possible result was to settle the dispute without resolving it.

One of the dangers in mediating sexual harassment disputes is that beneath stories of sexual mistreatment lie a number of subtle, complex, hidden issues. These involve the deceptive nature of much sexual communication, differences in how women and men interpret the meaning of the same communication, and the effects of unequal power between those who are communicating about sexual issues.

In trying to understand conflicting stories about sexual communication, it is useful to step back from the details and consider what sexual harassment is, both in the legal context and in terms of conflict resolution. The way we define the term *sexual harassment* is a function of our purposes, which are not the same in mediation as in law.

One of the main purposes of the legal definition of sexual harassment is to establish a category of persons to whom money must be paid or who must take action to correct the problem. Rarely does the legal purpose include drawing lessons about what has happened so that the parties can avoid future instances of harassment and initiate a healing process.

There are two legal categories of sexual harassment: quid pro quo harassment (that is, the explicit or implicit demand for sexual favors), and hostile environment harassment (that is, the creation of an unreasonably sexually hostile work environment). In order to prove sexual harassment, the complainant has to show that the sexual attention was unwanted. This is a claim that can be negated by evidence that the complainant has participated in or initiated the behavior.

In addition, there are a number of nonlegal definitions of sexual harassment that have practical value in mediation. They help us understand more about what actually happens in cases of sexual harassment, and they offer greater possibilities for learning. In our view, sexual harassment can involve any of the following factors:

- An inability to hear the word *no* when one is communicating sexual interest, or an inability to say no in a way that will be heard
- Any combination of unequal power and sexuality, as when sexuality is used as a way of exercising power over employees
- An uncensored, subconscious aggression expressed through sexuality, and the use of sexuality as a way of insulting, humiliating, or degrading others
- Perfectly appropriate expressions of affection or humor that are used in an insensitive way or in the wrong context (as, for example, when jokes that might be appropriate in an informal, intimate setting are told in a work setting where they are inappropriate or offensive, or when touching that would be appropriate between friends is used with subordinates)
- Any action or statement that creates a genuine feeling in another person that he or she has been sexually harassed

In mediating incidents of sexual harassment, it is useful to remember that sexual communication is extremely subtle and often indirect, especially in the workplace. Sexuality and the meaning of sexual communication are rarely discussed openly, even between couples, and we often attribute different meanings to the same gestures or phrases.

Communication of sexual intent takes place mostly beneath the surface of normal discourse; sexual feeling is internal and invisible to other people except when it is communicated through overt statements or behavior. Nevertheless, hidden feelings often slip through, even when they are not meant to be communicated.

To complicate things even more, sexual communication is directly affected by social and cultural mores, which differ enormously, not only across genders but also across nationalities, ethnicities, religions, and ages. Wherever such differences exist, sexual communication can go awry. In many cultures, sexual communication is equated with pornography, while in other cultures, it is considered erotica.

Historically, across cultures, men have tended to initiate sexual communication, whereas women have tended to interpret it and make choices. As a result, initiators often pick up different meanings from sexual communication than do the interpreters.

Commercialism and popular culture have also created a pervasive climate of sexual objectification, acquisition, appropriation, and immediate gratification, which has distorted sexual feelings and encouraged insensitive behavior. In the workplace, hierarchy and unequal power have equally distorted sexuality and sexual communication. There is an undeniable erotic element in the exercise of power, and a feeling of harassment often occurs when power is not reciprocal. Regardless of what is intended, sexual harassment of women can be seen as revealing and recapitulating women's unequal status in the workforce.

The essence of sexual harassment, then, is insensitivity to the wishes of others, lack of awareness of what is appropriate in different environments, and a combination of sexuality and hierarchical power, which allows coercion to replace consent. To avoid initiating, engaging in, condoning, or modeling these offensive interactions, one needs to be willing to invite, listen to, and reward honest feedback. Asking for feedback demonstrates respect for other people's feelings. Openness to honest feedback in sexual communication is helpful in personal relationships as well as in work environments, as it allows one to learn instantly what is and is not offensive to others. In this way, experiences are exchanged and discussed before they have time to harden into stories of demonization and victimization.

In this mediation, we were somewhat successful in helping the organization learn from both sides' stories about what happened. We compiled the following recommendations for improvement in policies, procedures, and responses from our separate meetings with the parties, and we presented them to the board of directors:

- All managers, supervisors, and employees should receive training in the issues surrounding sexual harassment and sexual communication, as well as in informal problem solving, respectful communication, and conflict resolution.
- Internal mediation, peer counseling, and conflict resolution systems should be introduced to encourage informal problem solving and to support interventions by other employees when they feel someone has not been treated fairly.
- Employees should be encouraged to point out sexual harassment, and the organization should set up an employee sexual

harassment hot line and hire a sexual harassment compliance officer.

- Top management should send a clear message that it will not retaliate against anyone for calling attention to sexual harassment issues.
- Personal coaching and counseling should be provided to accusers as well as to those accused of sexual harassment.
- More women and minorities should be hired into executive positions, and the board of directors should set an example in their commitment to gender equality by ensuring that the board's composition reflects the values it upholds.

We also recommended that the organization design a multi-level conflict-resolution system and encourage prevention, early intervention, scaled problem solving, and interest-based resolution of any disputes that might otherwise result in litigation. We proposed that the organization assess and analyze what employees (especially women) thought of its organizational culture, and that it consider ways of bringing the culture into greater conformity with its espoused values.

Learning and conflict resolution are ultimately not up to others; they are personal choices and cannot be compelled. Nevertheless, they can be encouraged by helping the parties deeply analyze their experiences, making recommendations for the future, using honesty and empathy to get below the superficial stories that the parties have told about their opponents, and creating a third story about learning, growth, and redemption.

The goal of mediation is to draw people who have been divided by adversarial stories into a community of learning. In such an environment, stories describing pain, shame, anger, and forgiveness can be told, heard, and merged to form a third story. Mediation encourages people to understand these conflict stories and tell them to each other without unnecessary demonization or victimization. It encourages both sides to transcend pain and humiliation by transforming them into lessons learned. This is the best way of responding to, recovering from, and preventing future instances of sexual harassment.

# Neighbors in Spite

The Browns and Peg Smith had lived next door to each other on a quiet block for more than seventeen years, without incident. They were not friends, but they were not enemies, either.

Peter Brown was a retired scientist with a meticulous concern for the appearance of his home and his person. Sarah Brown was also retired, but she was much younger than her husband and in better health.

Peg Smith had worked most of her life in a variety of secretarial and office management jobs. A widow for many years, she had been her family's sole support. She had recently married Bill, a practical man with lots of construction know-how. Bill created sets for the motion picture industry, and he painted as a hobby.

The trouble began when Bill lost his studio contract because of what he described as "internal politics" in his union. He had been forced to give up his studio, declare bankruptcy, and move whatever he could salvage into his and Peg's backyard. There were two routes into the Smiths' backyard. One ran through a side passage, which had several ups and downs and turns. The other was shorter and more direct and ran across the Browns' driveway.

According to Peter Brown, the Smiths began to move lumber and equipment across his property, blocking his driveway and parking in it for long periods of time, without ever coming to him or asking permission. According to Peg Smith, she did not initially ask Peter for permission because she didn't think the disruption would last very long. When he objected, she did ask permission, telling Peter that her husband had lost his job and studio and needed to move his lumber and equipment into their backyard. She said she had asked Peter nicely but he refused.

According to Peter, Peg's attitude toward him was angry and insulting. He claimed she never mentioned Bill's unemployment or their desperate economic condition, and he said he certainly would have given them permission to use his driveway if they had done so. Peg said it was Peter, not herself, who had been insulting, refusing permission to use his driveway despite her earnest pleas for help.

Bill was then forced to move many items of heavy equipment from his business into the backyard by going through the difficult side passage. In the process, he injured his back and was laid up for several weeks. Meanwhile, Peter put up a concrete wall separating his driveway from the Smiths' backyard, something Sarah, his wife, had been asking him to do for a long time. The wall was high and sat directly on the Smiths' and Browns' common property line.

That Christmas, the first act of escalation was initiated when the Smiths left a candy box filled with dog excrement on the Browns' front porch and piled lumber and equipment up against their side of the wall that Peter had built, so that the pile could be seen from the Browns' house and yard. Bill constructed a shed in his backyard to house the lumber and equipment, and Peter called the building department to report the construction as illegal. While Bill was tearing the shed down, he fell from a ladder and hurt himself again.

Next the Smiths put a radio in the window of their den, directly opposite the Browns' kitchen, and played it extremely loudly, even when they weren't home. The Browns claimed that the Smiths monopolized the parking spaces in front of both houses. They called the police about the cars and had tests done on the decibel levels produced by the radio. Finally, they called an attorney and were preparing to sue when they were asked by friends to try mediation. They had decided that they would sell their home if they had to rather than continue to live next door to the Smiths.

At the first mediation session, after we discussed ground rules and explained the mediation process, Peter Brown recited his story of what had happened. While he spoke, Bill Smith remained silent and Peg kept interrupting with hostile or angry remarks. We asked Peg to hold her comments for later, when she and Bill would have a chance to tell their story. In the interim, she could take notes or try to listen in order to gain a better understanding of Peter's position. Peter was hostile and angry in his presentation, but Sarah was more reasoned and gentle, and she spoke directly to Peg. Peg responded sympathetically to this move, and her voice calmed somewhat.

We went back and forth several times, letting each person tell his or her story and describe the events that were most bothersome. We then asked each person what his or her goals were for the mediation process or what he or she wanted to achieve. We wrote their answers down on a flip chart for all to see. The Browns' goals were to eliminate the noise from the radio, reduce the level of hostility, get their parking spaces back, and remove the construction materials stacked against the wall. The Smiths' goals were to get the charges dropped that the Browns had filed against them, be able to access their yard through the Browns' driveway if they needed to, improve communication, and have the Browns call them before complaining to the authorities.

Because the time scheduled for the session was running out, we asked them if they would be willing to agree to a one-week cease-fire so that the tension would not continue to escalate before our next meeting. At first Peg refused, saying, "I wouldn't give them the satisfaction." We said we were not asking her to agree to a cease-fire for them but for herself, and she quickly gave her consent. Everyone then assented to the following interim agreement, which they decided would be in effect only until the end of our next meeting:

- Neither side would call any governmental agencies, including the police, to complain about the other side.
- Both parties would try to keep the noise level down on their radios.
- Before either party took any action affecting the other party, the acting party would first communicate with the other party.

We encouraged them to give the cease-fire a chance, and we asked them to use the time between sessions to think of possible solutions that might be acceptable to the other side. We congratulated them on having reached a very good first agreement and suggested they call us if they got into trouble.

At the next meeting, we asked for a report on how the cease-fire had worked. Everyone agreed it had worked well. The radio had been kept down, and the Browns had called to find out whether they could drop the charges they had filed against the Smiths. Given their success in reducing tension during the cease-fire, the second session easily became a problem-solving exercise, with both sides willingly collaborating to solve their problems. We were able to reach the following agreements quickly:

- The Browns agreed that the Smiths could use the Browns' driveway to remove or cut down trees or in similar activities if the Smiths requested permission in advance.
- The Smiths agreed to remove the items stacked against their side of the wall that were visible to the Browns on the other side.
- The Smiths agreed not to use the Browns' parking spaces unless there were no other spaces available on the street.
- The Smiths agreed to keep their radio at a normal volume.
- The Browns agreed to drop all charges and, if necessary, to appear in court and withdraw their complaint regarding the noise.
- The Browns agreed to let the Smiths build a shed in their own backyard without complaining to the building department.
- The Smiths agreed to create a back entrance to their yard that would not require them to use the Browns' driveway.
- Both sides agreed not to call the authorities to complain about any future problems they might have before discussing them directly with one another.
- Both sides agreed to try to cooperate in solving future problems.
- Both sides agreed to use mediation if they were unable to resolve any future disputes.

We complimented both sides on reaching these agreements and pointed out that all the goals they had originally identified had been achieved. We told them we felt they could continue to improve their relationship in the future. They did not need to become the best of friends, but they could if they wanted to. We ended by asking to be invited to their next block party and by asking them, if they really agreed that the conflict was over, to shake hands as a way of burying the hatchet. Everyone shook hands warmly, thanked us for our efforts, and left.

In subsequent conversations, both couples told us the agreement was working and they were getting along extremely well. They said they had learned from the session how to be better neighbors with one another. Although they had not become the best of friends, they no longer believed the negative things they had said about each other when they first told their stories, and they saw their relationship as continuing to improve in the future.

## Observations

Robert Frost's line "Something there is that does not love a wall" aptly accounts for the parties' responses to one another in this case. In fact, the Browns and the Smiths had built many walls to keep each other out—walls of silence and of noise, walls of blame and of shame, walls of rationalization and of hate. For each real wall they created, another was contrived in their stories.

This mediation provides us with an excellent example of how a small, simple misunderstanding can escalate into a major war, and of how stories parties create to describe events can tell far different tales than the ones they intend. In fact, when both stories are added together, the demonizations and victimizations are removed, and neither story is labeled true or false, the conflicts melt away.

Each couple in this case, by cutting, pasting, and creatively coloring the facts, had assembled a convincing story, a collage of gravely inhumane treatment, injustice, and calculated disrespect on the part of the other side. The external stories portrayed unnecessary boundary creations and violations in which they could discover ample evidence of hostile intentions.

One of the purposes of all conflict stories is to create boundaries. Another is to invite their eradication. All boundaries face in two directions: they keep outsiders out, and they keep insiders in. From the outside, they announce hostility. From the inside, they trigger fear. They declare, simultaneously, safety and isolation, independence and loss of community. In this way, external boundary stories reflect internal ones. Stories of cruelty are often simply the outward image of inward pain. The opposite is also true, and more tellingly so in conflict stories: inward pain can drive people to create outward images of cruelty, as the best way of answering the question "Why did they do this to us?" In this way, people protect their egos from the fear that they deserve to be treated poorly, are unworthy of respect, and are receiving their just rewards.

People have a natural desire to protect themselves from repeated experiences of pain, fear, shame, and guilt. This desire leads them to invent simple explanations that promise simple solutions. People's own pain, in addition to other people's cruelty, causes them to distance themselves and erect emotional boundaries to protect themselves from harm. Yet the very act of hiding, screening, masking, covering over, burying, and suppressing parts of who they are communicates their own potential for cruelty. As people withdraw from others, they trigger withdrawal in those from whom they have withdrawn. In this way, a cycle is formed.

In the conflict just described, this cycle had degenerated into a petty exchange of accusatory stories essentially consisting of "You did" and "No, I didn't." If the parties or the mediator slip into trying to decide "who did" and "who didn't," perspective is lost, and there appears to be no way out. For this reason, we shifted the conversation onto more useful terrain by assisting the parties in creating a story of deescalation and successful cease-fire. We then encouraged them to identify what they wanted from their relationship. This allowed them to become both separate and interrelated, to create themselves as good neighbors, and to negotiate solutions to each of their problems. The process of identifying their goals *automatically* revealed who they were and instilled respect for what they wanted.

Once the parties became willing to drop their stories and externally drawn boundaries, they were able to communicate their internal uniqueness, which is its own boundary and needs no defense against violation.

# An "F" in Problem Solving

At the request of the district superintendent and the president of the teachers' union, we were invited to a high school to assist the staff in resolving a problem that we were told was threatening to destroy the school. We were informed that this was an emergency, and consequently there was no time for us to prepare or gather information about the issues. We had no chance to find out what was expected of us, to interview key players, or to speak personally with any of the parties before our arrival. To make matters worse, only a few days were left to resolve the conflict before summer vacation. Consequently, we had to move very quickly. We met privately with several groups in the morning, before an afternoon problem-solving workshop was to begin. Because the faculty and staff had scheduled a party for two retiring teachers, which was to be held the same afternoon as our intervention, we were left with only two and a half hours for the entire afternoon workshop.

In several, quick morning meetings, we sought to conduct an informal needs assessment process, to determine the level of conflict, and to design a program for the afternoon session. Our goals were to draw out the underlying problems, create a sense of trust in us and in the process, develop a willingness among the parties to address and jointly solve their problems, create a feeling that solutions were possible, identify what needed to be communicated to whom, outline future steps, and begin to resolve the conflict.

We first met with one faction of teachers, counselors, and others, who indicated that the conflict was being caused by the new principal because he had violated their trust on numerous occasions. The group expressed cynicism about the usefulness of mediation or any other kind of problem-solving process, and they told us that the atmosphere in the school was one of complete demoralization. To top it off, there was widespread fear of impending layoffs among the faculty and staff because a school funding measure had been voted down in a recent election. One teacher who was strongly resistant to our intervention circulated a petition against our coming and secured twenty faculty signatures. The petition expressed the belief that mediation was useless and that the group's time could be better used for other purposes.

We then met with the principal who informed us that a number of volatile incidents had already taken place at the school: There was a raging controversy over the strip search of a student. An unpopular policy had been instituted by the faculty, to ban students from wearing hats at school. And a disastrous meeting to explain the policy to the students had ended in a fistfight, with one of the students being hospitalized. We were faced with dozens of conflicting stories, ideas, attitudes, and characterizations regarding the nature and causes of these conflicts, all of which seemed to indicate a lack of respect for other people's boundaries.

At the same time, ironically, this school was preparing to participate in a project designed to increase cooperation and trust between unions and administrators. The school was being asked to establish a more collaborative working relationship among faculty, staff members, and administration. Therefore, it was important that the parties find some way of regenerating a sense of trust and open communication; otherwise, the entire project, and desperately needed funding, would be canceled.

We started the afternoon meeting, which was attended by the principal, two vice principals, and approximately fifty teachers and staff members, with a few words about conflicts in general and the natural tendency to sweep them under the rug or deny that they exist. We said we wanted to start by acknowledging that there was a conflict over our even being there. We did this to acknowledge and defuse their opposition as well as to let them know we wanted their full participation, were willing to model honesty and openness in solving our own problems, and were unwilling to force them into a process for solving theirs. We went on to say that, as in the proverbial example of the unacknowledged rhinoceros in the living room, enormous energy can be wasted in denying the existence of conflict. In the process of denial, trust gets lost along with open and honest communication. We invited them to stop sweeping their conflicts under the rug and to use this opportunity for resolving them. We asked them to live in the paradox of hope and doubt regarding their future success, and we offered to leave if they thought there was a better way to use their time.

We asked everyone to introduce him- or herself and indicate one constructive thing we could do with the time we had left. We asked them to say whether they thought the session would be a waste of their time and promised that if they felt that way, we would all adjourn and go home. Everyone wanted to use the time con- structively, to resolve the conflicts, increase cooperation, improve communication, and rebuild trust. We asked the group whether there were any common themes in the suggestions they had made, and several people shared their sense that problems needed to be discussed openly, differences resolved, and trust regenerated; oth- ers said that efforts in these directions needed to be appreciated by the administration. We asked for and received unanimous agreement that we should try to solve the problems rather than adjourning the session.

In order to ensure that the participants would not be seated together with their closest allies, we assigned them to teams of five by having them count off. We then asked each participant to write down, anonymously, the three primary problems in the school. The purpose of this "secret ballot" exercise was not only to iden- tify problems but also to encourage the participants to tell deeper, riskier stories than those they had told so far. We wanted to allow the participants to quickly tell their deeper stories without fear of disagreement or recrimination. We also wanted to normalize talk- ing about deeper issues, equalize participation so that less vocal participants would be heard, and include everyone in the process of defining what we were going to work on. We wanted to demon- strate that even those who disagreed about whether there were problems could think of ways to improve the school.

It did not take long for the participants to complete their indi- vidual lists and for each team to pass the collected lists forward to us. We then shuffled the lists to ensure anonymity and gave them out again to different teams. We asked each team to have its mem- bers read the lists aloud, jointly analyze the problems cited, group the problems broadly by category, select the top three to five by consensus, and report its results to the rest of the group. We did this to distill individual gripes into single, manageable lists of three top priorities and to create a sense of distance from individuals' stories by having the stories analyzed by third parties. We also wanted to break up cliques, create a team dynamic, give the participants practice in solving problems and reaching consensus, and encourage a sense of accomplishment through task completion. We wanted to defuse the emotional content of the stories about the violation of trust and demonstrate that collaboration can make a third story possible.

Before the teams reported on their results, we asked the participants how it had felt to use this process. We told them we wanted to make our process transparent, develop their awareness of the importance of process, create new stories of trust building, and encourage them to ask process questions (such as "How did that feel?") when problems began to arise. Several people said that it had felt great to talk openly about their problems instead of gossiping. Each team then reported its results to the group as a whole, and everyone was able to identify broad similarities in the various teams' priorities.

We asked whether any of the participants, while working in their teams, had personally experienced *any* of the problems they had identified. Not one person had. We asked how this was possible, given the number and depth of the problems. In response, several people pointed out that most of the problems concerned communication and broken trust, and that teamwork, collaboration, the presence of facilitators and recorders, the use of an inclusive round-robin process and consensus decision making, and open discussion of real life problems had automatically helped them work better. We agreed, and we told the participants that they could have the same experience they had just had every single day.

With the consensus of the group, we combined and refined the teams' separate lists into five primary issues on which they needed to work:

1. Communication
2. Improving trust in the relationship between the staff and the administration

3. Student discipline
4. Involvement of parents and community
5. Faculty governance

We asked the participants if they were ready to solve these problems—to take responsibility not just for pointing them out but also for coming up with and implementing creative solutions. When we obtained the participants' unanimous agreement to push ahead, we asked each of them to join one of five problem-solving teams, whose task would be to take one category of issues and brainstorm as many solutions as possible for solving this part of the overall problem. The purposes of this exercise were to give the participants some practical experience, develop skills in finding collaborative and creative solutions, defuse the emotions that had been stimulated by complaints, demonstrate that more than one solution was possible to each of the problems, encourage teamwork in problem solving, demonstrate that even entrenched and long-standing problems could be solved by consensus, move the group in the direction of strategic thinking and planning, and transform adversarial stories into stories of trust.

Everyone agreed to join a problem-solving team and start the brainstorming process. We asked the teams not to discuss or censor their ideas or decide whether or not an idea would work until all the ideas had been expressed.

Before presenting their ideas to the group as a whole, every problem-solving team reported that morale was higher and feelings were far more positive than when we had started, and there was much more optimism about the possibility of solving the problems. The problem-solving teams came up with specific, concrete suggestions, many of which could be implemented immediately (see Exhibit 6.1). It was clear from the overwhelmingly positive and specific nature of these suggestions that the group wanted the conflicts to end. The participants wanted the kinds of relationships that they had once had in their school and the positive experiences that they had had in their problem-solving teams. The mood in the room was extremely positive.

Because we had gone past the time for ending our session, the group quickly reached consensus on the next steps that needed to be taken. These included having the problem-solving teams meet

## Exhibit 6.1.    Brainstormed Solutions.

- Reduce put-downs and aggressiveness in discussions; have dialogue rather than confrontation or attacks.
- Increase people's ability to communicate honestly by reducing fear of repercussions and hopelessness.
- Increase commitment to involvement and open up to personal friendliness.
- Have more socializing at lunch and breakfast.
- Increase team teaching and intracurricular cooperation.
- Create a "secret pals" program.
- Give more positive strokes, hugs, and "warm fuzzies."
- Show more caring and support for others.
- Follow through on decisions.
- Involve all affected parties in decisions.
- Speak up when it is time to speak up.
- Be more creative in solving problems.
- Reinstate birthday celebrations.
- Relax and laugh a little more.
- If there is a problem, discuss it with the principal.
- Have regular TGIF parties at a local restaurant.
- Be personal with the principal so that she can be personal as well.
- Empower teachers to develop policies and procedures, and have the administration communicate them more effectively.
- Develop short- and long-term goals for the school.
- Show respect for the teachers as professionals, and put them in charge of their own destiny.
- Exhibit greater professionalism, and eliminate snide comments to other professionals and to students.
- Regularly say "good morning" to others.

again before the end of the school term, to come up with more concrete recommendations for action, and developing a process for reaching consensus during the following school year.

As we ended, we asked the participants to indicate what they had done that made the day successful. They felt that they had brought their underlying problems out into the open, where they could be discussed. They had worked to classify and categorize their problems and group them under headings that would make these problems seem more manageable. They had seen that there were many solutions to each of their problems. Through brainstorming, they had identified a number of solutions, some of which could be implemented immediately by anyone. They had recognized that through teamwork and collaboration they could reduce their feelings of anger and isolation and support one another in solving even their most difficult problems.

We recommended that they begin the next school year by getting together to plan, by consensus, what they wanted to do and how they wanted to interact with one another. We asked whether anyone had any difficulty with our communicating the substance of his or her concerns to the district administration, and there was consensus that we should do so. We recommended that the teachers meet again to discuss how they could resolve their issues with the administration, and that they identify their shared values and agree on ground rules to use in their communications and conflicts.

We told them that we were impressed with their shared dedication to teaching, to their school, and to its students. We asked for their feedback and thanked them for their courage, honesty, and willingness to address their common problems. We asked them to compare how they felt now to how they had felt at the start of the session and whether they preferred their stories of broken trust or the stories they would tell about what they had done today. Everyone stood and applauded at the end, and several of the participants, including the teacher who had circulated the petition against the session, came up to us to say how useful they thought the session had been.

Immediately afterward, we met with the district administration, the principal, and the assistant principals. We reviewed the activities of the session and summarized the most critical problems that needed improvement. We read them the problems that had been identified by the participants, together with the recommended solutions, and we discussed ways for the district and the school administration to respond immediately, implement the suggestions, and improve their own communication and management styles. They agreed to do so before the end of the term. On reflection, we realized there were a number of issues that needed immediate administrative attention, and we made a number of concrete recommendations to the administration (see Exhibit 6.2).

In the fall, we held a joint follow-up session with administration, teachers, and staff to identify and reach consensus on a set of shared values for their work together. These included:

- Making a commitment to put the interests of students and learning first
- Working to make the school a true learning community
- Listening actively and respectfully to what others say, without yelling, blaming, intimidating, or gossiping
- Communicating directly, openly, and honestly
- Focusing on issues and interests rather than on positions and personalities
- Acknowledging work well done
- Modeling the behavior expected from others

The participants agreed to give each other regular, direct, and honest feedback if they were not acting according to these values and to discuss one of these values at each monthly staff meeting, monitor how they were doing, and try to improve.

The teams we had formed to brainstorm solutions to the school's problems continued working to implement changes. Two years later, the teams were still functioning. Although conflicts continued at the school, they were more manageable because methods for addressing them and stories that celebrated them had been created.

## Observations

The conflicts, problems, and stories of violated trust in this school had existed for years. By contrast, all the resolution and problem-solving processes we have described took place in one brief half-day session, followed by another half-day session several months later.

**Exhibit 6.2.  Recommendations for Administrative Action.**

1. Communication problems attributed by many teachers and staff to the administration, and particularly to the new principal, needed to be admitted, and steps needed to be taken to correct these problems, regardless of who was "in the wrong."
2. Stress and accumulated discomfort over changes in rules, management styles, and so on, needed to be addressed immediately.
3. There was irritation over what many teachers perceived as ill-informed, top-down, adversarial, inconsistent, arrogant, noncollaborative, inexperienced, inflexible management, and it needed to be resolved through greater staff involvement in governance and through team-based problem solving.
4. Inadequate support was felt to be coming from the district and the community, and this needed to be communicated and corrected.
5. Divisions within the faculty and the staff, based on attitudes toward the new principal and changes in policies and procedures that she had initiated, needed to be addressed through direct and frequent communication.
6. Training was needed in active listening, collaborative group process, team building, leadership styles, motivation, encouragement of participation and responsibility, managing change, and other areas.
7. The district needed to meet with the school staff to clarify policies and procedures.
8. A mentoring system was needed for new principals.
9. An additional session needed to be held in the fall with the administration and the staff, to establish common goals and shared values and develop an action plan to implement creative changes through consensus.
10. The principal needed to hold individual fence-mending meetings with critical staff members, establish a system of open feedback, increase trust, and repair damaged relationships.
11. The administration needed to support more social events in the school and mix socially with the school's personnel to further each side's understanding of the other as people.

We managed to do a great deal in the time we were given, but brief interventions such as this one often result in temporary improvements rather than lasting change. It takes follow-up, realignment, and continuous renewal to change an embedded organizational culture and move people out of the dysfunctional ruts, routines, and stories they have accumulated for years.

Asking people what they want to do, or what kind of relationship they want to have, is asking them to create the stories that redefine their future, as opposed to most conflict stories, which redefine their past. These are the stories that they would like to tell about themselves, the stories that show who they are, as opposed to the ones they have been telling about others. In the process of telling these new stories, they recreate not just their past but their future as well. By telling us what they want, they describe what they do not want, and vice versa. By working collaboratively in teams, they build their commitment to creating radically new stories.

Using the force of honesty, we began by reversing the parties' expectations in order to generate the energy necessary to cut through their defenses. We were willing to call their bluff, adjourn, and let them go home if they felt that mediation was not the best use of their time. We were also willing to be open and honest with them about what they were doing to each other and to go right for their core stories. By our willingness to violate their cultural norms and do something different, we showed them that they could, too, and that we could be trusted.

Every violation of trust is automatically felt as a boundary violation, although the boundary is usually internal and based on expectations. The boundary violation in this case was subtle and indirect, yet it was devastating and thorough. It consisted of crossing the invisible line of trust that separates leaders from followers and breaking the implicit promise that power will be used benevolently for the common good, that there will be no retaliation for honest communication, and that words will be congruent with deeds.

In this case, we chose not to process the stories but instead to create new ones that answered the request hidden in the accusation. We gave the parties a choice: continuing to experience the violations of trust they had been inflicting on one another for years, or working openly and honestly to solve their problems and learning to treat each other with respect. They opted for the future, although they did not really believe it would be possible to get there. They chose to have the conflict stories stop, not by separating but by coming together.

In order for the parties to come together, we had to help them create a third story—about solutions rather than problems, a story grounded in direct experience rather than in ideas or words. They were shocked into a new pattern by realizing that they had been able to work together without experiencing any of the problems they had identified, that they had been respectful of each other without even trying, and that they had collaborated and solved their problems naturally, without rancor or violations of trust.

We have worked in hundreds of schools to solve similar problems, and the process we have described here does not always work; indeed, there is not a single mediation technique we know of that works always and everywhere. In some schools, a simple strategic planning or envisioning exercise will move people forward. In others, stories of abuse and powerlessness, demonization and victimization, cynicism and apathy are so thick, and the time and support available for conflict resolution is so meager, that there is little we can do. In many schools, teachers tell stories about violations committed by principals and about their own powerlessness in the face of an unresponsive, bureaucratic hierarchy. At the same time, principals tell stories about passive, negative, irresponsible teachers who are out to get them, and about unsupportive school districts. In these stories, each side is misunderstood, and each is powerless to solve its problems without the cooperation of the other. Both sides are stuck, and neither is willing to take responsibility for making the first move. Our strategy is to create an environment and an experience, followed by storytelling and dialogue, in which each side can empathize with the other and reveal its core story.

The core story and deepest truth in every school is always a commitment to students. In this mediation, once the staff and administration realized that there was a way for them to be heard and work with each other to solve their common problems, the desire to meet the needs of the students took over. As the teachers described their problems with the principal, the issue became not only her style of communication and management but also their own unwillingness to meet with her and work on their problems.

All conflict stories present the same two faces, the same mutual descriptions. When teachers discover that their stories of bureaucracy and intransigence are also stories of their own apathy, acceptance of the way things are, and lack of follow-through, the solutions become clear. In this case, both sides came to realize that their stories were standing in their way, keeping them stuck, and frustrating their desire to be of service. The solutions they designed were really just ways of reminding themselves that they had a common story to tell, a story of how they could cut through their problems and work together to educate their students.

As important as the solutions, however, was their mutually supportive, team-based, collaborative process that the staff and administration used in order to experience a new way of learning from their problems. By using this process to tackle their issues, they were able to solve the deepest problem of all: the problem of feeling stuck and demoralized by their conflict. Our role was simply to encourage them to participate in this process and to allow them to discover and return to their own core stories, which were the same for everyone: stories about the desire to help children learn, about the willingness to contribute, about the exercise of real leadership, about real actions to improve relationships, about the willingness to change old stories and behaviors, about the ability to work collaboratively with others to solve problems, about the eagerness to take responsibility for what they created in the ongoing process of improving the quality of their lives, and about their ability to change their stories. This is what they taught each other.

# Conclusion
## Living Happily Ever After

We all dream that our conflict stories will come to magical conclusions. We long for endings that will relieve our pain, renew our lives, and revitalize our relationships with one another. We admire our mediation clients, whose stories we have told here, for their willingness to participate in a risky, unknown process that offered no guarantees.

In each of the conflicts we have narrated, we encouraged people to act as though magic was possible and to make themselves vulnerable before their adversaries. We asked them not only to tell their deepest stories and share their most vulnerable emotions but also to listen to their antagonists' stories and to risk compassion. They knew that happiness might elude them. While only a few of them reached fairy-tale endings, most put their conflicts to rest and gained a deeper sense of peace and self-knowledge as a result of the mediation process.

As mediators, we also have dreams about happy endings, yet in our practice the "happily ever after" we seek is not one in which the parties merely end their conflicts. To desire this would be to seek what is not ours to decide. Instead, our dream is that we continue to learn from each moment of each mediation, that we grow more connected and more willing to explore our conflicts and the forces within and between us that drive them. In this way, it becomes clear that whenever we come to grips with a single problem, we come to grips with the whole of human history.

As we conclude our examination of conflict stories, we invite you to reflect on the strategies we used and the results we achieved. The anecdotes we have shared reveal successes as well as failures. We do not recommend that you copy our styles or solutions. Rather, we hope you discover better approaches, which feel comfortable and compatible with your own style. We hope you will reflect on what you have read, filter it through your own experiences, and create a synthesis of understandings that will make you more successful in working with conflict stories.

What is most important is that you engage in a self-reflective practice. We encourage you to work with partners, coaches, peers, and support groups to find opportunities for continuous learning that will improve your skills, uncover the subtle truths contained in your conflict stories, and assist you in your reflection and growth.

No real-life conflict story has a predictable ending. No conflict is the same as any other. No story is exactly repeated. No textbook can tell you what to do. No reaction can be planned. The challenge is to be ready for *anything* at any time, to be able to respond skillfully to whatever someone may do or say. To do so, you need to observe, through empathy and honesty, your own reactions and responses to the twists and turns of each unique story and dialogue.

The challenge is to move both the conflict and the story that expresses it in fresh and unexpected directions and to be constantly and deeply aware of what is taking place inside us as conflict resolvers. In this way, every conflict we address becomes a learning opportunity of the sort described by John Dewey, who informs us, "Just as no man lives or dies to himself, no experience lives and dies to itself. Wholly independent of desire or intent, every experience lives on in further experiences."

Mediation practice is a continuum, a cyclical and iterative process in which each encounter lives on in future engagements. In our learning process, each mediation, each story, and each individual has led us to truths we carry with us into our next experience.

In this sense, every conflict story is a parable that contains a hidden truth. We hope the stories and parables we have recounted here have left you with tools, insights, and suggestions that will live on in your own future encounters. We wish you great adventures, and we hope that each conflict story you hear will challenge you and ask you to grow. We hope that in doing so you will live happily, in conflict, ever after.

# Index

**A**

Acknowledgement: of differences, 168; failure to provide, 96

Acting out, 47

Action plans, developing, 139, 140, 152

Actions: justifying, 7; rationalizing, 35; responsibility for, 53

Ad hoc board-staff committees, forming, 142, 143

Adam and Eve conflict story, 52–56, 57

Addiction mediation, 115–122; observations of, 122–123

*Alias Grace* (Atwood), vii

Alignment, 47, 203

Allusion, 17

Ambiguity, effect of, 48

Anger: in boundary violations, 169, 170; exploring, 41, 46; nursing, 98–99

Anger problem mediation, 95–100; observations of, 100–101

Anima and animus, 171

Apology: distinctions in, 137; requesting, uses for, 67, 69, 78

Archetypal roles: changing, 29–32; examining, 27–29; recognizing, 34

Archetypes: boundary violations and, 170–171; cultural, 49; transformation in, 57

Assisting, implication of, 33

Assumptions: cultural, 21–22, 44; in demonization, 89; emotional, 15; hidden, 7; mistaken, 10, 23–25; questioning, 45, 46

Attack, main method of, 39, 40

Atwood, M., vii

Audience approval, forms of, 29

Authentic experience: mistaking stories for, 40; recapturing, 41

Authentic self: loss of, 6–7, 31, 60, 61, 87; reaching, 17, 62; revealing, 8, 36

Authenticity: creating, 63; defense against, 40; need for, 61–62; returning to, 41, 42; sacrificing, cost of, 87

**B**

Background information, obtaining, 12–13, 157

Blame, shifting, 53

Board-staff mediation, 130–143; observations of, 143–144

Boundaries: creating, 8, 154, 171, 172, 192–193; eliminating, 192–193; need for, 167; rebuilding, 169, 170; unnecessary, 168

Boundary violations, 167, 168, 169–170, 203

Brainstorming, using. *See* Teamwork

Bridging, 8, 58, 168

Buddhist expression, 8

**C**

Campbell, J., 32

Cease-fire, use of, 190–191

Ceremonies, 57

Change: charting, 44; impending, sign of, 124; long-term, creating, 163, 164, 203; in mediators, 32–33; renewal to, 203; through listening, 2; transformational, 36

Childhood experiences, impact of, 38, 70, 113

Choices, 63

*Chorus of Stones, A* (Griffin), 62

Clary, K., 124

Coaching, 151, 154

Codependency, 31

Collective stories, usefulness of, 10

Collusion, 11

Commonalities: awareness of, 5; discovering, 67, 71, 146, 168; and discrimination, 4; example of, 204, 205

Communication: deepening, 61; forms of, 48; increasing effectiveness of, 13; in organizational culture, 180; responsibility for, 183

Communication techniques, observing, 93

Compassion: developing, 170; disarming, 39; evoking, using stories to, 3–5. *See also* Empathy

Confidentiality agreement, use of, 160

Conflict: defining, 167, 168; as feedback, 94; as opportunity, 57, 124, 125

Conflict, organizational. *See* Organizational conflict

Conflict stories: components of, 13–15, 34; dual role of, 39–40; as fairy tales, 3; functions of, 13–14, 15–17, 34; power of, 2–3, 35; purpose of, 48, 168–169, 192–193; as symbols, 40, 41; system of, 49; types of, defined, 7–8. *See also specific mediations; specific story types*

Conflict triangle, 27–28

Connections, 6, 58, 61, 166–167, 169. *See also* Interrelatedness

Context: awareness of, 12; and childhood experiences, 38; questioning to provide, 74; in sexual banter, 182; ways to elucidate, 12–13

Contexts: alternative, inventing, 33; hidden, 17, 44

Contextual elements, 12, 13

Contrasting, 45, 56

Core stories: bottling up, 60; defined, 7, 8; discovering, 8–10, 12, 36, 41; failure to process, 114

Correcting process, 45

Costs, measuring, 93

Counterattack, 39, 40, 169

Cultural assumptions: as a lens, 21–22; revealing, 44

Cultural heritage, impact of, 51–52

Cultural meaning, 39, 49, 50

Cultural mores, and sexual communication, 185

Cultural norms, 126–127

Cultural patterns, breaking, 127

**D**

Dangers, 10–12, 14, 32, 36, 89, 184

Date rape mediation, 73–79; observations of, 79–80

Deflating, 51

Dehumanizing, refusal to, 52

Democracy, loss of, 61

Demonization: assumptions of, 89; focus on, 7; getting past, 60; omitting, 43, 180; reinforcing, 33

Denial, 29, 44, 195–196

Devil's advocate role, use of, 82–83

Dewey, J., 208

Dialogue, importance of, 61

Differences, acknowledging, 168

Discrimination, 3–5

Disrespect, subconscious, 181–182, 183

Distortions, 22, 24, 43, 177

Diversity, 3–5

Divorce, fuel for, 46

Divorce metaphors, 17–18

Divorce, paternity issue in. *See* Paternity mediation

Dragons: roles of, 27–32; transformation in, 57

Drug problem mediation, 115–122; observations of, 122–123

Dulany, P., 168

Dysfunctional systems: breaking, 92–93; dance in, 91–92

**E**

Eliot, T. S., 1
Emotional assumptions, 15
Emotional boundaries, 193
Emotional truth, 178
Emotions: acknowledging, 61; as a lens, 21–22; locked in, 26
Empathy: as a choice, 63; developing, 170; disarming, 39; evoking, 3–5, 61; and judgment, 172; in mediators, 36; turning away from, 60
Enabling, 31
Eskimo carver, 59
Expectations: as a lens, 21–22; questioning, 16; unrealistic, 20, 23–25
External stories: defined, 7, 8; getting past, 60; inconsistency and, 48; and inflating, 51; and interpretation, 19; probing beneath, 36

**F**

Fact, separating, from interpretation, 18–19, 33, 56
Facts, linking, 15
Failure, fear of, 99, 100
Fairy tales: archetypes in, 27–32; conflict stories as, 3; transformation in, 57; truth and, 37
Falsity, examining, 36–37
Families of origin: archetypes in, 171; effect of, 50, 71–72, 113, 118
Family mediations. See Paternity mediation; Siblings' mediation
Family realities, 72
Fear: assuaging, 6; exploring, 41, 46; of failure, 99, 100; in relational silence, 60–61
Feedback: conflict as, 94; from mediators, asking for, 142; in sexual communication, 186; written, use of, 135–136
Fields, 46–47

Filters, 20–21, 23–25, 33
Firing, effect of, 88
Foerster, H., 167
Follow-through, 154
Follow-up, 201, 203
Forgiveness: achieving, 58; as a boundary, 172
Freud, S., 21
*From the Beast to the Blond* (Warner), 31, 166
Frost, R., 168, 192
Future, separating, from past, 40, 172

**G**

Gender inequalities, 46, 186
Ghost roles, discovering, 47
Goals: as a lens, 22; listing of, 190, 193
Gossip, reasons for, example of, 127
Grievance systems, forming, 97
Griffin, S., 62
Ground rules, 74, 81, 171
Group assessment, use of, 137–138
Group work. See Teamwork
Guilt, apology as expression of, 137

**H**

Happy endings, 17, 58, 207, 208
Hegi, U., 35
Helping, implication of, 33
*Hero with a Thousand Faces, The* (Campbell), 32
Hidden meanings, 3, 7, 35, 50, 170–171
Hierarchy, effect of, 46, 186
High school mediation, 194–201; administrative recommendations in, 201, 202; observations of, 201–205
History. See Past
*History of Danish Dreams, The* (Hoeg), xi
Hoeg, P., xi
*Hollow Men, The* (Eliot), 1
Honesty, 63; in mediators, 36, 195; turning away from, 60

Human resources, working with, 90–91, 164
Hypnotic effect, 89, 91

**I**

Illusion, 57
Impasse, cardinal element of, 59
Improvement, continuous, 154
Inactions, justifying, 7
Inconsistency, effect of, 48
Inequality, of women, 46, 186
Inflating, 51, 61
Influence, 12
Inner self. *See* Authentic self
Intention: discovering, 48; in sexual banter, 182
Interconnection. *See* Interrelatedness
Interests: questioning, 16; separating, from positions, 171–172
Internal stories: defined, 7, 8; getting past, 60; inconsistency and, 48; and inflating, 51; probing beneath, 36; seduction of, 11
Interpretation, 48; methods in, 44–45; separating fact from, 18–19, 33, 56
Interpretations: backing away from, 44; multiple, eliciting, 56; revealing nature of, 19–20; types of, 56
Interrelatedness, 2, 167, 168, 170, 171, 172. *See also* Connections
Intimacy: desire for, 41; inviting, 62; negative, 43, 169
Isolation, 61
Issues: listing, reason for, 66–67; organizational, 182–183; revealing deeper, 50; revisiting, 154. *See also* Problems

**J**

Judgments: effect of, 45; opposite of, 172
Jung, C. G., 171
Justifying, 8, 35, 39, 51; in boundary violations, 169; focus on, 7, 26; rein-forcement through, 89; in workplace conflicts, 90

**K**

Kafka, F., 1
Kelly, G. B., 87
Kerr, W., 172

**L**

Lao-tzu, *xviii–xix,* 129
Leaders, organizational, 128–129, 182
Leadership style, 129
Learning: community of, 187; in mediators, 154; method of, stories as, 2; organizational, 125, 179, 183
Lenses, 23–25, 33, 43; defined, 21–22; recognizing, 20–21
Limits. *See* Boundaries
Listening, invoking, 2, 3
Listening skills, 57, 58
*Long Day's Journey into Night* (O'Neill), 172
Long-term change, creating, 203; example of, 163, 164
Love, possibility of, 172

**M**

Mapping, 45, 47
Martyrdom, way to, 89
Masks: removing, 8, 62; stories as, 1; wanting, 61
Meaning: as fluid, 48; ideas about, 38–39; inverting, 33; layers of, 50; rituals and, 49; understanding, 60
Meanings, hidden, 3, 7, 35, 50, 170–171
Mediating: along two tracks, 46–47; dangers in, 10–12, 14, 32, 36, 89, 184
Mediation: as a continuum, 208; goal of, 187; involving others in, 90–91; methods of, 100; power of, 168, 169; trust in, 64
Mediation agreements, use of, 91, 99
Mediators: attitude of, 25; change in,

32–33; as devil's advocates, 82–83; feedback from, 142; goal of, 58; learning in, 154; role as, 7–8, 36, 56–57, 63, 171, 195; trusting, 64; withdrawal by, 161

Metameanings, 47–50, 54–56

Metamessages. *See* Subtexts

Metaphorical truth, 3, 15, 38, 178

Metaphors, 15; arranging, 25; creating new, 18; and cultural meaning, 49; inverting meaning of, 33; language of, 17–18; and reality, 8; truth of, 38; use of, 57. *See also* Symbols

Mirror image, 3, 15

Moral structure, identifying, 45

Murder, way to, 89

Myths, 49

**N**

Narrative structure: archetypal roles in, 27–31; eliciting alterations in, 42–47; restructuring, 32–33; understanding, 25–26

Narrative therapy, adapting, 40

Needs assessment, use of, 194

Needs, questioning, 16

Negative intimacy, 43, 169

Neighbors' mediation, 188–192; observations of, 192–193

Nelson, F. B., 87

Nursery school mediation, 145–153; observations of, 153–155

**O**

Objectivity, losing, 89

Omnipartial role, 63

O'Neill, E., 172

Openness, requiring, 62–63, 170, 186

Opportunity, conflict as, 124, 125

Options, listing, example of, 110

Organizational conflict: defining, 124–125; dysfunctional system in, 91–92; justifications in, 90; reasons for, 88, 143; as systemic, 94

Organizational culture: capturing, 94; communication of, 180; dysfunctional aspects of, identifying, 128; hierarchical, 46, 186; long-term change in, 203; revealing, 126, 127, 183; role of, 125–126

Organizational issues, revealing, 182–183

Organizational leaders, 128–129, 182

Organizational learning, 125, 179, 183

Organizational responsibility, 93–94

Organizational success, 125

Organizations: archetypes in, 171; creating support systems in, 128, 155; feedback for, 94; inequality of women in, 186; recommendations for improving, 186–187; subconscious disrespect in, 181–182, 183

Overstating technique, 44

**P**

Parables, 49, 56, 57

Paradigms, as a lens, 22

Past, 38; as a lens, 22; separating future from, 40, 172

Paternity mediation, 81–85; observations of, 85–86

Perception, angle of: acknowledging, 61; as a lens, 21–22; and truth, 37, 38, 177

Perpetrators. *See* Dragons

Personalities, defining problem as, 142

Plumbers' mediation, 156–163; observations of, 163–165

Positioning, reasons for, 26

Positions, 8; separating interests from, 171–172

Power: erotic element of, 186; reclaiming, 31; of stories, 2–3, 35; trading, for sympathy, 26

Prejudice, 3–5

Princes: roles of, 27–32; transformation in, 57

Princesses: roles of, 27–32; transformation in, 57
Problem-solving teams, using. *See* Teamwork
Problems: defining, as personalities, 142; listing, examples of, 66–67, 68, 131, 146–147; redefining, 43; separating people from, 171. *See also* Issues
Process awareness, 67
Process questions, encouraging, 197
Progoff, I., 51

**Q**
Questioning, reasons for, 57, 74
Questions: to facilitate responsibility, 92–93; to identify story components, 14–15; to understand story functions, 15–17

**R**
Rabbi story, 51
Rationalizing: in boundary violations, 169; reinforcement through, 89
Readiness, need for, 208
Realignment, 203
Reality, 5, 6, 8, 38, 63, 72
Reflective space, 67
Reframing, uses of, 43, 57, 148, 180
Reinforcement, creating, 89
Relational silence, 59–61; breaking through, 62, 63
Relationship: and context, 13; death of, 61; as a lens, 22; questioning, 16
Relationships, 5, 63, 166, 167
Relief, feeling of, 61, 63
Reluctance, getting past, 60
*Repetitio ad absurdum,* 44
Repetition, 16
Rescuers. *See* Princes
Resignation acceptance mediation, 102–113; observations of, 113–114
Resistance: example of, 156–157, 195; overcoming, 63, 64
Resolution: defining, 58; expectation of, 57; source of, 32

Resolution triangle, 30
Responsibility, 14, 172; apology as, 137; in archetypal roles, 29–32, 34; for communication, 183; for continuous improvement, 154; denial of, 26, 53; focus on, 7; organizational, 93–94; questions to facilitate, 92–93
Risks. *See* Dangers
Rituals, 16, 49
Roles, archetypal. *See* Archetypal roles
Roosevelt, E., 94
Rybarczyk, B., 44

**S**
Sacrifice, 90; costs of, 87
Safe environments, creating, 63–64, 80
Safety, in stories, 6
School mediations. *See* High school mediation; Nursery school mediation
Sculpturing technique, use of, 134–135
"Secret ballot" exercise, 196
Secrets, revealing, 57, 62, 63
Seduction, 11, 32, 89, 91
Self-concept, as a lens, 21–22
Self-esteem, 16; damage to, 87–88; as a lens, 22
Self-managing teams, suggesting, 162
Separations, 18–19, 33, 56, 171–172
Settlement, settling for, 36, 89
Sexual banter, 182
Sexual communication, 184, 185, 186
Sexual harassment, 46; costs of, 179; defining, 184–185, 186; preventing, 186–187
Sexual harassment mediations, 9–10, 173–183; observations of, 183–187
Siblings' mediation, 66–71; observations of, 71–72
Silence, relational, 59–61; breaking through, 62, 63
Silko, L. M., 2
Similarities. *See* Commonalities

Single parents, support for, 46
Social mores, and sexual communication, 185
Stagnation, 61
Standards, as a lens, 21–22
Stepping back, 63, 64
Stereotyping, 28
*Stones from the River* (Hegi), 35
Stories: power of, 2–5; shaping of, 1–2
Storytelling: broadening process of, 128; and deflating, 51; feeling unheard in, 59; purpose of, 61–62; reasons for, 5–7, 35, 38, 48
Strategies, and implementing vision, 139, 140, 152
Subconscious disrespect, 181–182
Subconscious mind: influence of, 8–9, 37, 60; speaking directly to, 18
Subtexts: exploring, 47–50, 54–56; universal, 26
Success: fear of, 99, 101; organizational, 125
Summarizing, use of, 57
Support, ongoing, 128
Suppression, price of, 61
Symbolical truth, 38
Symbolism, 17; example of, 54–56; ideas about, 37–38; use of, 57
Symbols, 15; conflict stories as, 40, 41; and cultural meaning, 49; truth of, 38. *See also* Metaphors
Sympathy, trading power for, 26, 28
Synergos Institute, 168
Synthesis stories: and alignment, 47; creating, 39, 57–58, 204; substituting, 62; working towards, 42

**T**

*Tao Te Ching* (Lao-tzu), 129
Teamwork: continuation of, 201; examples of, 131–132, 139–140, 148, 149, 196–198
Termination, effect of, 88
*Testament to Freedom, A: The Essential Writings of Dietrich Bonhoeffer* (Kelly and Nelson), 87

Therapy, suggesting, 79, 82, 84, 99, 152
Third stories. *See* Synthesis stories
Transcendence, 32, 34
Transformation: defined, 36; possibility of, 50–51, 57, 58; processing, 114; source of, 32
Triggers, 46
Trust, 64, 168, 203
Trust-breaking behavior, reason for, 114
Truth: determining, in sexual harassment, 177–178; distorting, 24; emotional, 178; ideas about, 1, 37–39; issue of, examining, 36–37; metaphorical, 3, 15, 38, 178; questioning, of assumptions, 45; through collective stories, 10
Truths, deeper: discovering, 3, 7, 35, 60, 62; synthesis stories and, 57, 58

**U**

Unheard stories, effect of, 59, 61
Union representatives, working with, 90–91; mediations involving, 102–112, 115–122
Unpredictability, 10–11

**V**

Validation, use of, 41–42
Victim, positioning as, 14, 26
Victimization: assumptions of, 89; getting past, 60; omitting, 43; reinforcing, 33
Victims. *See* Princesses
Visions, describing, 139
Von Foerster, H., 167
Vulnerability: assumption about, 24; as a choice, 63; defense against, 40, 41; encouraging, 32, 61, 170; risking, 50; turning away from, 60

**W**

Warner, M., 31, 166
*Who Whispered Near Me* (Clary), 124
Wilde, O., 61

Wishes: example of listing, 68, 138–139; listing, purpose of, 67, 146; revealing, 16
Withdrawal, by mediators, 161
Wittgenstein, L., 11
Women, inequality of, 46, 186. *See also* Sexual harassment

Workplace conflict. *See* Organizational conflict
Workplace metaphors, 18
Workplace rules, broken, 90

**Z**

Zen, language of, 40

# About the Authors

KENNETH CLOKE is director of the Center for Dispute Resolution in Santa Monica, California, where he is a mediator, arbitrator, consultant, and trainer specializing in resolving complex multiparty conflicts, including grievance and workplace disputes, organizational and school conflicts, sexual harassment and discrimination lawsuits, divorce, family, and public policy disputes, and in designing conflict resolution systems for organizations. His consulting and training practice also encompasses issues of organizational change, leadership, team building and strategic planning. He is a speaker in the field of conflict resolution and author of many journal articles and books, including *Mediation: Revenge and the Magic of Forgiveness*. He also is the coauthor (with Joan Goldsmith) of *Thank God It's Monday! 14 Values We Need to Humanize the Way We Work* and, most recently, *Resolving Conflicts at Work: A Complete Guide for Everyone on the Job*.

JOAN GOLDSMITH has been a management consultant and educator for the past thirty years, specializing in leadership development, organizational change, conflict resolution, and team building. As a principal with CSC Index, she assisted *Fortune* 500 clients in leadership development, change management, and human resource development.

She is the author of *Learning to Lead: A Workbook on Becoming a Leader* (with Warren Bennis), *Thank God It's Monday! 14 Values We Need to Humanize the Way We Work*, and *Resolving Conflicts at Work: A Complete Guide for Everyone on the Job* (with Kenneth Cloke).

In the nonprofit sector and the field of educational reform, she has been an advisor on organizational issues, school change, curriculum development, and teacher education. She is the founder of Cambridge College and a former member of the faculty of the Harvard Graduate School of Education.

Printed in the United States
83049LV00002B/187-204/A